Twayne's English Authors Series

EDITOR OF THIS VOLUME

Kinley E. Roby

Northeastern University

J. B. Priestley

TEAS 283

J. B. Priestley

J. B. PRIESTLEY

By A. A. DeVITIS
and
ALBERT E. KALSON

Purdue University

TWAYNE PUBLISHERS

A DIVISION OF G. K. HALL & CO., BOSTON

Published in 1980 by Twayne Publishers,
A Division of G. K. Hall & Co.
All Rights Reserved

Printed on permanent/durable acid-free paper and bound
in the United States of America

First Printing

Frontispiece photo of J. B. Priestley © by Mark Gerson

Library of Congress Cataloging in Publication Data

De Vitis, A. A.
J. B. Priestley.

(Twayne's English authors series ; TEAS 283)
Bibliography: p. 243 - 51
Includes index.
1.   Priestley, John Boynton, 1894–   —Criticism
and interpretation.   I.   Kalson, Albert E., joint
author.
PR6031.R6Z564   828'.9'1209   79-22492
ISBN 0-8057-6774-6

for Rose, Mollie, and Fred

Contents

About the Authors

Preface

Chronology

1. Backgrounds 17
2. The Novels: Themes and Directions 29
3. First Efforts 39
4. "Hit or Miss" 51
5. England at War 64
6. Following the War 77
7. Novels of the 1960s 87
8. Miscellaneous Pieces 110
9. The Plays: Influences and Motifs 116
10. Celebrated Apprenticeship 126
11. Early Comedies 136
12. Chekhovian Drama 144
13. Time Plays 153
14. Mature Comedies 166
15. Experiments and Innovations 179
16. Wartime 193
17. Cautious Optimism 205
18. Last Plays 218
19. Conclusion 229

Notes and References 233

Selected Bibliography 243

Index 252

About the Authors

A. A. DeVitis, Professor of English at Purdue University, is the author of two other TEAS volumes, *Graham Greene* and *Anthony Burgess,* as well as a book on Evelyn Waugh. His articles and reviews of modern British literature appear in *Renascence, College English, Twentieth Century Literature, Saturday Review,* and *Western Humanities Review.*

Albert E. Kalson is an Associate Professor at Purdue University, where he teaches dramatic literature and film. His studies of David Storey, Harold Pinter, and Tennessee Williams have appeared in *Modern Drama,* and he has published articles on Restoration drama and reviews in *Studies in English Literature, Theatre Survey, Restoration and 18th Century Theatre Research, Theatre Journal,* and *Modern Language Review.*

Preface

John Boynton Priestley does not like the expression "Man of Letters," although the term fits him well; nor does this cheerful, pipe-smoking Yorkshireman care to be called "Jolly Jack." He wishes that the English had an equivalent for the French "Maître," a term which might serve to indicate his prodigious literary achievement. And if the English, as do the French, had a National Academy, Priestley might just conceivably wear its garment but with a half-ironic grin. For Priestley, despite his protestations to the contrary, is one of our language's best natured and most sensible writers, one who has never been above a good joke whether on himself or on someone else. He is, according to John Braine, the distinguished novelist and fellow Bradfordian who has himself written on Priestley, one of our most "normal" writers; and it is perhaps this very normality that distinguishes his achievement.

In more than a half-century of professional writing, J. B. Priestley has produced over 150 volumes of distinguished literature ranging through literary criticism, the novel, the drama, the critical and discursive essay, the travel account, to radio broadcasts of the most persuasive nature, as well as several compelling books of autobiography and reminiscence. From his earliest publications, those well-reasoned studies of Thomas Love Peacock and George Meredith, his work has demonstrated an unerring ability to deal incisively with the idiosyncrasies of the English national character. It is for this reason that he has often been compared to Dickens, a comparison which Priestley labels odd, since he feels that more pronounced influences on his work are Henry Fielding and Laurence Sterne.

Shrewd, intelligent, relishing a good fight cleanly fought, enjoying his satirical thrusts at pretension and stupidity, Priestley in his work reveals above all a logical mind taking delight in communicating an essentially optimistic view of man in nature and society. But this does not mean that Priestley's view of man in the twentieth century is Pollyanna's. His novels and dramas reveal a deep awareness of the darker aspects of human behavior, but he does not dwell on them. There is simply too much in life to be enjoyed if the individual will only accept himself and acknowledge the richness which the world has to offer. What he reveals in his art is an unshakable belief that no obstacle is insurmountable if individual men will unite to work in community.

It has not been possible in this introductory study to do complete justice to Priestley's accomplishment. His erudition and humanity perhaps shine forth most fully in such later works as his superb volume of literary criticism, *Literature and Western Man*, published in 1960, as well as the probing philosophic musings of *Man and Time* in 1964. His most recent volumes, erroneously called "cocktail-table books," *The Prince of Pleasure and His Regency 1811-20* (1969), *The Edwardians* (1970), *Victoria's Heyday* (1972), and *The English* (1973), reveal a far-ranging and sympathetic intellect exploring those aspects of human character that individualize a time through an understanding of the people who lived it.

This study, however, has had to be limited to those works that can fairly be called "creative"; that is, some eighty novels and plays from the late 1920s past the 1960s on which Priestley's reputation securely rests, creative writing which explores the social, political, and moral forces at work on his time, and offers as well a provocative theory of time itself. After a look in Chapter 1 at the backgrounds which influence all of Priestley's work and an introduction to his idiosyncratic view of time, Chapters 2 through 8 deal chronologically with the form, content, and themes of the novels. Chapters 9 through 18, again for the most part in chronological order, concentrate on the plays, their style and craft. Wherever possible we have introduced material from the other genres which Priestley has mastered to support an argument or add to an interpretation of a novel or play. Even so, the task has been tremendous, for Priestley, actively writing in his eighties, hardly allows his admirers and his critics to pull abreast of his current output.

We should like to express our gratitude to Mr. Priestley for answering a number of questions that perplexed us, for his graciousness in showing us Kissing Tree House, and, most especially, for a memorable walk through his garden. We should

Preface

also like to express our indebtedness to the Purdue Research Foundation for a grant toward the study of Priestley's drama, and to Cherylynn Knott and Robert Petersen, who helped so much with the entire manuscript. We are also grateful to the following for permission to quote from Priestley's works and from commentararies about those works: William Heinemann Ltd; Heinemann Educational Books Ltd; A. D. Peters and Co. Ltd; Samuel French Ltd; Aldus Books Ltd; David Hughes and Granada Publishing Ltd; as well as Routledge & Kegan Paul Ltd for permission to quote P. D. Ouspensky.

A. A. DeVitis
Albert E. Kalson

West Lafayette, Indiana

Chronology

(Dates of single plays refer to first production; dates of play collections refer to publication)

1894 Born September 13 in Bradford, Yorkshire, England.

1910– Employed by Messers. Helm and Co., Bradford, in the
1914 wool trade.

1914– Duke of Wellington's and Devon Regiments, commis-
1919 sioned lieutenant.

1918 *The Chapman of Rhymes.*

1919– Married Pat Tempest (died 1925); Trinity Hall, Cam-
1922 bridge, B.A.

1922 *Brief Diversions; Papers from Lilliput.*

1923 *I For One.*

1924 *Figures in Modern Literature.*

1925 *The English Comic Characters;* edited *Essayists Past and Present.*

1926 *Talking; George Meredith;* edited *The Book of Bodley Head Verse.* Married Mary Holland Wyndham Lewis (divorced 1952).

1927 *Adam in Moonshine; Benighted; Open House; The English Novel; Thomas Love Peacock.*

1928 *Apes and Angels.*

1929 *Farthing Hall,* with Hugh Walpole; *The Good Companions; The Balconinny; English Humour.*

1930 *Angel Pavement; The Town Major of Miraucourt.*

1931 *The Good Companions,* adaptation with Edward Knoblock.

1932 *Faraway; Dangerous Corner; Self-Selected Essays.*

1932– Forms production company for his own work under the
1938 name English Plays Ltd.

1933 *Albert Goes Through; I'll Tell You Everything,* with Gerald Bullett; *Wonder Hero; The Roundabout; Laburnum Grove.*

1934   *Eden End; Four-in-Hand; English Journey.*

1935   *Duet in Floodlight; Cornelius; Three Plays and a Preface.*

1936   *They Walk in the City; Spring Tide*, under the pseudonym Peter Goldsmith with George Billam; *Bees on the Boat Deck.*

1937   *Mystery at Greenfingers; Time and the Conways; I Have Been Here Before; Two Time Plays; People at Sea; The Bad Samaritan; Midnight on the Desert.*

1938   *Music at Night; When We Are Married;* cofounder of the London Mask Theatre; *The Doomsday Men.*

1939   *Rain Upon Godshill; Johnson Over Jordan; Let the People Sing; Our Nation's Heritage.*

1940   *Britain Speaks; The Long Mirror.*

1940–   B.B.C. "Postscripts" broadcasts; *Postscripts.*
1941

1941   Chairman, Committee on War Aims; *Out of the People.*

1942   *Black-Out in Gretley; Britain at War; Good Night Children.*

1943   *Daylight on Saturday; The Man-Power Story; British Women Go to War; Desert Highway; They Came to a City.*

1944   *Four Plays; Here Are Your Answers; The New Citizen; How Are They at Home?*

1945   *Three Men in New Suits; Three Comedies* (includes *The Golden Fleece*, performed earlier as *Bull Market*).

1946   *Bright Day; Russian Journey; The Secret Dream; Ever Since Paradise.*

1946–   U.K. delegate to UNESCO conferences.
1947

1947   Chairman, International Theatre Conference, Paris; *The Rose and Crown; Three Time Plays; The Arts Under Socialism; Theatre Outlook; The Linden Tree.*

1948   Chairman, International Theatre Conference, Prague; Chairman, British Theatre Conference; *Home Is Tomorrow; The High Toby.*

1948–   *The Plays of J. B. Priestley*, three volumes.
1950

1949   President, International Theatre Institute; *Delight; Summer Day's Dream; The Olymians.*

1950   *Going Up; Bright Shadow; Last Holiday.*

1951   *Festival at Farbridge; Treasure on Pelican.*

1952   *Dragon's Mouth,* with Jacquetta Hawkes.

1953   Married Jacquetta Hawkes; *The Other Place; Private Rooms; Mother's Day; Try It Again.*

1954   *Low Notes on a High Level; The Magicians; A Glass of Bitter; The White Countess.*

1955   *The Writer in a Changing Society; Journey Down a Rainbow,* with Jacquetta Hawkes; *The Scandalous Affair of Mr. Kettle and Mrs. Moon; The Golden Entry.*

1956   *Take the Fool Away.*

1957   *Thoughts in the Wilderness; The Art of the Dramatist; The Glass Cage; Now Let Him Go.*

1958   *Topside, or The Future of England; Doomsday for Dyson.*

1959   *The Story of Theatre.*

1960   *William Hazlitt; Literature and Western Man.*

1961   *Saturn Over the Water; The Thirty-First of June; Charles Dickens.*

1962   *The Shapes of Sleep; Margin Released.*

1963   *The Pavilion of Masks; A Severed Head,* adaptation with Iris Murdoch.

1964   *Sir Michael and Sir George; Man and Time.*

1965–
1967   Member, National Theatre Board.

1965   *Lost Empires.*

1966   *Salt is Leaving; The Moments.*

1967   *It's an Old Country.*

1968   *Out of Town* (Part I of *The Image Men*); *London End* (Part II of *The Image Men*); *Trumpets Over the Sea; Essays of Five Decades; Anyone for Tennis?; All England Listened.*

1969   *The Prince of Pleasure and His Regency, 1811–1820; The Wonderful World of the Theatre; Time and the Conways and Other Plays; When We Are Married and Other Plays; Linda at Pulteney's.*

1970   *The Edwardians;* Doctor of Letters, Bradford University; *Anton Chekhov.*

1971   *Snoggle.*

1972   *Victoria's Heyday; Over the Long High Wall.*

1973   *The English;* Freedom of the City of Bradford.

1974   *Outcries and Asides; The Carfitt Crisis and Two Other*

Stories; A Visit to New Zealand; eightieth birthday celebrations.

1975   *Particular Pleasures.*

1976   *Found, Lost, Found; The Happy Dream; English Humour* revised and expanded.

1977   *Instead of the Trees;* Order of Merit.

CHAPTER 1

Backgrounds

I *Life*

JOHN Boynton Priestley, born on September 13, 1894, in the wool-merchandizing city of Bradford in Yorkshire, has described his career as essayist, novelist, and dramatist in several books of autobiography and recollection: *Midnight on the Desert* in 1937, *Rain Upon Godshill* in 1939, *Margin Released* in 1962, and *Instead of the Trees* in 1977. In *Margin Released,* subtitled *A Writer's Reminiscences and Reflections,* Priestley, while recounting his earliest memories, writes of the sounds and sights and forces that shaped a young man of simple origins into the professional writer who from 1922 to the present time has written over one hundred and fifty books.

Priestley's mother died soon after his birth, and he was reared by a stepmother who defied tradition by being kind and loving. His father, the son of a mill worker, was a schoolmaster devoted to the cause of education. Priestley describes him as "unselfish, brave, honourable, public-spirited . . . the man socialists have in mind when they write about socialism,"[1] a description that applies to Priestley himself.

The early years at Bradford were rich in the discoveries that a sensitive and romantic boy could draw upon to feed an imagination and to people a world later on, and Priestley has relied upon his memories of this season of youth to texture several of his best works. *Bright Day* (1946), for example, recreates the romance and illusion of a pre-World War I time in hues of mellow and elegiac nostalgia. And *The Good Companions* (1929), his first popular novel, as well as *When We Are Married* (1938), his most successful comedy, draw upon his memories of Yorkshire and the Yorkshire character for both scene and character.

17

Life in Bradford was surprisingly full, especially for a boy who dreamed of becoming a writer. The young Jack Priestley went as often as he could to the town's two theaters, which offered everything from *Oedipus Rex* to *The Merry Widow,* and to its two music-halls, where among many comedians he saw Grock and W. C. Fields and Little Tich perform. The plays he could not see he read as a member of the Playgoer's Society and the Arts Club. He attended concerts where he heard Kreisler, Casals, and Bauer; this was the "era of Ysaye and Kubelik, Pachmann and Rachmaninov and Busoni, men who appeared to have more dominating and warmer personalities than the technical perfectionists who came later" (MR, 29). Music subsequently became for the man a passion, one that is reflected in many of the works.

The years before the First World War were for the boy Priestley a period of first love and excitement and discovery best symbolized by Bradford's busy Market Street, with its "metropolitan look, an air of massive opulence . . . its solid buildings of smoke-blackened stone," and the square into which the street opened with "a brightness, a bewildering dazzle, that was a promise of adventure and ultimate triumph" (MR, 19). Just off Market Street was the grand-scale Swan Arcade and the wool office where the boy may have been "the worst junior clerk in the history of the wool trade."[2] There he wrote poetry and short stories into small, handmade notebooks that he perched on his knee as he furtively stole time away from the firm's wool tops and noils in the combination office and sampling room with its own peculiar Dickensian air. Nature also enchanted the youth, especially the Yorkshire Dales and the moors, "only a tuppenny tram-ride away,"[3] where a walk of twenty miles was an habitual weekend recreation.

One of the most important of the intellectual influences to the development of the artist that the boy would become was that of his English master, Richard Pendlebury, "tall, intensely dark, as handsome and commanding as an ideal Spanish grandee" (MR, 6), an appearance Priestley would later employ to describe one of his most striking protagonists, Cosmo Saltana of his large-scale novel *The Image Men* (1968). Pendlebury awakened the boy's interest in literature and encouraged the development of his own unmistakable gift for *writing,* a word the West Riding folk could invest "with a dreadful irony and mockery you had to face like a January east wind," Priestley claims.[4]

The youth defied the wind, and the first published piece for which Priestley received payment—one guinea—appeared in *London Opinion,* a popular weekly (MR, 67). Inspired by the appearance in neighboring Leeds of three young American jazz musicians, the Hedges Brothers and Jacobsen, Priestley's imaginary interview in the form of a topical skit entitled "Secrets of the Ragtime King" impressed his cautious father who, until then, had thought his son's ambitions a bit outlandish since they seemed to have more to do with entertainment than education. As both a congratulatory and conciliatory gesture the elder Priestley offered his son a cigar. For several months in 1913 Priestley regularly contributed a cultural column entitled "Round the Hearth" to *The Bradford Pioneer,* a Labour weekly, and occasionally placed other pieces in periodicals with a national circulation.

In 1915, at twenty, Priestley enlisted in the Duke of Wellington's West Riding Regiment, also known as "The Havercake Lads" and "The Dirty Duke's" (MR, 83). After his indoctrination he was sent to France where, near Souchez, he was wounded and invalided back to England. After his recuperation, in 1917, he applied for and, a year later, received a commission as lieutenant in the Devon Regiment. In France again, he was gassed, then sent to a recuperation depot, which serves as setting for the single fictional piece that deals directly with his experience of the war, the haunting short story entitled "The Town Major of Miraucourt" (1930). Significantly, except in the story and in *Desert Highway* (1943), a play about a lost tank crew in World War II, war does not figure directly in the novels or dramas, yet its influence is pervasive. By and large a romantic, Priestley's world-view may be an attempt to put war and devastation in a proper long-range perspective, an attitude which even marked his eagerly awaited weekly "Postscripts" broadcasts during the Second World War.

At the war's end, Priestley entered Cambridge to study literature, history, and political science, augmenting his ex-army grant by writing pieces for regional and London newspapers. Yet summarizing this period of his life, Priestley writes in *Instead of the Trees,* "The truth is, Bradford from 1911–1914 gave me more than Cambridge did from 1919–1922."[5] His first book, "undergraduate odds and ends" called *Brief Diversions* (1922), received good reviews but did not sell. "Nothing happened," Priestley writes in *Margin Released*. "My career began with an enormous anti-climax" (MR, 144).

Twenty-seven, his army grant running out, Priestley, now married to Pat Tempest, expecting a family, gave up the idea of teaching abroad "in places so small or remote that their currency was never quoted in *The Times*" so that he could not discover what the jobs were worth (MR, 145). Offered some extension work near Bradford, he decided instead to go to London to try his luck at freelance writing with fifty pounds in his pocket.

In London he was given a hand up by J. C. Squire, whom he had met at Cambridge, and he found himself writing for Squire's *London Mercury*. In 1924 he published *Figures in Modern Literature*, a work of criticism, and in 1925 *The English Comic Characters*. In 1926 his study of the Victorian poet-novelist George Meredith appeared, and the following year his study of Thomas Love Peacock. During this period he also wrote for the *Daily News* and became a reader for the Bodley Head. Among the novels he recommended to that press were the early works of Graham Greene and C. S. Forester. Meanwhile, at night, in spare hours, he worked on his first novel, *Adam in Moonshine* (1927). His first play, *Dangerous Corner*, appeared in 1932, following the huge commercial success of *The Good Companions* in 1929, which gave him security and thus the time to turn his attention to the stage. In *The Georgian Literary Scene* (1935) Frank Swinnerton records Priestley's entrance into the literary world of the thirties, summing up a good deal of critical response as he does so: "Before he began to write novels," Swinnerton writes, "he was a reviewer and essayist, and when he first wrote a novel all the critics said it was the novel of an essayist, just as when he first wrote a play all the critics said that it was the play of a novelist."[6]

After a long illness, the first Mrs. Priestley, whom he had married in 1919, died in 1925. A year later he married Mary Holland Wyndham Lewis, from whom he was divorced in 1952. The two marriages produced five children—four daughters and a son. In 1953 he married the distinguished anthropologist Jacquetta Hawkes. Since his early years in Bradford, Priestley has lived in London, and, for a time, on the Isle of Wight; presently he and Mrs. Priestley occupy a lovely Georgian home, Kissing Tree House, in Alveston, just outside Stratford-upon-Avon.

Priestley has traveled widely in Europe and the United States. He has visited Mexico, Africa, the Soviet Union, Australia, and Japan, and he has used his travels not only as backgrounds for his fiction, such as *Faraway* (1932), with its South Seas setting, but also as the basis for some of his most challenging and cogent works. His *English Journey* (1934), for example, a masterpiece of its kind, recounts his impressions of England in the throes of economic depression, while *Midnight on the Desert* and *Rain Upon Godshill* record his observations of the United States, and the more recent *A Visit to New Zealand* (1974) considers "two remote islands" as an outpost of European civilization.[7]

Throughout his life Priestley has not merely written about man's responsibility to his fellows; he has demonstrated his commitment to community. Together with his second wife he ran a hostel for evacuated children during World War II. After the war he campaigned vigorously for nuclear disarmament, and he has served as UNESCO delegate. A long-standing belief that the establishment of a National Theatre could "do little for the general theatrical activity of the country,"[8] that government subsidy should be divided equally among a number of companies, did not prevent him from serving on its board once such a theater was founded; realizing, however, that the board was consulted more frequently on financial matters than on artistic policy, the area in which he could contribute, he resigned the position after a year. Having refused a knighthood and a life-peerage in the past—"I started as J. B. Priestley and I'll finish as J. B. Priestley," he says[9]—in 1977 he accepted membership, restricted to twenty-four persons, in the Order of Merit. But perhaps he is even prouder of the conferment upon him in 1973 of the Freedom of the City shortly before his native city lost its authority to award such honors under a redistricting plan. Savoring the ironic implications, Priestley says, "I am the last Freeman of Bradford."[10]

II *Priestley on Time*

World War I brought the destruction of a generation, and Priestley has ever since been haunted by a world that was, or, perhaps, a world that has never been. Despite his subsequent disclaimer, "For every ounce of nostalgia and longing in my work there are several pounds of humorous realism,"[11] a slightly imbalanced personal view, biographer Susan Cooper suggests that "a longing for the way things could be . . . a sense of the unfulfilled capabilities of man" infuses his work and "is woven closely into his recurrent fascination with the nature of Time."[12] That sense of loss was partially assuaged by a reading of J. W. Dunne's *An Experiment with Time* (1927) which fueled his own thoughts on the coexistence of all time in one time as he pondered man's mortality. Priestley has frequently acknowledged that Dunne's theories, and, to a lesser extent, the time-recurrence theory formulated by P. D. Ouspensky in *A New Model of the Universe* (1931), are motivating factors in his own works. Their concepts influence the structure as well as the themes of his plays, notably *Time and the Conways* and *I Have Been Here Before* (both 1937), and are pervasive to the novels as well, especially *The Magicians* (1954). While many readers and theatergoers have obviously relished the work without knowledge of Priestley's theories on the subject of time, no student of Priestley can fully comprehend the novels and plays without sharing their author's interpretation of Dunne's and Ouspensky's quasi-scientific philosophies.

In *Midnight on the Desert,* Priestley reveals that in 1937 he had already considered writing a book on the subject of time even though his qualifications were "magnificently inadequate." He wanted to undertake the task, he writes, "to see what would happen to me in that dark forest of speculation. . . . For several years I had had a hunch . . . that this problem of Time was the particular riddle that the Sphinx has set for this age of ours, that it was like a great barrier across our way and we were all squabbling and shouting and moaning in its shadow, and that if it could be solved there might follow a wonderful release and expansion of the human spirit."[13] A fantasy by E. A. Abbott published in 1884 had piqued his curiosity and even confirmed some of his speculations. *Flatland: A Romance of Many Dimensions* is an ironical tale about a two-dimensional square in a world called Flatland. The square meets a stranger, a three-dimensional sphere, who tells him about his own three-dimensional world: "The two-dimensional creature is bewildered by the three-dimensional one, who has the power of moving in a new and inconceivable direction, and also the power of seeing everything that is happening in Flatland because he has only to look down on its two-dimensional plane to possess all its secrets" (MD, 249). Priestley presses the analogy:

We can read with sympathy the account of the Flatlander who suddenly found himself in Spaceland, because lately we have begun to see ourselves as spacelanders who have been granted a vision of Space-Timeland. We are beings with a three-dimensional outlook who are called upon to make sense out of a fourth dimension . . . compelled to regard the shape of things along their fourth dimension as a series of changes in Time. I could understand, though not very clearly perhaps, that what we call Time—or part of what we call Time—might be simply our mode of apprehending a fourth dimension. . . . In other words, we never see things as they really are, but see a series of three-dimensional cross-sections of them. Our minds cannot conceive the other dimension except as movement, change, the flow of Time. (MD, 249–51)

In 1964 Priestley finally wrote the book he had been thinking about for so many years: *Man and Time,* a highly personal consideration of man's view of time through the ages, his understanding, and his misunderstanding of time based on scientific theory and fanciful conjecture, as well as its handling in literature. The work contains a succinct statement of Priestley's distress with and distrust of the too-limiting conventional view of the reality of time:

Common sense still tells us that everything is real only when it is Now, in the present moment. Whatever is not-Now does not exist. Reality is served to us in these thin slices of Nows. . . . And common sense . . . has settled down with the notion that everything is real only when it is Now, so let the world keep on destroying and re-creating itself every fraction of a second or so. . . .
    There is an opposite view. . . . Everything is solidly there, whether we call it past, present, or future. We experience things in time because our Now, so to speak, goes steadily forward, as if we were traveling through a dark landscape with a searchlight, or we were staring at a bright scene through a slit in a moving barrier. We invent Time to explain change and succession. We try to account for it out there in the world we are observing, but soon run into trouble because it is not out there at all. It comes with the traveling searchlight, the moving slit. . . . There is, however, one snag. How can the searchlight, the moving slit, steadily revealing what we call the present, be manipulated to light up, to offer a slitful, of the future so much further on or of the past that has been left behind? If Time is really our name for this steady forward movement of consciousness over the fixed scene, then what are we going to call this jumping about?[14]

Priestley first discovered some answers to his questions in a book which both stimulated and stretched his imagination. Published in 1927 by J. W. Dunne, "a hard-headed military engineering type, whose hobby was not fantastic speculation and juggling with ideas but fly-fishing," *An Experiment with Time* enabled Priestley "to escape from the bondage of chronological time" (MT, 245). The designer of Britain's first military aircraft, Dunne began to speculate about time after some disturbing dreams convinced him that he was experiencing precognition, a foreknowledge of future events *"displaced in Time."*[15] His experiments and investigations led him to believe that his own experiences were by no means unique, that all men have past and future time revealed to them in the distortion of dreams, but "the waking mind refuses point-blank to accept the association between the dream and the subsequent event."[16] Since Priestley too had experienced *déjà vu,* had himself had some startling dreams which seemed to come true, he was intrigued by Dunne's revelations which comprise the easy-to-grasp first part of the work and persevered through the more complicated, somewhat abstruse theorizing of the rest.

For Priestley's readers, what finally matters is Priestley's own interpretation of the basic theory. Dunne believes, Priestley explains,

that each of us is a series of observers existing in a series of Times. To Observer One, our ordinary fully-awake sharp selves, the fourth dimension appears as Time. To Observer Two, which is the self we know in dreams when the first observer is not functioning, the fifth dimension would appear as Time. This second observer has a four-dimensional outlook, and this fact explains the fantastic scenery and action characteristic of dreams, in which everything seems to be so fluid. . . . Dunne says this is because we try to interpret in our ordinary three-dimensional fashion these strange images gathered by our four-dimensional selves. . . . Now Dunne holds that the dreaming self, now moving Time Two, has a wide length of Time One, the fourth dimension, stretched before it, and so contrives to telescope into the fantastic narratives of dream both images from the Past and *images from the Future.* (MD, 253–54)

One reason that the theory, Serialism as Dunne calls it, may appeal to Priestley is its provision for immortality: Observer One may die in Time One but still live within Observer Two in Time

Two and so on. Another reason may be Dunne's concentration on self-consciousness as well as on time: "There had always been something bewildering to me about the idea of self-consciousness. We observe something, and we are conscious of our observation, and we are conscious of the observation of the observation, and so forth" (MD, 252). But it is the "and so ons" and the "and so forths" which create problems, for Dunne requires for both self-consciousness and time a regressive series; "that is," in Priestley's words, a "series beginning with a unique first term, and then going off into infinity with all their terms in identical relations with each other" (MD, 253). This aspect of Serialism, the regression to infinity, Priestley cannot accept:

There is no such infinity of selves. Self-consciousness does not lead to an infinite regress. . . .
There is Self 1, which, because we are self-conscious, is always an object. There is Self 2, which may be a subject or an object. This self observes Self 1, but can be in its turn observed by Self 3. This last self is never an object; there is no other self to observe it; we can put Self 3 on paper, as I am doing now, but we are not in practice aware of our own Self 3; it is ultimate. (MT, 253–54)

And Priestley notes that all of Dunne's detailed accounts of the workings of his theory "were confined to the first three terms of the regress: Times 1, 2, and 3; Observers 1, 2, and 3. They were in fact all he needed" (MT, 256).[17]

Despite parting company with Dunne on this point, Priestley nevertheless insists on giving him his due: "He opened a way, and, whatever my reservations may be, I think it is the right way . . . because he rejects the idea . . . that our lives are completely contained by chronological uni-dimensional time" (MT, 245). Yet there was still another aspect of Serialism which left him ill at ease: the possibility of intervention. If man experiences precognition, can see the future, he has the possibility of intervening to change that future. Yet Dunne theorizes that precognition is possible because of a time plane in which past, present, and future coexist. If man changes his fate, intervenes in his own future, what had he seen in his precognitive dreams? Can dreams reveal alternatives to the future? Dunne's theory paradoxically posits a fixed universe offering alternatives, supporting at once the case for free will and the case for determination (MD, 266–67).

By chance or by some grand design, Priestley found in a bookshop in Santa Barbara the work that might help him out of the maze, *A New Model of the Universe* by P. D. Ouspensky, "a Russian journalist, author, lecturer, who had some acquaintance with the sciences and mathematics but was chiefly interested in what he called 'the miraculous'" (MT, 265). Reading the book in Death Valley, a setting as intriguing as the work itself, Priestley was immediately drawn into the extraordinary world of the Russian mystic.

What first attracted him is Ouspensky's belief "that Time, like Space, has three dimensions, and only three" (MD, 273), thus avoiding Dunne's troublesome regression to infinity:

The three dimensions of time can be regarded as the continuation of the dimensions of space, i.e. as the "fourth," the "fifth" and the "sixth" dimensions of space. . . . Time is the boundary of our senses. Six-dimensional space is reality, the world as it is. This reality we perceive only through the slit of our senses, touch and vision, and define as three-dimensional space. . . . Every six-dimensional body becomes for us a three-dimensional body *existing in time,* and the properties of the fifth and the sixth dimensions remain for us imperceptible.[18]

The fourth dimension presents man with his line of conventional time. The fifth dimension, forming a surface in relation to that line, is eternity, not unending movement along the line, but a perpetual now. More startling is the sixth dimension, or the final third dimension of time:

The sixth dimension will be the line of the actualisation of other possibilities which were contained in the preceding moment but were not actualised in "time." . . . But these possibilities are actualised in the sixth dimension, which is an aggregate of "all times." . . .
Until now we have taken all the lines of the fourth, the fifth and the sixth dimensions as straight lines, as coordinates. But we must remember that these straight lines cannot be regarded as really existing. They are merely an imaginary system of coordinates for determining the spiral. (O, 429–30)

"The moving finger writes," comments Priestley. "But Ouspensky would say that the moving finger goes on writing the same thing over and over again, and can be induced to change a word or two" (MD, 275), for, according to the most novel aspect of the theory, time's wavelike movement allows for eternal

recurrence. The line of the fourth dimension is circular. It returns to its starting point; therefore, a man dies only to be born again. But Ouspensky's recurrence must not be confused either with Nietzsche's eternal return or with reincarnation. Man dies because his time ends. Future life requires a tomorrow, but there is no tomorrow after death—no time, no after. Eternity, however, demands repetition. Life ends and begins; time ends and begins:

This means that if a man was born in 1877 and died in 1912, then, having died, he finds himself again in 1877 and must live the same life all over again. In dying, in completing the circle of life, he enters the same life from the other end. He is born again. . . . He will make the same mistakes, laugh and cry in the same way, rejoice and suffer in the same way. And when the time comes he will die in exactly the same way as he did before, and again at the moment of his death it will be as though all the clocks were put back to 7.35 a.m. on the 2nd September 1877, and from this moment started again with their usual movement. (O, 477)

Ouspensky, however, allows for intervention through the possibility of inner development, a modification to his basic theory of recurrence which, as Priestley understands it, is the most intriguing part of the entire work: "Some people, those comfortable creatures of custom we all know, live identically the same lives over and over again. Others, such as madmen, suicides, criminals, go through the same tragic performance with a dwindling inner life until at last there is nothing vital left in them. . . . A few, the esoteric élite, learn to live, evolve properly, and so finally, in some mysterious fashion, turn the circle into a spiral, and escape" (MD, 276-277). Ouspensky writes, "Evolution. . .is connected with recollections. . . .The evolving individual remembers, although vaguely, his previous lives. But as evolution means escaping from the wheel of the fifth dimension and passing into the spiral of the sixth dimension, recollection has importance only when it bears an active character in a certain definite direction, when it creates discontent with what exists and a longing for new ways" (O,485).

If *I Have Been Here Before*, Priestley's play directly based on Ouspensky's ideas of recurrence and intervention, explains rather than dramatizes, *Time and the Conways*, the work most closely associated with Dunne, is Priestley's most successful rendering of theory into literature and better exemplifies his method. The world of his own past is revisited and infused with an awareness of the effects of time on all men, and Priestley brings that understanding to all of his work. Yet neither biographical details nor obsessive ideas dominate that work. Instead, they form the focus through which a writer, demonstrating his own humanity, views a world around him.

"In half a century of professional authorship," Priestley writes, "I have never spent ten minutes planning a literary career or even wondering about one."[19] The author of scores of books has had little time to plan. For J. B. Priestley, to live is to write: "When you get to my age, if you stop writing you may die," he told an interviewer shortly before his eightieth birthday.[20] But for those readers who seek only the man and his obsessions in his work, who believe "that real literature . . . is indeed more or less disguised autobiography," he offers some words of caution: "The fiction and drama that last longest come to us out of larger-than-life and not out of neurotic odder-than-life. They are born of imaginative breadth and generosity and not of do-it-yourself psycho-therapy. They are created when the ego is forgotten and not when it dominates the scene."[21] What follows is a study of a writer who has over the years proven himself a professional in the best sense of the word, and has himself stated, "Whatever else I have written, I have to be considered first in terms of my plays and novels and the vast distances they have travelled."[22]

CHAPTER 2

The Novels: Themes and Directions

A NY assessment of fiction written in the twentieth century must inevitably be made against the accomplishments of such masters of the form as James Joyce, Virginia Woolf, D. H. Lawrence, Joseph Conrad, Henry James, and William Faulkner. J. B. Priestley has written no novel equal in intellectual capacity to *Ulysses* (1922), no novel illustrative of the intuitive faculty equal to *To the Lighthouse* (1927), no novel displaying the pulse of the body and its urges equal to *The Rainbow* (1915), no novel of moral and ethical concern equal to either *The Secret Agent* (1907) or *The Golden Bowl* (1905), no novel displaying the mythical dimensions of sin and redemption equal to *The Sound and the Fury* (1929) or *Light in August* (1932). In more than thirty novels, however, Priestley has in his own way contributed both pleasure and knowledge to at least two generations of novel readers. His place in the scale of literary achievement may be lower than Joyce's and Faulkner's, but by and large his audience has been vaster, and it has been both appreciative of and grateful for his contributions not only to the novel but also to the literature of our times. Today it is difficult to imagine with what enthusiasm his novels and plays and essays were received in the thirties and the forties, or with what gratefulness his radio broadcasts were listened to during the period of the Second World War. Colin Wilson calls these broadcasts "magnificent stuff—patriotic without being jingoistic, propaganda in the very best sense of the word."[1] And he adds that these talks made Priestley as great a hero as Winston Churchill.

Styles change and tastes alter, and Priestley is as a novelist in many ways of and for his time, the 1930s—which may account for the fact that his achievement has been largely neglected by the more intellectually oriented critics. No Priestley novel makes its way with any regularity into syllabuses for courses on the

29

English novel, with the possible exception of *Angel Pavement* (1930), which can be still read as an excellent example of romantic realism. It may be quite simply that Priestley has gone out of fashion, along with such early contemporaries of his as H. G. Wells, Hugh Walpole, and Arnold Bennett. Yet his achievement as a novelist is staggering. In *The Novel Now* Anthony Burgess points out that Walter Allen makes no room for Priestley in his *Tradition and Dream*, putting the omission down to the fact that Priestley makes no experiments in his novels, preferring to leave experimentation for his drama—an observation not altogether true. Burgess more correctly points out that Priestley contents himself in his fiction with a no-nonsense, nonintellectual approach to life and concludes that "it would be foolish to disregard his achievement and make little of his vast creative energy."[2]

Priestley's novels, in effect, do not lend themselves to critical exegesis. Their themes are straightforward, their procedures for the most part uncomplicated, the characters immediately recognizable as types rather than as "round" projections of life in the Forsterian sense. But there are exceptions to this general rule. *Bright Day* (1946), Priestley's finest novel, for example, indicates both experimentation in form and roundedness of character; and it employs music and memory as constitutive symbols that give the activities of the novel both resonance and texture. And *Daylight on Saturday* (1943), a novel very much for and of its time, makes equally startling use of stream of consciousness and related techniques for which other novelists have been lavishly praised. Ivor Brown correctly points out that for the critic Priestley is indeed a bad subject: "All his life he has read widely and absorbed rapidly; but other writers' ideas and methods, however much appreciated, may affect, but do not dominate, his own. A man of such various gifts and such multifarious practice in the arts belongs to no 'school.' He creates, and recreates, in his own way. Classifications do not contain him. He is immensely, unquenchably, himself."[3]

There are in fact only a handful of critical books on Priestley's novels, and the best of these are David Hughes's *J. B. Priestley: An Informal Study of his Work* (1958), and Susan Cooper's *J. B. Priestley: Portrait of an Author* (1970). These studies of the novels, and the plays, are largely complimentary, yet they do propose proper critical emphases toward an assessment of

Priestley's accomplishment. Colin Wilson has pointed out that Priestley belongs to the great tradition of the English novel, along with Dickens, Trollope, Meredith, Thomas Hardy, and Arnold Bennett. And he adds that, like Dickens, Priestley is "immensely interested" in certain things, certain people, and certain places, especially his native Bradford and the Yorkshire character: "You have only to read *The Good Companions . . .* to realize that Bradford means as much to Priestley as 'Combray' did to Proust."[4] High praise indeed.

The best criticism of his works, however, is that made by the author himself. In such books of autobiography and critical statement as *Midnight on the Desert, Rain Upon Godshill,* and *Margin Released,* Priestley has indicated clearly and forcefully what he intended in his novels, why the techniques that he attempted either failed or succeeded. In commenting on the quality of his novels, Priestley reveals himself very much a traditional critic, knowledgeable of the fiction and drama of the past; and he reveals this wisdom in his witty and erudite treatment of literature, *Literature and Western Man,* which was published in 1960, one of his finest books.

In some ways Priestley's achievement—in *Midnight on the Desert* he admits a wish "to be an all-round man of letters on the 18th Century plan"[5]—comprising over thirty novels, forty plays, and at least twoscore more publications which include books of reminiscence, collections of short stories and essays, travel books and edited works, such as those on Dickens and the Edwardians, seems to have been lost in the shadows of Bloomsbury and Joyce's Dublin, and absorbed in the aftermath of revived interest in the works of Conrad, Lawrence, Ford Madox Ford, and others. His reputation seems to have declined not only along with those of Bennett and Wells, but also with those of Chesterton and Belloc, Walpole, and even to an extent that of Aldous Huxley. Yet Priestley has continued, indeed continues, to write, as a glance at his bibliography will prove; and in the 1960s he published at least a dozen works, among which are some of his most "modern" novels. It is true that he does not aim his fiction at professors of literature—he seems to have a friendly contempt for them, perhaps because he himself might have become one—or at coteries; and he is not the least bit interested in novels that make the agony of novel-writing their chief concern. The antiroman and the novel of so-called "metafiction" in no way interest him;

rather his interests are the roman policier, as reflected in *Salt is Leaving* (1966), and the satirical comedy, his long novel of 1968, *The Image Men*, serving as an example.

In *Midnight on the Desert*, Priestley answers those critics who maintain that his novels have been largely works of reporting, and he states: "They may well be right when they hint that the higher, grander, subtler forms of imaginative writing are quite beyond me; I have never made any great claims myself for my fiction, beyond protesting once or twice that there might be a little more in it than met the top-speed reviewer's eye, and that because I wrote one jolly, hearty popular novel [*The Good Companions*] it does not follow that everything I have written since is exactly the same" (7-8). He adds that he has always had a genuine interest in all forms of literature and in the technical problems that writing involves. He has indeed become in the twentieth century a modern counterpart of the eighteenth-century man of letters, although he publicly has lamented the fact that the English language does not have an equivalent of the French "maître," which he would prefer. Only Graham Greene approaches him in exhibiting variety as well as quality of performance.

In his novels Priestley more often than not portrays a romantic view of life, a view which inevitably colors his characters and transforms his fictions into either fantasies, detective stories, novels of social criticism, or comic adventures. Even in some of his darker works, *Angel Pavement* and *Black-Out in Gretley* (1942), for example, the sympathetic imagination is forcefully at work. When he is said to reflect Dickens in his novels, Priestley bristles, feeling that his novels more rightly belong with those of Fielding and demonstrate the tone of the romantic essayist William Hazlitt, "whom I read with passion in my early years."[6] Yet the comparison with Dickens is appropriate, for no writer of our time demonstrates in the same way an enthusiasm and delight that peoples an eccentric and yet recognizable world. One of Dickens's best-loved works is his *Pickwick Papers* (1836-37), a book distinguished by a kindly view of the comic vagaries of life but a view that denies neither aberrant human conduct nor the grotesque attitudes that the human personality can demonstrate. Priestley's *The Good Companions* is like *Pickwick Papers* in that it too portrays a gallery of caricatures and rogues, as lovingly, as charitably.

Yet Priestley is correct: an influence more persuasive than Dickens on his created world and on his world-view, but one more difficult to limit, is that of English Romanticism generally, and of William Wordsworth specifically.

In his Preface to *Lyrical Ballads*, Wordsworth speaks of the necessity that the poet feels to produce immediate pleasure, that the production of such pleasure should not be considered a degradation of his art; and he continues: "It is an acknowledgement of the beauty of the universe, an acknowledgement more sincere, because not formal, but indirect; it is a task light and easy to him who looks at the world in a spirit of love: further, it is a homage paid to the naked dignity of man, to the grand elementary principle of pleasure, by which he knows, and feels, and lives, and moves."[7] While not a poet, Priestley in his novels approaches the poet's ground. His chief aim is to look upon man in a spirit of love and compassion, but he does not always do so indirectly. At times his romantic attitude betrays him into sentimentality, but it also justifies the happy ending that characterizes the majority of the novels. More importantly, it helps to define the many themes that the novels attempt to portray and the kinds of novels upon which Priestley attempts to impress his imagination.

In the third stanza of "The Solitary Reaper" Wordsworth categorizes the two great subject matters of romance:

> Will no one tell me what she sings?
> Perhaps the plaintive numbers flow
> For old, unhappy far-off things,
> And battles long ago:
> Or is it some more humble lay,
> Familiar matter of today?
> Some natural sorrow, loss, or pain,
> That has been, and may be again?

The "old, unhappy far-off things, / And battles long ago" describe both the historical novel and, to a lesser extent, the Gothic romance. In the historical aspect of romantic literature Priestley demonstrates an academic interest. *Adam in Moonshine*, his first novel, is in many ways a spoof of the historical novel, Thackeray's *Henry Esmond* (1852) in particular; both *Adam in Moonshine* and *Henry Esmond* are concerned with the Stuart return to the English throne. Here Priestley handles the aspects of the historical romance farcically; the disguises, assumed identities, and outlandishly conceived confrontations are superb comic commentaries on the form. Yet the vibrant enthusiasm and the vitality centering on the chase are the more important aspects of the whole.

More significant perhaps is the Gothic influence on Priestley, and some of his best works are in that tradition; *Benighted* (1927), his second novel, in part spoofs Charlotte Brontë's *Jane Eyre* (1847), until the farce gives way to the psychological demands of characterization and to the sheer excitement of the confrontation between a madman and a jaded romantic. *The Doomsday Men* (1938) and *Saturn Over the Water* (1961) portray science outlandishly, yet convincingly, in its man-made-monster attributes, while *The Magicians* (1954) and *Jenny Villiers* (1947), in a way unique to Priestley, recreate the past in order to make the present viable.

The desire to recreate the past in several novels modulates into the desire to escape into the faraway and the exotic, which is what *Faraway* (1932) succeeds in doing. There the allure of Tahiti, the Marquesas, Easter Island, itself a barren vestige of a mysterious yesterday, Ozymandias-like, is given full reign in an unlikely adventure that brings its central character back to England and to the ease and complacency of middle-class suburban life.

But escape in Priestley's fictional universe is not to be found only in a search for hidden treasures in the South Pacific; romance can also be found at home, in England, the "familiar matter of today" of Wordsworth's poem. And this is the area in which Priestley's imagination spreads itself to create some of his most remarkable works. The familiar, everyday world of the small town, with its pubs and clubs, and most of all with its theaters, provides the setting for the discovery of enchantment as rich as any that Tahiti affords. And this occasions Priestley's great theme—England, beneath whose surface romance and mystery lie at hand, if the seeker can only realize that true enchantment lies within the self; that enchantment transforms into meaningful existence the mundane activities of life. The deep-down freshness that lies beneath the everyday is the theme that distinguishes Priestley's comic epics, chiefly *The Good Companions* and *Festival at Farbridge* (1951), the former his best-known novel, the latter one of his largest and most satisfying canvases.

The romantic imagination also, to a degree, shapes the characterization, for Priestley's best-drawn portraits are of those who are aware of themselves as creatures of enchantment. Adam in *Adam in Moonshine* realizes that the magic of his adventure is that with which he endows it. And Baron Roland is, as is Commodore Tribe of *Festival at Farbridge,* like Falstaff, a giver of life. There are god-figures and devil figures in many of the tales, figures ordering, determining, defining the essential nature of experience. And at times a sinister aspect is allowed to assume control of the portrait of the charismatic character; yet the portrayal of evil in Priestley's novels is never as convincing as is the portrayal of good.

The romantic impulse also helps to define Priestley's women; and there are two types which figure prominently in his fiction, the anima figure and the maiden. Of the two, the seductress, a contemporary *belle dame sans merci,* is the less convincing, perhaps because Priestley does not attempt to more than minimally characterize her. She is the Countess Nadia Slatina of *Saturn Over the Water:* "The old original wicked lady from a far countree. She wasn't at all lusciously sexy, the pêche Melba type; that would have been too easy. It wasn't the flesh in sex but the devil in it that she suggested, one ruined spirit to another. . . . She spoke rather slowly in a low seductive voice, and could ask for a match as if she was about to give you the key of her turret in the castle."[8] She is also the Countess Helga of *It's an Old Country* (1967) who laughs at Tom Adamson when he realizes that she is merely an ordinary woman and not the mysterious enchantress into which his romantic nature has transformed her.

The maidens generally are more successfully portrayed in the novels than are the anima figures; yet they are like the *femmes fatales* in that they are largely unbelievable as "round" characters. They are pert, ingenuous, stubborn, capricious, lovely; they insist that they are aware of their sexuality, but they remain unconvincing as they protest their knowledge of the ways of the world. They are perhaps more convincing in such frolics as *Low Notes on a High Level* (1954) than in the larger, more seriously conceived works. Their sexuality, necessary primarily because of the happy endings that Priestley is given to, becomes a matter of social convenience and fictional necessity. For in Priestley's fictional world the happy ending presupposes a marriage, as it does in the novels of Jane Austen. Both the seductress and the maiden are better portrayed when their derivation from romantic convention is permitted to show through the plot and the action of the pieces in which they appear. In other words, they succeed better as symbolical characters. There are, however, two remarkable exceptions to this general rule: Freda Pinnel of *Daylight on Saturday*, and Maggie Culworth of *Salt is Leaving*. The young Rosalia Arnaldos of *Saturn Over the Water* is, however, no more convincing than is her older counterpart, Elfreda Drake, of *The Image Men*, and they are both more typical. In that novel, however, Primrose East, former model, is a delightful example of Priestley parodying himself. Although she is a fantasy figure for many of the young men in the novel, she herself falls for the false glamour of a useless young man, and she awakens to reality in time to be saved from a "happy" marriage.

The romantic imagination also colors some of Priestley's most unsuccessful efforts in the novel form: *Wonder Hero* (1933) and *They Walk in the City* (1936). These pieces go wrong chiefly because the fairy tale does not coalesce with or successfully counterpoint the social criticism, which is handled heavily, as the conviction behind the presentation reduces to dogmatic and aggressive assertions that the evil of the world corrupts the innocent and the good; noble children are defiled by a corrupt society.

The desire to be free in society is, however, one of Romanticism's greatest concerns, as it is Priestley's. Freedom from want, freedom from too much government control, freedom to discover the human potential, freedom from fear and coercion: these are themes that lend stature to all of Priestley's novels without exception, and most especially to those in which England seems to be a final repository of the free spirit in the world. *Let the People Sing* (1939) serves as an example. Yet even this great admiration for England modulates as Priestley moves from the romantic ardor of the late twenties that characterizes *Adam in Moonshine* into the fuller awareness of the giant destructive potential in the hands of power maniacs after World War II. These maniac figures may not, in fact, be too far removed from the evil magi of Gothic convention. In *It's an Old Country*

Tom Adamson, unlike several of his predecessors, decides to put his trust in the world, rather than in England.

Even Priestley's concern with the nature of experience in time, to which he gives a semiscientific scaffolding through reliance on the time theories of J. W. Dunne, can be explained as a romantic manifestation. The ability to transcend present time is an integral aspect of the romantic agony, and its successful representation is called a "time spot" or "epiphany," depending on which critic one happens to read. To see, as Wordsworth puts it in the "Simplon Pass" episode of "The Prelude," the forms of nature as the "types and symbols of eternity" is also Priestley's concern. And he too, like the great romantics, believes in amelioration, learning through mistakes how to form a better future.

It has already been mentioned that Priestley in his fiction portrays in what can be called modern humanistic terms an essentially optimistic world view. In politics this reduces to what he calls "Liberal Socialism." He appears to be convinced of the inherent goodness of the race, of its potential to make a better world. And it is to this end that he employs his most forceful character, the god-figure, who is portrayed as the organizer, the master of ceremonies, or the celebrant. This is by no means to say that Priestley is unaware of the threat of power, the allure of evil; indeed almost capriciously he gives his reader his clearest statement of the fascination of evil in one of his thrillers, *Saturn Over the Water*, in which he portrays a power cult determined to enslave and destroy. Yet salvation, the novel insists, is possible if men join together to project their desire for tolerance and harmony through a common cause.

And it is this aspect of human understanding that marks his major plot device: more often than not he throws people of different backgrounds and classes together into a common endeavor, and democratic action follows as a result. The plots of the majority of his novels employ the common cause, and it is shown to be merely emblematic of the desire of the many to live in harmony and tolerance.

Priestley's fiction falls naturally into three major categories. The first is that of the seriously conceived and executed novel, which employs symbolical structures and attempts characterization of depth. The best novel of this group is *Bright Day*. The second category can be termed the thriller or entertainment, which is short on believable characterization but long on suspense and puzzle. The best example of this group is *Saturn Over the Water*. The third is the frolic, or lighthearted satirical romp. Farce, pace, imagination distinguish this category, and one of the best of many excellent romps is *Sir Michael and Sir George* (1964).

CHAPTER 3

First Efforts

BETWEEN 1927, the year of the publication of his first novel, *Adam in Moonshine*, and the present time, J. B. Priestley has been responsible for the appearance of over thirty novels. Besides those novels for which he is sole author, Priestley has collaborated with Hugh Walpole in *Farthing Hall* (1929) and with Gerald Bullett in *I'll Tell You Everything* (1933). He has also, in a sense, collaborated with Ruth Holland, who has written the novelized versions of the plays *Dangerous Corner* (1933) and *Laburnum Grove* (1936), and with L. W. Taylor, who has also "retold" *Laburnum Grove* (1941).

Any attempt to characterize J. B. Priestley's achievement in the novel must, however, rest primarily on those works for which he is solely responsible and must begin with an evaluation of his first novel, *Adam in Moonshine*, a romantic escapade reminiscent of the lighthearted adventures of G. K. Chesterton no longer popular today. *Adam in Moonshine* reveals Priestley as an essentially romantic writer, yet one whose imagination is tempered by an awareness of the more desperate activities of life.

I Adam in Moonshine

Priestley describes his first novel in *Margin Released*, one of several books of autobiographical and critical reminiscences, as "all fine writing and nonsense, a little coloured trial balloon . . . [that] moves stiffly, creaking with self-consciousness."[1] Written at night, after the labors of a strenuous day of journalistic work, *Adam in Moonshine* is an attempt on the artist's part to come to terms with the demands of narrative form as well as with the essential imaginative qualities that form will embody.

The adventure, "half poetry and half lovely farce," as the protagonist Adam Stewart will label it toward the novel's end,

39

describes an outlandish plot to restore the Stuarts to the English throne. But the plot in itself, as Adam realizes from the moment that he sees the lovely girls, with whom he will soon be involved, boarding the train at St. Pancras Station, is less important than the spirit of romance which subsumes it. The reviewer for the *Times Literary Supplement* upon the publication of the novel rightfully assessed the book as a "piece of high spirits" needing to be read in "a not too critical mood." He complained, however, that the narrative was too often marred by the author's intervention into the escapades of his central character. He found Adam's personal reflections "so richly indulged in that some readers will feel a little cloyed."[2] But it is precisely Adam's predilection for introspection that makes the novel interesting to a contemporary reader and critic; for in the definition of Adam's character can be seen the basis for much of the characterization of Priestley's later protagonists. Adam's imagination is a compound of romantic illusion and a practical awareness of the limitations of romance; and he realizes that the romance and illusion that he savors is largely in himself. Toward the novel's end, recalling his marvelous adventure with the girl Peter over the Yorkshire Dales, Adam tells himself:

Everything . . . was just beginning, but now he had a sudden premonition that everything was soon to end too, that these very moments now shredding away were those above all others that he would return to in wonder once they had grouped themselves, radiant in lost sunshine, in his remembrance.[3]

No two novels could be less alike in form and theme than *Adam in Moonshine* and Evelyn Waugh's *Brideshead Revisited* (1945); yet both Waugh and Priestley present the same romantic awareness of the wonder of life in the characters of Sebastian Flyte and Adam Stewart. Sebastian as he lives his Arcadian interlude in the company of his teddy bear Aloysius and his friend Charles Ryder is fully aware of the moment of happiness, its evanescence, and he wishes that he could bury the moment, at the end of a rainbow, to be unearthed in later years as proof that once there did exist a time of grace and beauty. Essentially a romantic doctrine, "food for future thought" is precisely that which Adam is most aware of as he moves into the richly textured pathways of romance and self-discovery.

Mistaken at St. Pancras for the returning prince—the similarity between Adam Stewart and the prince who never appears being one of surname only—young Adam soon finds himself involved with a strange group of mysterious conspirators who call themselves Companions of the Rose. The leader of the group is Baron Roland, large, affable, a trifle sinister, a combination of Shakespeare's Falstaff and Wilkie Collins's Count Fosco. Baron Roland has organized a group of dilettantes, Scots millionaires, and leisured aristocrats into the society which has gathered for an important occasion in a stately country house in a remote section of the North Country. Attracted to the lovely young girls Peter and Helen, who are themselves involved in the adventure for its romance, Adam enters wholeheartedly into the intrigue but finds that he is challenged not only by his awareness of its preposterous demands, but also by Inspector Hake of Scotland Yard and his associates, Ruddell and Siddell. Adam's attempts to enter fully into the romantic adventure are challenged by the outrageous and farcical attempts of the policemen to use him, yet outwit him. Disguises, assumed identities, misleading clues, false beards, all the elements of farce are introduced into the action to counterpoint and heighten the illusion and gaiety of the escapade.

Adam soon finds himself in love with Helen Maythorn, only to discover at the adventure's conclusion that she is married. But married or not, she is the stuff of Adam's dream, the sweet cheat who will soon dissolve into the vapors of memory, never to be forgotten, always to be cherished, even though the Companions of the Rose suffer a loss of dreams when they are apprehended by the police on the very eve of the triumphant return of their prince. She is, of course, the anima figure who reappears in various guises in the majority of the novels. Baron Roland throws Adam and Helen his briefcase at the moment that Inspector Hake and his disguised subordinates arrest the conspirators; they flee over the dales in Helen's car, open the briefcase, only to discover that it contains a ham sandwich, which they gratefully eat. If *Adam in Moonshine* does not fully succeed in combining romance and farce, it is still nevertheless a remarkable work, for it all but succeeds in combining the two modes; it is indeed an attempt of great merit for a first novel.

As important as Adam's romantic nature to a consideration of Priestley's developing artistry is the character of Baron Roland, the organizer, the manipulator, who is, like Falstaff, not only comic in himself but the cause of gaiety in others. Part charlatan, part master of ceremonies, the character will reappear time and again in Priestley's novels, occasionally as a theater impressario, occasionally as a sinister and bewildering manipulator of souls. He is in essence a Byronic figure of romance, given special direction and purpose within the tale in which he appears. As a master of ceremonies, a celebrator of life, an organizer of dreams, the figure assumes special symbolic proportions in Priestley's fictional world. He appears as the Magicians in *The Magicians*, as the organizer in *Festival at Farbridge*, and as Professor Saltana in Priestley's large-scale novel of the 1960s, *The Image Men*. If Baron Roland has become Professor Saltana in *The Image Men*, then Adam Stewart has become Dr. Owen Tuby in that same novel. Both Baron Roland and Adam grow older as Priestley moves through the thirties, past the years of the Second World War, and into the years of its aftermath. Yet the figures that derive from them remain creatures of fantasy, and for the most part they are innocent and good. The sinister aspect of Baron Roland, however, becomes a not inconsiderable aspect of the character's appeal, an aspect which in some of the more realistic novels, such as *Salt is Leaving* and *Lost Empires*, symbolizes menace rather than light. "More Baron and less Adam would have been our preference," commented the *TLS* reviewer in 1927, failing to note that Adam and Baron Roland are in effect two aspects of the romantic self,[4] perhaps of the author himself.

Despite his failure to fully combine romance and farce, Priestley demonstrates in his first novel those abundant qualities of wit and inventiveness that characterize his people in his best and most entertaining works. Drenched in moonlight, Adam, straightforward, upright, decidedly English, looks forward to the more psychologically convincing protagonist of Priestley's finest novel, *Bright Day*. The novel also reveals another strong component of Priestley's art: his delight in the countryside, his ability to render scene; he confesses in *Margin Released* that what is truest in the novel is his feeling for its backgrounds, the Yorkshire Dales (MR, 181). And indeed the chase that is the novel's climax—Peter and Adam's flight through the rain-drenched countryside in an attempt to checkmate Inspector Hake—is the finest writing in the novel, especially since it introduces at its denouement the mad cleric Canon Drewbridge, who imprisons Adam and Peter in his lumber room, leaving them to summon the police by peddling his bicycle through an inundated countryside, his priestly skirts aloft.

II Benighted

Published in 1927, *Benighted*, Priestley's second novel, following his limited success with *Adam in Moonshine*, was, like *Adam*, written late at night. "I didn't see myself as a born novelist," Priestley writes in *Margin Released*. "Had I been, obviously I would have been writing novels from the first, nothing would have been allowed to stop me" (MR, 177). It is, like *Adam*, a further attempt to come to terms with the modes of the novel, in this case its Gothic form.

Benighted is an attempt, "familiar enough now but unusual then in the Twenties," Priestley writes, "to transmute the thriller into symbolical fiction with some psychological depth" (MR, 181). Priestley feels he did not succeed in this, although the book sold 20,000 copies in the United States under the title of *The Old Dark House* and Hollywood later transformed it into a successful motion picture (1932). Priestley, however, succeeds in this novel better than he knew.

It is the attempt to add psychological depth to a basically farcical situation that distinguishes the book, for in the character of Roger Penderel, Priestley attacks honestly and straightforwardly the problem of the post–World War I malaise in the educated and sensitive but largely rootless upper middle class, thus anticipating the angry young men of post–World War II years. Using again the device of the common cause—throwing people of different classes into a unifying experience—Priestley portrays in melodramatic terms the theme that purposive action liberates the psyche and allows the individual to come to terms with himself and the society in which he has lost his identity. " 'Anyhow, do something, and then you won't know yourself,' " says the chorus girl Gladys to the cynical young Penderel, and for a moment the young man dreams of a future with the good-hearted but equally misused girl.[5]

The symbolical action of the novel is its chief asset: as Penderel finds himself protecting the group, which includes his friends, Philip and Margaret Waverton, Sir William Porterhouse, a rich industrialist, and his mistress, as well as the members of the

Femm household where the two groups are forced to take shelter during a torrential rain and flood, the isolation of the Gothic house suggests not only the atmosphere of *Wuthering Heights* (1847) and *Nightmare Abbey* (1818) but also that of Noah's Ark. The theme of survival is psychologically projected over the sensationalism and violence that frequently characterize the Gothic form. Penderel places himself in control of the situation that develops at the novel's end as Saul Femm, the mad inmate of the household held imprisoned in the upper regions of the house, is released from his room by drunken Morgan, the brutish and dumb servant of the household. On a staircase, Penderel and Saul grapple with one another for the lives of the household and perish together in the plunge from the staircase. The relationship between real madness—Saul has an apocryphal vision of fire cleansing the world—and the madness born of disillusionment is symbolically made. The sacrifice of young Penderel assumes full significance without Priestley's having to bring in unnecessary Christ-as-victim commentary, the action itself fulfilling the purpose.

The Gothic elements of the novel, the storm, the darkened house, the suggestion of evil and depravity, of sin and lack of forgiveness, do create the proper ambience of horror and delight. But what gives the novel more than the status of an entertainment, besides Priestley's handling of Penderel's psychology, is the awareness of a love that becomes meaningful as the chic and bored Margaret and her kind and generous husband Philip are reconciled. Equally significant is Priestley's ability to keep the element of farce under control, something he had not been able to do in his first novel. Delighting in the Gothic trappings, Priestley early in this second novel enjoys them for what they in essence are—props, devices, diversions. As the action of the novel progresses, however, positive virtues of characterization and theme force the elements of farce into the background and the work succeeds largely because of them.

III   Farthing Hall

Perhaps the most revealing of Priestley's collaborations for purposes of this study is *Farthing Hall*, written as a result of Hugh Walpole's generous offer to a struggling young writer of a publisher's advance based on his name, an advance that would enable the younger writer to carry on with his own more important work. Within the epistolary form of the novel—two friends correspond—Priestley assumed the persona of the older, more studious correspondent, although he was neither old nor studious at the time. The epistolary form made it possible for Walpole and Priestley, two busy and serious writers, to collaborate profitably (MR, 173). In the novel, a mixture of both Jane Austen's domestic comedy and her Gothic parody, *Northanger Abbey* (1817), a romantic tale is juxtaposed with a domestic dilemma, both episodes coming to a single and happy conclusion as the villainess of the comedy is transformed into the heroine of the romance. What the novel reveals, more importantly, is Priestley's professionalism, his ability to assume a voice and a persona alien in large measure to that which characterized the author of *Adam in Moonshine* and *Benighted*.

IV   The Good Companions

Susan Cooper rightly points out in her *J. B. Priestley: Portrait of an Author* that in *Benighted* Priestley managed to lay to rest a number of the ghosts that had haunted him as a result of his army service. Through Penderel Priestley's memories of war and death were given an objective reality that the dramatic symbolism of the novel not only enhanced but even justified, albeit melodramatically.[6] At any rate, the Gothic ambience satisfied in Priestley the need to explore another aspect of his romantic temperament, one that can perhaps be called Byronic, as *Adam in Moonshine* had allowed him to explore the mystery that is immediately beneath the surface. Walpole's generosity had, in addition, given Priestley the time to experiment with the larger canvas, to write a long novel in an old-fashioned mode—the comic picaresque—a mode that would inevitably align Priestley alongside the masters of the long novel—Fielding, Dickens, Thackeray.

Refusing the advice of his editors, and against the odds that the novel would please his readers, perhaps remembering the excitement and romance of the tuppenny gallery at Bradford's Empire Theatre, Priestley set about collecting the information necessary to present convincingly a group of traveling performers in the 1920s. Written in a mood of relaxation, *The Good Companions*, in Priestley's words, "might be contemporary and

realistic . . . but what happened in front of it did suggest one of
the cosier fairy tales" (MR, 185). Giving himself release from
"anxiety and strain and tragic circumstance," Priestley shaped
and colored "a long happy daydream" (MR, 186).

Following the device used in both *Adam in Moonshine* and
Benighted, a disparate group of people are brought together and
united into a common cause—the survival of a Concert Party, or
Pierrot group. Elizabeth Trant, a spinster of thirty-seven years,
finds herself in possession of a small sum of money after the
death of her father, whom she had nursed for fifteen years.
Together with Mr. Oakroyd, a Yorkshireman of kindly habits and
handyman abilities, Miss Trant befriends and becomes responsible for a group of stranded players, the Dinky Doos. The group
includes a number of old-timers who do old-fashioned special-
ties, but also Miss Susie Dean and Mr. Jerry Jerningham,
soubrette and leading juvenile, both of undisputed talent and
ambition. Miss Trant also enlists the help of Inigo Jollifant,
onetime schoolteacher discharged from his position because of a
drunken episode who has a facility for composing sprightly tunes,
and Morton Mitcham, banjo player and liar extraordinary. The
group, under Miss Trant's determined leadership, now called the
Good Companions, embarks on a tour of the provinces to bring
fame and fortune to all, especially to Susie Dean and Jerry
Jerningham.

In many ways Dickensian in its descriptions of both character
and setting, *The Good Companions* moves through areas of
sentimentality and romance, and, at its best, into areas of deft
social analysis. For Priestley, although he lavishes attention and
affection on his entertainers, is fully aware of the fact that the
life they prefer is coming to an end, that soon the traveling
parties and concert groups will be replaced by the motion
picture. The new cinema and the old provincial theater come to
old-fashioned grips in the Gatford Hippodrome, where the hired
rowdies of the impressario of the Triangle New Era Cinema Co.
turn a sell-out performance of the Good Companions into a riot.
But Miss Trant's brief victory is mere time-serving, for the
Pierrot groups are out of place in an automated world. Soon she
leaves the company to marry an old admirer; Susie and Inigo go
off to London's West End to pursue glamour and illusion in the
musical theater, where personal happiness eludes them; Mr.
Oakroyd goes to Canada to join his daughter Lily; Jerry

Jerningham finds himself a suitable patroness; and the older members of the company go off to a coastal resort, lingering yet awhile before finding a livelihood in another arena.

Although the novel appears largely nostalgic today, what distinguishes it for a contemporary reader is the hard core of realism that lies immediately beneath the sentiment and the comedy. Theater glamour is dissected and analyzed and shown to be hard work and determination, family life and responsibilities to be largely matters of convention, and kindness and good nature to inhere only in those who understand the reality of getting a living while at the same time doing the work that gives greatest pleasure. The individual adventures, as in most picaresque novels, delight and entertain in themselves, and the good humor that they portray does much to make the novel one of Priestley's most successful works. Yet it is in areas of social analysis that Priestley comes nearest to the early Dickens in both tone and feeling. Although the novel teems with comic characters and inventive episodes, its meaning lies essentially beneath its romantic surface, which, in turn, is reflected by the disciplined substructure that can be discerned beneath the seemingly disparate episodes. The novel is, in effect, constructed in three large movements, resembling in some ways the structure of a symphony. The first movement brings together Miss Trant, Mr. Oakroyd, and Inigo Jollifant, three lonely people joined together by a mutual need to fly from unwanted and inhibiting responsibilities. The organization and deployment of the Pierrot group, the second movement, first called the Dinky Doos and then transformed into the Good Companions, comprises the ups and downs of getting engagements, putting on performances, pleasing crowds. The third movement reaches the romantic chords sounded earlier, as it sends the good companions back into the world that they had briefly escaped, Miss Trant to her Scottish admirer, Oakroyd to a new land, and Inigo Jollifant to the West End to live within crying distance of Miss Susie Dean, his romantic, unfulfilled dream of youth and love. Above this three-part structure the eccentric characters, some caricatures, some more deftly drawn than others—Morton Mitcham, Jimmy Nunn, Elsie Longstaff—perform their comic turns.

The theater and the provincial traveling parties, furthermore, serve as a unifying metaphor for the activities of the whole. Illusion and romance, as Adam Stewart discovered in Priestley's

first novel, reside chiefly in the individual, who is himself
enchanted and enchanting. The romance that Inigo Jollifant finds
in Susie Dean is the romance that is in himself, which in turn
finds expression in the songs that he writes with such deceiving
ease.

V   Angel Pavement

The Good Companions, a runaway best-seller in 1929,
presents a cozy fairy tale against an essentially realistic
background, England in the 1920s. It presents, furthermore, an
optimistic view of man and society, one that many of Priestley's
readers and admirers still attach to him, calling him "Jolly Jack"
and "a good companion," much to his dismay (MR, 185).
Published in 1930, *Angel Pavement* appears at first view to be a
departure from the interests that characterize Priestley's first
three novels; yet, on closer scrutiny, it appears more properly as
a dark reflection of a still essentially romantic world-view. If
Baron Roland is more outrageously humorous than he is sinister
in *Adam in Moonshine,* more Falstaff than Count Fosco, then the
charismatic figure of Golspie in *Angel Pavement* is the portrayal
of Roland's more sinister aspect, an aspect held in abeyance by
the demands of the romantic escapade that Adam finds himself
involved in as a peripheral Companion of the Rose. "A thick
figure of a man but now slow and heavy," Golspie enters into
London's business world catalyzing action, exciting emotion, only
to leave the city as mysteriously as he had appeared there.[7] His
daughter Lena his only commitment, Golspie galvanizes a dying
business, creates life and hope in those he encounters, although
his motives for doing so seem entirely selfish. He is, as was Baron
Roland, the master of ceremonies, except that his celebration in
this instance is one of the darkness rather than of the light that
resides in the individual.

Whereas *The Good Companions* had dealt with the romantic
life of actors on provincial roads, *Angel Pavement,* like the later
play *Cornelius* (1935), describes the London-bound lives of what
today is called the "white collar" population. Into the offices of
Twigg and Dersingham, dealers in veneers used in the manufac-
ture of furniture, strolls the lavishly mustached and balding Mr.
Golspie, "one of those men who are difficult to place," attracted
to Twigg and Dersingham only by the fact that the office is

located on Angel Pavement, an all-but cul de sac in the heart of London's business section (2).

The location of the office and the sale of veneers afford the novel its symbolical pattern, as Golspie, something of a confidence man and racketeer, as was Baron Roland, challenges the class consciousness of those to whom he brings a new supply of Baltic merchandise at half the price of the domestic supply. In less than six months Golspie, who is joined in London by his daughter, Lena, takes over the Twigg and Dersingham office. He is immediately challenged by Mrs. Dersingham at a disastrous dinner at which Lena makes an uninvited appearance, and is labeled a crude and vulgar man by the politer segment of London mercantile society.

It is perhaps because of his daughter's ungracious reception that Golspie decides that strictly fair play is unnecessary in a society that puts too much store on old school ties and polite table manners. His manipulation of Twigg and Dersingham at first breathes new life into the office staff: Lilian Matfield, head secretary, is fascinated, but waits too long to admit her attraction for the life of adventure he represents; Henry Smeeth, head bookkeeper, a careful husband and father, at first incredulously accepts a pay boost, only to discover that Golspie has brought Twigg and Dersingham to bankruptcy by the end of six months, and that he, Smeeth, at fifty, is jobless in a period of general unemployment. Lena Golspie enchants Turgis, the officeboy, in a bored evening, and makes him feel the anguish of jealousy, Priestley suggesting Turgis as a comic Othello.

Perhaps what most distinguishes *Angel Pavement* is its ambience—London in the first pangs of the Great Depression: the pubs, tearooms, tobacco shops, music halls, and motion picture palaces become aspects of characterization. For the city is the novel's center, as it dominates and then enervates its citizens, as does Joseph Conrad's London of *The Secret Agent*. The setting may outwardly be Wordsworth's London as seen from Westminster Bridge, but its great heart seems dull and apathetic, closed to romance. Golspie can stand its suffocation for only six months, and although he has attempted to bring freedom of flight to several of the inhabitants of Angel Pavement, they find it impossible to do more than stumble over the city streets. At the novel's end Golspie and Lena are shown sailing away from London to South America, to new adventure.

As an exercise in romantic-realism, one in many ways reminiscent of Arnold Bennett's *Riceyman Steps* (1923), *Angel Pavement* is both an exciting and challenging novel, one that largely succeeds in escaping its time, as *The Good Companions* does not. It succeeds primarily because of its technique, a third-person narration that largely refuses to do more than comment minimally on Golspie's motivation. A confidence man but not exactly a charlatan, Golspie locks the novel to a seemingly pessimistic view; but the dramatic action of the whole—the confrontation of character and event, as in the Dersingham dinner party scene—reveals the romance beneath the banal. Furthermore, the wood veneers, the mysterious inexhaustible Baltic supply, incorporate structural as well as symbolical and imagerial motifs which are more than mere garnish. What *Angel Pavement* finally portrays is a convincing view of the modern metropolis as a prison which destroys the romance of life. As a result, it is one of Priestley's most successful works.

CHAPTER 4

"Hit or Miss"

FOLLOWING the success of *The Good Companions* and *Angel Pavement*, Priestley found himself in the early 1930s with both the opportunity and the means to travel, to look about, and to devote himself to whatever literary endeavors pleased him. He describes himself at this period as "a kind of three-ring circus" and adds that everything he wrote was either "hit or miss."[1] The period of the early 1930s marks, nevertheless, his earnest entrance into the theater, and some of his surest "hits" were achieved in that arena. The novels of the same decade are, however, lackluster when compared with those that had come earlier, in part explained by the simple fact that Priestley never saw himself as a "novelist or nothing"; and when he turned from the theater it was not always to fiction (MR, 179). Some of his finest works of the time are in fact books of travel and personal reminiscences, excellent pieces such as *English Journey* (1934) and *Midnight on the Desert* (1937), a form which has frequently involved him since he first became a professional writer.

One superb short story, "The Town Major of Miraucourt" (1930), one collaboration with Gerald Bullett, *I'll Tell You Everything* (1933), and six novels appeared between 1930 and 1938, the calm before the storm of Priestley's—and England's—second world war. They are *Faraway*, 1932; *Albert Goes Through*, 1933; *Wonder Hero*, in the same year; *They Walk in the City*, 1936; and *The Doomsday Men, An Adventure*, in 1938. *Faraway* begins with a search for uranium ore; *The Doomsday Men* ends the period with the atomic engine designed for global destruction.

I Faraway

Planned as a symbolical tale of a treasure hunt, *Faraway* was unfortunately interrupted in the writing while Priestley visited

51

the South Seas, where some of the novel's action is placed (MR, 191). It is one of Priestley's least successful works, although it does contain several passages of fine description. The third-person narrative flags as Priestley abandons his tale of romantic adventure to describe the sights and sounds he observed in his travels. Ivor Brown has remarked, however, that the novel was in some ways ahead of its time, concerning itself as it does with the international search for pitchblend and the ethical implications of the discovery and use of atomic energy.[2]

A Stevensonian adventure of discovery and lost love, the narrative of *Faraway* carries the reader from Suffolk, England, to New York, to San Francisco, to Tahiti, where a motion picture company is busily engaged in making a film that recalls *Mutiny on the Bounty,* to the Marquesas, to Easter Island, where the symbolical meaning is most forcefully portrayed as the survivors of the expedition view the gigantic graven images of a devastated culture, and back to Suffolk.

A staid and seemingly conservative bachelor, William Dursley, a malter of Buntingham, is visited by his uncle Baldwin who, just before his death, gives William information about a rich vein of pitchblend to be scooped out of the earth of an uncharted South Pacific island which he, Uncle Baldwin, has named Faraway. The legacy is to be shared with a retired naval officer, Commander Ivybridge, and an American, P. T. Riley, both of whom had once done Baldwin good turns. The forty-year-old William, in accordance with his uncle's wishes, bypasses the claims of a sinister piratical figure called Garsuvin, enlists the aid of Ivybridge and Ivybridge's colleague Ramsbottom, who finances a part of the expedition and largely serves for comic relief, and P. T. Riley—Terry—, a lovely San Franciscan, the daughter of the man whom Baldwin had wanted to share the legacy. Terry Riley becomes for William the personification of his romantic dreams, as his adventure becomes his means of securing self-knowledge.

The plot device, the same that Priestley had employed in *The Good Companions,* the common cause, places a group of diverse people into close proximity, to discover their humanity, or its lack, as they struggle to realize the goal of their odyssey. In love with Terry, who succumbs to the spurious glamour of American motion-picture making, William would give the pitchblend when found to the League of Nations, or some such international organization; Commander Ivybridge to England; and Ramsbottom would exploit the mineral commercially and keep the profits for the group. But Garsuvin, an unconvincing descendant of Golspie and Baron Roland, forestalls all possibilities, and the pitchblend becomes his to exploit in conjunction with the Chilean government which, since Baldwin's time, has laid claim to the island.

William Dursley, the protagonist of the piece and the one through whose consciousness the majority of the plot episodes are recounted, is an evolved version of both Adam Stewart and young Penderel of *Benighted*. There is some attempt made to define him through the foil characters, Ivybridge and Ramsbottom—"'As for you, Dursley, you're about half-and-half, Ah fancy, somewhere between us,'" says Ramsbottom—but the consideration is developed neither through narration nor dramatic interplay, more than likely because any such consideration would complicate an essentially simple allegory.[3] It does, however, become clear that William's unspoiled English nature will subdue his romantic heart, which is indeed the plot resolution that forces the adventure to its anticlimactic conclusion. William marries a comfortable widow, whose courage and nobility of spirit he has remarked on Tahiti. He returns with her to Buntingham, to his maltings, to raise a family, yet always to be haunted by the image of the beautiful perfidious Terry who comes to call on him one rainy night while he is sitting with his wife and chess companion in his "snug" study.

Predictable in the majority of its plot situations, the narrative is largely redeemed by its descriptions of places and people encountered by the adventuresome quartet on their ramshackle quest. The narrative is also reclaimed by some deft and purposeful satire as Priestley leads William through a night of New York Prohibition-era fun and several nights of San Francisco glamour. Besides the descriptions of Tahiti, the Marquesas, and most especially those of the Easter Island sequence, and by the satirical thrusts leveled at Americans at home or in the process of making a movie, the various characters encountered by the group do much to make the novel palatable: the senile adventurer who believes that the World War has destroyed the majority of the great cities of the earth; the spoiled Oxford scholar (perhaps a romanticized combination of

Arnold's scholar gypsy and Gauguin) who has resigned from the struggle in order to criticize it from his remote South Seas vantage point; the grotesque Hollywood location crew; Purvis, the practical English supervisor on Easter Island who goes about his job in sensible English fashion, nevertheless aware of the real glamour of the environment he lives within; and most especially the "mystic" who makes Ramsbottom believe that his old long-lost sweetheart, Maggie Armitage, returns to him in the form of a Polynesian girl.

Ultimately *Faraway* is an example of Priestleyan optimism at its least convincing. Although the novel portrays the same theme that *Adam in Moonshine* and *The Good Companions* had, that the good in life far outweighs the bad, the spirit of romance in this novel, although indestructible in William—he keeps Terry's night-time visit a secret from his wife—becomes an inadequate means of gauging the value of dreams. One is at the end left with a sensible view of things, William by his hearth, at home with his family, in his country, at his work.

It is difficult to say exactly when the influence of J. W. Dunne first enters Priestley's fictional world, for even in those novels which make no explicit mention of Dunne or serial time, there is still to be discerned an implicit commitment to the recoverability of time in order that human experience might be bettered in a future period. Again, this aspect of time can be put down in the fiction to a romantic impulse, perceived by readers of Wordsworth as a "time spot" or by later readers of Marcel Proust and Virginia Woolf as an "epiphany." Indeed, this aspect of time recovered may be the chief factor contributing to Priestley's essentially optimistic view of man and society. Things can be improved in the corridors of time.

One of the most perplexing of the minor characters in *Faraway*, however, is the nature man, a Russian—" 'Ah fancy he said he'd been a count or a prince,' " says Ramsbottom of him—a character who appears in the brief sequence which returns to Ramsbottom the Maggie Armitage of his lost youth (227). Chiefly an aspect of the rich comedy that Ramsbottom, with his Yorkshire accent, affords, the sequence can be explained as a simple exercise in hypnotism. Yet when it is considered alongside one of Priestley's most finely wrought works, "The Town Major of Miraucourt," such simple dismissal becomes difficult.

II   "*The Town Major of Miraucourt*"

A first person narrative, its style more finely honed than is usually true of Priestley's fiction, "The Town Major of Miraucourt," published in 1930, relates an adventure that occurred ten or twelve years before the time of narration. The fantasy, dreamlike, fluid, suggests an oasis in time distilled from the pressures of the present and from submerged memories of war and death. The narrator sees a figure from his youth and remembers the period when he was recuperating from the effects of a gas shell thrown at him in 1918. Sent to a fantastic, surreal "depot" responsible for sending entertainers to the troops, the young officer-narrator is ordered to a corps subsidiary depot. Unable to return to his billet, except by "independent" means, he finds that he has to spend a day and a night in a hamlet called Miraucourt, where he observes a derelict group of soldiers whose appearance and comportment seem to defy the modern world. The narrator soon discovers that they are in fact the soldiers of Shakespeare's *Henry* plays, Falstaff, Bardolph, Pistol, and Nym, all called "Smith" in the still moment that the story recreates. As remarkable for its creation of mood as it is for its convincing portrayal of a tunnel of time, the narration allows access to emotion that exists out of time yet is dependent for being upon the events of daily living. More like Bergson than Dunne at this point, the concept will be modified in *The Magicians* and *It's an Old Country.* Yet two significant plays of the 1930s, *Time and the Conways* and *I Have Been Here Before*, depend structurally on Dunne and his concept of serial time and on Ouspensky and his theory of recurrence.

III   Albert Goes Through

A lighthearted satirical fantasy, *Albert Goes Through* is more long story than novel, although published as such. Like Gore Vidal's later *Myron* (1974), it demonstrates Priestley's firsthand observation of Hollywood motion pictures, their sameness, their illogicality, their banality. It is, to use Priestley's term, a "frolic," yet in comedic terms it too comments on the fluid nature of time, anticipating the more serious concerns of the time plays of the 1930s.

In love with the Hollywood sex goddess as portrayed by Garbo, Dietrich, and Kay Francis, Albert Limpley, who works for T. Birtley and Sons, Auctioneers, Puddyworth, transfers his allegiance to Felicity Storm, Hollywood's latest and newest heartthrob. As a result of an overdose of a patent medicine called "Thunderbolt," a feverish Albert finds himself magically transported into the time and life of the film when he attends Felicity's latest showing. *Albert Goes Through* is in many ways reminiscent of Hollywood's *Sherlock Jr.* (1924), in which Buster Keaton goes through the silver screen.

Albert finds himself moving importantly into a spy-romance, then a western, a gangster war, and finally a musical comedy—all with the identical plot: in all four sequences Felicity is not so much a spy as a misunderstood younger sister gallantly attempting to rescue her brother first from western badmen, then from ruthless gangsters by paying off his debts, meanwhile vamping young Limpley, in each episode her put-upon, and, finally, reluctant rescuer. Albert awakens in the theater-manager's office to discover himself more at ease with lisping Nellie Weedon, who also works for Birtley's, than ever he was with Felicity Storm.

Whimsical, slight, lighthearted, the fable nevertheless underscores Priestley's conviction that romance sweetens life, for Nellie and Albert continue to go to the movies even after the adventures that Albert has lived through in the film.

IV Wonder Hero

Wonder Hero, also published in 1933, returns to the London of *Angel Pavement* while alternating scenes of North Country life to offer suitable counterpoint for the essentially polemic theme. Priestley describes *Wonder Hero* and *They Walk in the City* as "journalistic, social-moral fables" (MR, 192), admitting that both novels are relative failures because of their inability to express his deeper purpose. David Hughes shrewdly suggests in his study of Priestley's works that the novel's failure may be put down to the fact that Priestley could no longer suppress, as he had in his earlier novels, "a political demon which required only a slight relaxation of . . . interest in character and situation for their own sake."[4] The novel nevertheless found readers in its time and, more importantly, indicates today Priestley's intelligent awareness of the pressures placed on the lives of the ordinary person in the throes of economic depression. His *English Journey* perhaps better accomplishes the same purpose in a more resonant fashion, since it eschews sentiment for direct social criticism and journalistic observation.

In *Midnight on the Desert* Priestley describes the process of creation for a novel which, he says, pleased the workman in him but when completed largely displeased the artist. The process, nevertheless, demonstrates Priestley's method in orchestrating the aspects of his fiction. Furthermore, the phrase "wretched compromise between my fine ambitious plan and my modest ability" all but describes the narrative technique of both *Wonder Hero* and *They Walk in the City:*

My immediate task was to find the right setting, the most suitable scheme of action, the best manner of narration, for what seemed to me an attractive and not unworthy idea. This was to take two simple young people, typical specimens of the exploited and helpless class, to bring them together, part them, bring them together again, in the fashion of the oldest and simplest love stories, but to place them and their little romance within a strong framework of social criticism. The two youngsters would be symbolic figures rather than solidly created characters. Much of what happened to them would be symbolic of the special difficulties and dangers of the large class they represented. Like a scarlet thread running through the narrative would be the fairy-tale of young love, as this boy and girl saw it; but the reader's mind would be constantly yanked away from their viewpoint to a wide and critical survey of the social scene. If, for example, they met in a tea-shop, I would try to convey the wonder and glow of that meeting, but at the same time I would examine the institution of the tea-shop itself, relating it to a sharp analysis, which would develop with the story, of our modern urban life. This would not be easy: it meant a double point of view throughout, but as one could not have the simple romance and the social criticism at the same time, there would have to be frequent transitions and these would have to be very artfully done. And I would have to work out a story that could be enjoyed on two different levels.[5]

Wonder Hero considers the world of journalism and aims both sardonic and caustic satire at the means that large newspapers used in the 1930s to keep up mass circulation. Behind the manipulations of the *Daily Tribune,* the newspaper which turns Yorkshireman Charlie Habble of Utterron into the wonder hero of the week, lie the threats of communist and fascist ideologies at

war with one another, the theme that Graham Greene employs
in his novel of the same time, *It's a Battlefield* (1934). Although
the truth of Priestley's social observations as he follows exploited
Charlie Habble and his Ida Chatwick, winner of a North Country
beauty contest, is constantly evident, the love story and the
social commentary fail to harmonize. The coming together of
young, bluff, honest Charlie and pretty Ida, instead of being
symbolical first and pathetic second, is largely sentimental; and
the sentimentality dissipates the effects of social realism, the
chords that the novel strives to maintain in counterpoint largely
through supporting characters such as the communist agitator
Kibworth and the press columnist Hal Kinney.

V   They Walk in the City

Written while Priestley was in the Arizona desert, *They Walk
in the City* is, like *Angel Pavement* and *Wonder Hero,* set in an
economically depressed city; it too is a proletarian novel, and one
that like *Wonder Hero* sacrifices character and setting to thesis.
The events of the plot, as are those of *Wonder Hero,* are largely
conceived as counterpoint, yet once again the two voices fail to
resolve themselves into a single meaningful composition.

They Walk in the City tells the story of Edward Fielding and
Rose Salter, both of Haliford, who find each other on a moor
overlooking a large industrial town, only to lose each other
because of a locked bathroom door. Rose goes to London,
Edward follows, finds her, loses her, and finds her again, with the
help of a group of unemployed and overaged men, in a
mysterious house of suspicious character in fashionable St. John's
Wood.

The fairy-tale motif of the two lovers lost on the concrete
pavements of a large and menacing city is contrasted to the
largely undefined menace to youth symbolized by the enameled
procuress who melodramatically abducts Rose in a large silver
car. The love story is overly romanticized to lend point to the
social criticism, but the fairy tale is so incongruous that the whole
degenerates into cloying sentimentalism. To bring the lovers
together Priestley introduces an unprepared-for and totally
unconvincing confrontation between the communists and the
fascists in Trafalgar Square, at which time the procuress seizes
Rose to use her for her evil schemes. Edward finally finds Rose in

the fashionable house, along with the dead body of a mysterious Mr. Antwill, another exploiter of the unwary and the decent. Edward insists on calling the police, for, as he says to Rose, " 'The police have got to know about the murder, and about this house, too, or else we'll never get any further. I don't mean just us— though I do mean us—but everybody. . . . What's it all about?' "[6]

What is best about *They Walk in the City* are the passages of description—the sights and nuances of the city—and the ironic commentary on the advertising claims made through the magazines and films, which Priestley will later call "Admass," to appeal to pretty girls of limited educational opportunity. Such passages as the one cited below do much to offset the generally sentimental tone of the fairy tale:

Nellie was quite happy paying ten shillings for ninepennyworth of lanolin, beeswax, borax, and a drop of almond oil. And Rose, who paid sixpence for exactly the same preparation under another and more plebeian name, envied her sister this and other luxurious aids to beauty. She was not envying her at this moment, however, being busy with a toothbrush rubbing potassium chlorate (a poison) into her dental cavities, happily convinced, for she had often read the advertisements of this toothpaste, that she was protecting herself against pyorrhea. The advertisers had warned her solemnly against this disease, but had not seen fit to add that neither their toothpaste, nor anybody else's, could prevent or cure it. Both these girls spent a good deal of their money on rubbish that clever advertisement copy writers either cajoled or frightened them into buying, and perhaps they were fortunate in not having more money to spend, otherwise even their powerful constitutions—and they were both as strong as horses—might soon have been wrecked by this search for health and beauty. (79)

VI The Doomsday Men

The Doomsday Men, published in 1938, is set in the Mojave Desert, in and around Barstow, California. It is a novel as remarkable for its descriptions of the desert as it is for its story of detection, intrigue, and scientific fantasy. Priestley has written that the book took just nineteen days to write, that it was for him a diversion from the more strenuous tasks of working on his experimental drama, *Johnson Over Jordan* (1939), and a discarded play-sketch from which only the title, *The Linden Tree*,

was salvaged.[7] Whether the novel was written in haste, or in the
spirit of relaxation, it reveals little carelessness in its composition.
Like *Benighted*, Priestley's earlier thriller, this time the inspiration being the science-oriented world of potentially destructive
apparatuses, the elements of the tale are held together within a
tightly paced narrative that is rarely allowed to lurch into farce,
as was the earlier Gothic tale. It is an "entertainment" in the
Graham Greene sense rather than a novel; that is, long on
suspense and incident, short on characterization.

The structure of *The Doomsday Men* is as simple as it is artful,
again illustrating Priestley's use of plot counterpoint. Although
there is some moralizing within the tale, this aspect is never
permitted to rise so far above the action of the whole that the
main purpose of entertainment is wrenched as a result.

A London architect called Malcolm Darbyshire meets the girl
of his dreams, mysterious, aloof, unhappy, a princess in obvious
distress, while playing a championship match of doubles with her
in the south of France. The match initiates the motif of serve and
return, which describes the action of much of the entertainment.
An American physicist, George Glenway Hooker, on leave from
his American university, by chance encounters Paul Englefield, a
brilliant atomic scientist who has been working along the same
lines as he, in a London shop that sells scientific apparatus. Jimmy
Edlin, investigating the murder of his newspaperman brother,
follows clues left by his brother in a notebook which take him to
the temple of a religious cult called the Brotherhood of the
Judgement in Los Angeles, where Jimmy ingratiates himself with
the brethren and learns that their chief stronghold is located
somewhere near Barstow. In Barstow, Jimmy combines forces
with architect and physicist who have been brought to the same
place by leads of their own.

The three searchers soon learn that they are on the trail of the
three rich and powerful MacMichael brothers, who have
themselves combined forces to create and fuse a gigantic
doomsday machine to destroy a world which, they are convinced, not only deserves but desires extinction. Darbyshire,
Hooker, and Edlin are contrasted to the three brothers who,
within the loose allegory of the tale, represent science gone
berserk, religious fanaticism, and great wealth devoid of altruism
or philanthropical enlightenment.

The three searchers are helped in their attempt to win the

match against the three brethren by Charlie Atwood, a
character in many ways reminiscent of Roger Penderel, the
bored soldier of *Benighted.* A hasbeen stuntman, Charlie is
sympathetically described by his sister-in-law as a sensitive boy
when he went into the army, a disillusioned man when he came
out; Charlie then substituted the spurious excitement of the
Hollywood adventure film for the life-and-death struggle of the
war. His arms and legs broken, as well as his spirit, as a result of
his exploitation by the makers of illusion, Charlie looks for
escape in alcohol. Summoned by Andrea MacMichael's desperate
phone call as her stepfather and her mad uncles are about to
detonate their destructive mechanism, Charlie does the only
thing he can—he dives his derelict airplane into the high tension
wires that feed the doomsday machine, perhaps saving the
planet as he does so.

If *Faraway* foreshadows world-wide political events as it
describes the search for uranium ore, as Ivor Brown has pointed
out, *The Doomsday Men* anticipates a form of escape fiction that
became popular as an aftermath of Hiroshima. The novel in
effect looks forward to the thrillers of Terry Sothern and Ian
Fleming, who made Dr. Strangelove and Dr. No familiar figures
of contemporary popular fiction and motion picture art. Priestley
anticipates, in addition, the tongue-in-cheek quality that characterizes Fleming's cartoonlike escapades. In *Rain Upon Godshill*
he points out that any plot involving the destruction of the world
must end in anticlimax, "for clearly you cannot destroy the world
and still tell the tale, and yet if you do not destroy it, people feel
disappointed." And he concludes that his novel did no one any
harm (137), implying, perhaps, that tongue-in-cheek helps solve
the novelist's dilemma. The tongue-in-cheek quality, furthermore, through narrative voice, extends wittily into the structure,
as Priestley, in motion picture fashion, cuts from descriptions of
young love flowering in a desert of cactus and joshua trees to
scenes of intense physical action. The similarities to the Sothern
and Fleming thrillers are, however, similarities of surface only.
For Priestley is a more serious writer than they. He is at his
stylistic and romantic best in sensitive descriptions of the desert
landscape where the Doomsday men have set their machinery of
destruction. He himself refers modestly to these "pretty bits of
writing" in *Rain Upon Godshill* and asks his readers to pay
particular attention to Chapter Eight (136). In these "pretty bits

of writing" the artist reveals his eye for the unique details of landscape and climate, details which suggest to the casual reader only the devastated planet that the doomsday men envisage; to the more observant eye the quiet and subtle life of the landscape suggests, as it does to Wordsworth, the renewing powers of nature—in a setting quite far removed from the English countryside of *Adam in Moonshine* and *The Good Companions*.

The Doomsday Men is also remarkable for the manner in which it insists on an optimism that in this novel stops far short of the sentimentalism that Priestley is sometimes betrayed into while advocating his simple Romantic doctrine of goodness, one which Wordsworth articulates in "Tintern Abbey," as the "still sad murmur of humanity." Malcolm Darbyshire says to Andrea MacMichael, as they sit on the desert sand looking out to the vistas beyond:

"We're not in Paradise, and have no right to expect to be. People fall out of love, children die, there are bestial wars, and everywhere there's ugliness and pain and misery, just as everywhere the sun goes down and the night comes. But people also fall in love, as we've done, and children grow up happily, wars come to an end or are avoided, bits of ugliness disappear—and it's our job not to whine that these things exist but to help them out of the world, and people have fun together, help each other in need, try to soften pain and drive away misery. Even now, in many ways, people are better than they were, and even if they aren't, we can't just sit about and moan that it's all hopeless. It's good— it's grand and glorious—for us to sit here together—as you admit yourself—"[8]

Malcolm's statement is a remarkable one, considering the time of the novel, the eve of World War II. Ironically the three demented magicians are concerned with the same things, and their desire is not to control the planet but to rid it of its human miseries. At the novel's end, Malcolm, who is at this point undoubtedly spokesman for the author, tells Andrea, who is conveniently discovered to be not the daughter but the stepdaughter of one of the mad brothers, that there is indeed a certain grandeur in the larger patterns of the lunacy that her stepfather represents. Malcolm and his two companions have succeeded in aborting doomsday by sacrificing drunken and noble Charlie Atwood to the cause of what can only be described as a belief that good fellowship produces right action. That these simple human accommodations to time and event need to be shockingly portrayed from time to time in the hope that men may be made newly aware of the potent forces within them that they too often let atrophy is the deeper meaning of the tale. Although there is no specific mention of the perfectability of experience in time, a theme that Priestley will advocate in novels much less compelling than *The Doomsday Men,* the thought is pervasive to the narrative, allowing the artist to strike the proper balance between the hopefulness of Malcolm and Hooker and Jimmy Edlin and the "enlightened" pessimism that the three Doomsday men espouse. The novel does not end echoing its beginning with "Game, Set, and Match", for, if it did, the result would be total destruction or universal peace.

CHAPTER 5

England at War

A plea for sanity in a darkening world reluctantly preparing for war, *The Doomsday Men* marks for Priestley the end of a generally sunny period. Even such didactically intended novels as *Wonder Hero* and *They Walk in the City* sacrifice social and political conviction to the fairy-tale ending. From 1939 to 1946 Priestley, however, published five darker novels, all of which are in one way or another concerned with England at war. They are *Let the People Sing*, published in 1939, *Black-Out in Gretley, A Story of—and for—Wartime*, published in 1943, *Daylight on Saturday*, 1945, *Three Men in New Suits*, 1945, and *Bright Day*, generally reputed to be Priestley's best work of narrative fiction, in 1946.

The period of war also marks Priestley's entrance into the world of mass media, for in 1940 he began making radio broadcasts for the BBC, his contribution to the immediate cause of the war. The "Postscripts" began after Dunkirk and came to an end when the Luftwaffe launched its blitz on the city of London. David Hughes in his study of Priestley writes of these broadcasts:

I never thought, and I do not think now, that it is possible to overrate the effect of these broadcasts at a crucial hour in history. As to their literary value, if one can speak of it in the same breath, they read now as evocatively as they were heard at the time; they re-create the tensions that were felt, and then at once relax them. It is odd that one should not even require to place them in historical context to return to the pleasure, and almost to the relief, of hearing them, for they make the context as they go along, and that is probably due to the fact that Priestley introduced much that seemed irrelevant to the immediate concern of war, always giving it a twist that brought it back to his theme. . . . Postscripts . . . was the first really effective barrage in the war Priestley was fighting; this time, rather different from the past, no one needed persuading, for it happened to be everyone else's war as well.[1]

The concerns of these broadcasts are largely reflected in the novels of the time.

In *Midnight on the Desert* Priestley recalls the argument of one of the talks he gave for the BBC, during which he discussed his concept of the state and outlined a program of government which he labeled "Liberal Socialism": "the individual," he writes, "should not be a cog in the great machine but the reason for the machine's existence, because it [my system] drew a sharp line between what properly belongs to a communal existence and what belongs to private life, because it denied men no right but that of enslaving other men. . . ."[2]

Priestley's ideal and, it must be added, romantically conceived state, perhaps what he was struggling to define in the subtext of his earlier novels of social protest, banishes exploitation and usury and withdraws from all departments of life which have nothing to do with the growth of the spirit: "The state owns all the vital necessaries of life, and distributes them gratis . . . and if you want luxuries and privileges, as most of us do passionately, then you must work. There is no having it both ways in my country, no grabbing all the luxuries and privileges, and not even working for them. And by necessaries, we mean necessaries; clean shelter, plain food, some clothing, and not drinks and cigarettes and money for gambling and visits to the films." (MD, 136). One cannot help but wonder if the last category includes money for theater and books. Nevertheless, it is such a state that serves as the ideal behind the struggle of *Let the People Sing,* one of Priestley's novels of the war period, as well as a play of the same time, *The Golden Fleece,* not published until after the war.

I   Let the People Sing

Let the People Sing makes use of the common cause as the means of catalyzing a community to insure democratic action. An out-of-work comedian, Timmy Tiverton, who had once been a leading halls entertainer, together with a refugee from the Nazis, Professor Ernst Kronak, temporarily without a visa, and Hope Ollerton, a young woman of no talent but incredible beauty, join together to bring a community to its patriotic senses.

The Market Hall, willed to the people of Dunbury as a place for musical activities, is being taken away from them by the city's Tory entrepreneurs who wish to let it either to the capitalists who run United Plastics, a company whose main offices are in the United States and who wish to use it as a display hall, or to the Foxfield group, who wish to house there a museum for the various trophies of a no longer viable aristocratic tradition. Timmy, Hope, and the Professor join Hope's uncle, Fred Hassock, a huckster-auctioneer who precedes his selling activities by providing his customers with modest entertainment, to stand against the Tories and fascists of the community.

The upsetting news of the witholding of the entertainment license for the little Market Hall causes old Fred Hassock to fall from a perch where he had been placing his decorations and to be hospitalized. Hope, Timmy, and the professor carry on with the venture despite police intervention, and the banner cry of the little group becomes "Let the People Sing."

Soon the factory workers, who sympathize and strike, and the townspeople, deprived of music and simple pleasure by the more powerful factions at work in the city, combine with them to withstand the wresting away of the Market Hall which is rightfully theirs. The matter is put to arbitration, and after getting the arbitrator, Sir George Denberry-Baxter, good and drunk (he is affable and human when drunk, despotic and unreasonable when sober, recalling the millionaire drunkard of Charlie Chaplin's 1931 film *City Lights* and anticipating Brecht's 1940 character Puntila), the people win the decision.

After the escapade, Timmy finds new employment in the halls, the professor is sent for by his son in the United States, and Hope finds romance and happiness with Roger Liss, the boy she had ignored until he had feigned indifference and thereby enraptured her.

Overly plotted, repetitious in its insistence on the theme that good will overwhelm greed and arrogance, unconvincingly Dickensian in its portrayal of character and comic event, *Let the People Sing*, despite the best of motives, fails. The character of Timmy Tiverton is overextended as he is asked to maintain the delights of the music halls and the values of decency and fair behavior. The caricature figure of Sir George Denberry-Baxter, the boorish-boisterous drunk; the mannish lady doctor, Miss

Buckie; the old halls trouper, Daisy Bailey, who runs the "Dog and Bells," an American-style roadhouse which employs down-and-out entertainers: all overemphasize the theme of democratic behavior. More successful, however, is the minor character Candover, a halfwit whose dreams mysteriously record the devastations of the past and in cinemalike terms foretell those of the future.

What is, perhaps, most remarkable about the novel is the analysis of the English character, rightly given to the good-natured refugee Professor to make:

"The great traditions of this country . . . are these. First, the liberty of the individual. So long as they do no harm to others, men must be allowed to develop in their own way. Second, that which goes with liberty—toleration. Third, voluntary public service. Fourth, a very deep love, a poetical love, rooted deep down in the unconscious, of England and the English way of life, of the fields and woods, flowers and birds, of pastimes, of the poets and story-tellers. Fifth, which you find everywhere among the common people, humour and irony and along with these a profound depth of sentiment."[3]

No better description of Priestley's central theme is to be found anywhere in his work, the celebration of those virtues of the English character which Shakespeare himself extols—stubbornness, decency, honor, and above all the desire to be free. It is Priestley's great theme and England is his great love.

II Black-Out in Gretley

A first-person narrative, *Black-Out in Gretley, A Story of—and for—Wartime*, introduces Canadian Humphrey Neyland, who has lost his wife and child in an accident in Santiago, Chile, to a gloomy, rain befogged, and grimy midlands town called Gretley. Ostensibly a tale of crime and detection the novel in reality fulfills the essential purpose of propaganda, encouraging its readers to beware of smalltalk while exhorting them to abide by wartime regulations.

Working "temporarily" for the British Secret Service, Neyland is sent to investigate Nazi espionage activities centering on the aircraft factory that is Gretley's main industry. Enormously successful "because the appetite for reading matter was at its sharpest in this dark period of the war,"[4] the novel, predictably plotted, deals, nevertheless, imaginatively and to a degree convincingly with the psychology of English collaborators. Even the gloominess and rain that constantly overwhelm the atmosphere of Gretley symbolically underscore the grayness of the motives that induce Englishmen to throw in their lot with the Nazis.

Chief among these collaborators are Diana Axton, whose cover is the proprietorship of an arty gift shop called Prue's (a character perhaps reminiscent of Unity Mitford), and Colonel Tarlington, the Tory aristocrat of the community (perhaps modeled on such collaborators as Oswald Mosley). Diana has aligned herself with the Nazi effort because of some romantic dream of Nordic superiority; Colonel Tarlington, to retain the privileges which he feels historically belong to his class. At the action's conclusion, when Neyland reveals to Tarlington that England has found him out, Tarlington takes the only "gentlemanly" way out of his predicament—he puts a bullet through his brain. But before he does so he is made to listen to Neyland's moralizing speech:

"When Hess flew over here, he was looking for people like you. It isn't that you're pro-German, unpatriotic in the ordinary sense. In the last war, which seemed to you a straightforward nationalistic affair, I've no doubt you did a good job. But this war, which is quite different, was too much for you. . . . But you're a bit more intelligent and a bit more unscrupulous than most of your kind, and so you realized that to keep all you wanted to keep, it meant that the people musn't win and that Fascism musn't lose."[5]

Black-Out in Gretley contains its full share of red herrings and sensational goings-on, most of them centering on the roadhouse called the Queen of Spades, run by an attractive black marketeer whose chief trait is a voracious appetite for young men. She is contrasted with young Sheila Castleside, a pathetic child-woman who has been pretending to be someone better than the lowly clerk she was before the war. Sheila refuses to betray her country. She is murdered, but Neyland avenges her death, and he is in turn rewarded with the love and admiration of widowed Dr. Margaret Bauernstern, who has never been under any suspicion by either Neyland or the reader.

Black-Out in Gretley needs to be read as an entertainment of and for its time, as its subtitle soberly suggests. It is in many ways a continuation of Priestley's romantic interest in the Gothic form, but when compared to *Benighted* and *The Doomsday Men* it rightly appears one of lesser achievement despite some fine passages of atmosphere and creditable nuances of characterization.

III   Daylight on Saturday

Published in 1943, *Daylight on Saturday* is a much more successful novel than *Black-Out in Gretley,* largely because its aspects of propaganda are subdued to more stringent considerations of character and symbol. In the tradition of romantic realism set by *Angel Pavement,* avoiding the robust sentiment of *The Good Companions, Daylight on Saturday* examines the psychology of the English at war, not the psychology of the soldiers and sailors and airmen but of the people who work the various factory shifts, attempting as they do so to find meaning for their lives through their contribution to the common cause of England at War.

In *Margin Released* Priestley points out that *Daylight on Saturday* was planned with considerable care; that he felt that he should take the same trouble with his work that the men and women whom he had observed in the various factories obviously took with theirs. "Whatever its value as fiction," he writes, "I hope it will not be altogether forgotten, for I should like to think that some English readers, during the next fifty years, might learn from it how people lived and worked in World War Two."[6] *Daylight on Saturday* is in fact one of Priestley's more successful works, rich in symbolical suggestion and character relationships.

Through a dexterous manipulation of point of view, Priestley moves from omniscient observation into the various echelons that make up the Elmdown Aircraft factory, delineating individuals through modified stream of consciousness, identifying their politics, characterizing their dreams. The action of the novel is locked to the factory, the only views of a world beyond the buildings and yards tied to the reveries of the various workers.

In charge of the plant is Mr. Cheviot, wise in his knowledge of power and the abuses to which power can lead, burdened with the knowledge of the guilt he shares with other engineers and men of business who have brought about the war indirectly,

simply by doing their jobs making the machinery of warfare.
Cheviot arbitrates between Blandford and Elrick, those immediately under him in the management of the works. The
philosophical center of the novel, Cheviot moves through all
levels of the plant's personnel, equally at ease with managers,
supervisors, handymen. At one point he talks to Sammy Hamp,
who does the sweeping up, about his aviator son who has been
reported lost in a mission, and about all the other fathers' sons
involved in the imbecility of war: " 'What were we doing to allow
all this, so that our lads, who were at school when we were telling
each other that Hitler didn't mean any harm, have to go and give
up their lives? There're machines down there, Sam, that I
bought myself in Germany, not six months before the war
started. And we were selling 'em engines, and would have sold
'em anything else we'd got. Good for trade. Nice business.' "[7]

Cheviot's sympathies as plant supervisor are largely with
Elrick, who has learned from experience about the running of
the works and the handling of men; and he has respect for both
the machinery and the skilled workers who produce respectable
goods from them. Burdened with a wife grown simple because of
a miscarriage, he compensates for his frustrations by drinking
and chasing women. He loses his temper easily, especially when
in the presence of Blandford, who represents both the upper
class and the opportunist late-entrant into the business world.

Blandford has his position largely as a result of education and
influence, but he is not without ability. Each man chooses to
misunderstand the other, Elrick feeling that Blandford cares
only about high production, to be brought about chiefly by
eliminating the quality brought to the product by the skilled
workman, whereas Blandford feels that Elrick overemphasizes
the human aspect and exaggerates the necessity of quality in the
manufactured product. Elrick feels that the workers have
forgotten to be proud of their accomplishments; Blandford
rationalizes that a victorious battle will raise morale and boost
production. At the novel's end Montgomery's victory over
Rommel accomplishes Blandford's purpose. And Blandford and
his view are preferred to Elrick and his.

Between the extremes of Elrick and Blandford stands Angleby,
the young, idealistic engineer who comes to understand the
genuine concern of Elrick while appreciating Blandford's more
logical and colder analysis of what limits production. Angleby is

attracted to Blandford's wife's cousin, Freda Pinnel, one of the few convincingly sexual women in Priestley's fictional world. A snob and malcontent, Freda finds Angleby's assurance and competence annoying at first, then challenging, and finally satisfying. Indeed, there is something of a Lawrentian dichotomy described in their mutual attraction and repulsion. They discover a curious happiness in their intellectual and emotional commitment to a cause which both can believe in. At the novel's end, they suggest a possible harmony between the different classes they represent.

Other characters are as skillfully and as economically drawn: Gwen Ockley, tragically attracted to Elrick, fully aware of his predilection for simpering, empty-headed girls such as Nellie Ditton, who feels that she is too refined for her job in the works; Sister Filey, easy and boozy, also attracted to Elrick; Alfred Cleeton, the intellectual; Miss Shipton, the reluctant mistress; and Mr. Bolton, who has lost his family in an air raid—all are skillfully presented as Priestley moves into their consciousness to describe their political hopes, dreams, their limitations, their concepts of duty. A fluid motion-picture-like technique, suggestive of filmic cross-cutting, allows Priestley to move easily from character to character, to contrast mood with mood, to transform into symbols the various offices, corridors, and machines of the works' premises. The fluid movement creates a rising tension, a mounting excitement, that culminates in a death struggle between Elrick and Stonier, a skilled workman driven insane by the pressures of the war. Stonier listens to the machines speak to him of sacrifice and blood as he looks at Nellie Ditton, the virgin he will sacrifice. Stonier and the cashiered Elrick grapple over the machinery, over Nellie. Elrick is crushed by the very machinery he respects.

In the character of Elrick, Priestley looks back to Roger Penderel of *Benighted* and directly anticipates the angry young men who appear after World War II—the young men of the great middle class who populate the fiction of John Wain, John Braine, and the drama of John Osborne. A man of action and foresight, up from the ranks, frustrated by his awareness of hypocrisy and fraud, Elrick is correctly identified by Cheviot, and by his author, as someone who has gone all wrong: " 'So he's angry inside all the time. The trouble in him joins up with any trouble outside.' "(222).

But the characterization of Elrick is by no means the novel's only triumph. Equally persuasive is the characterization of the works themselves, the microcosm reflecting the trouble outside its yards. Within the symbolical structure of the whole, Cheviot becomes a god-figure, Elrick the victim, and Angleby and Freda the future. Stripped of his comic attributes, deprived of his sinister and mysterious motives, Cheviot hardly resembles the organizer of the earlier novels. Elrick is also difficult to recognize as the quester, for his romanticism and idealism have gone sour. It is his romanticism, nevertheless, that propels him to rescue Nellie Ditton, a maiden in distress.

There is no forced optimism at the novel's conclusion, but there is an assurance of a future, a new beginning, earned through understanding and sacrifice. The romantic impulse is still strong in Priestley's imagination. The people sing in *Daylight on Saturday,* but quietly, as they leave their arc-lighted factory for the pallid daylight of their Saturday half-day of rest.

IV   Three Men in New Suits

Three Men in New Suits is a didactic tale concerning the postwar temper of Britain; it addresses the problems of returning service men once the peace has been established.

Dressed in his badly cut demobilization suit of clothes, Alan Strete represents an anachronistic landed aristocracy. He returns to his decaying large house to find his mother, Lady Strete, and his uncle Rodney pretending to a manner of life that was moribund even before the war. His sister Diana finds it difficult to accept her role as war-widow and daughter, let alone the times which have deprived her of a comfortable life.

Alan Strete finds himself in danger of succumbing to a prewar complacency, which appears as madness to him, when he accepts the offer of Lord Darrald, powerful owner of the *Daily Gazette,* to write a column on postwar psychology for the *hoi polloi* in a condescending manner they will be able to understand. But Alan is saved by the appeal made to him by two comrades, Herbert Kenford, son of a farmer made prosperous by the war, and Eddie Mold, a worker, whose homecoming is marred by the knowledge forced upon him by his neighbors of his wife's unfaithfulness. The three comrades talk heroically at the novel's end, realizing the need to cherish the unity and camaraderie engendered by the Nazi threat.

As the three veterans speak in the gathering dusk outside the Strete manor, they are overheard by Alan's sister Diana. The four decide that there is power in their understanding that a return to prewar complacency is tantamount to an admission of defeat, and that to make a better world each must pull his share of useful work. " 'We have at last to have faith in people, compassion for people, whether they have white faces, brown faces or black faces,' " says Alan to his friends. " 'Either the earth must soon be the miserable grave of our species or it must be at last our home, where men can live at peace and can work for other men's happiness.' "[8]

The chief problem with the novel, if indeed the book can be called a novel, is identical to that which mars a play of the same period, *They Came to a City* (1943): both preach rather than dramatize their message, and the solution offered for permanency after the war, a vaguely suggested socialism or mild communism, is neither developed nor, indeed, made explicit.

V Bright Day

Of all of Priestley's fiction *Bright Day* is most admired. David Hughes writes of the Jungian aspect of the work: "In a curious way this novel strikes behind specific memories and throws a little light on the memory that we might all be said to share in common, the sense of race, our roots in history; it is only a chink in the curtain perhaps, but it has the effect of making one feel more than human, more mortal yet more sharply alive. This is the condition of mind which the sight of hills or the sound of music inspires, a climate in which beliefs take root and one's convictions harden, growing a shade wiser."[9] Which is to say that *Bright Day* fulfills the highest demands of art.

In her study of Priestley, Susan Cooper writes at length about the technical accomplishments in the novel, commenting on Priestley's fluid use of the time shift, his reliance on music as an integrating motif, his ability to telescope past into present and thereby formulate a repeated and meaningful pattern, and his dexterity in "turning the present into the past which could not be called retrogressive."[10] And Ivor Brown has commented on the

felt experiences recorded in the novel, pointing out that the life
between the wars is "recorded in writing better than good."[11]
Bright Day is, understandably enough one of Priestley's favorite
novels, and he writes more perceptively about its accomplishment than any critic can:

> If I were to be judged on evidence supplied by one single novel, my
> own choice would not be *Angel Pavement,* in spite of the solid support
> it has had, but *Bright Day.* There are several good reasons for this. One
> of them is that in this novel I did not fail the idea with which I began, in
> spite of considerable technical difficulties, the constant shift of time,
> atmosphere, tone. Another is that although the story is not at all
> autobiographical—the first-person narrator, Gregory Dawson, is a
> writer, it is true, but both his work and his attitude towards it are quite
> different from mine—I was able to recreate, in the scenes recollected
> from Dawson's youth, something of the life I had known before 1914,
> and not, I believe, without colour . . . And here for once, try as I might,
> I cannot grumble, for *Bright Day* was generally received as I hoped it
> would be, and among the many people who read the book were some I
> was delighted to please. One of them was Jung, who wrote me a long
> letter about it. (MR, 195-96)

Published in 1946, *Bright Day* is the first-person account of the
life of a filmscript writer who is suddenly reminded of his early
years while working on a script for a motion picture to be called
The Lady Hits Back. More ambitious in its handling of technical
devices than any novel that had preceded it, Priestley here
reveals not only his craft but his artistry as well, for indeed, of all
his novels *Bright Day* is the one for which he will be
remembered.

Bright Day makes use of a Proustian or Bergsonian memory
device to set in motion in the present the life in the past that has
shaped Gregory Dawson into the middle-aged, successful-
though-unhappy screen writer who sits in a genteel hotel on the
Cornish coast wondering about his lack of interest in either life
or work. The sight of a desiccated couple suggests hauntingly a
forgotten memory, a wisp of youth; then the strains of a Schubert
trio reinforce the double illusion of strangeness and familiarity. A
train of associations, returning him to a past long forgotten but
still potent, follows, and Dawson recognizes the aged couple as
the Eleanor and Malcolm Nixey who had intruded themselves
into his first great love affair.

Eighteen and impressionable, orphaned, living with his aunt and uncle in wool-producing Bruddersford, wanting to be a writer, young Dawson had fallen in love with his employer's entire family, a charmed and gracious group not unlike the Conways of the earlier play *Time and the Conways,* comprising Mr. and Mrs. Alington, their beautiful daughters Joan, Bridget, and Eva, and their sons Oliver and the precocious David. The Nixeys had brought into the pattern of the carefree lives of the Alingtons, who had sentimentally attached the young Gregory, a future which spans not one but two world wars, a future that they cannot understand or even acknowledge as possible. The Nixeys introduce into the carefree family group a notion of living that allows for neither idealism, gracefulness, nor fair play; Malcolm Nixey's place in Alington's wool business is simply a ruse to allow him to take the business away from Alington, who is temperamentally unsuited to cope with "modern" business procedures. Alington even fails to sell the business at its peak value—ironically, the war will raise the price of the wool and Alington sells the business just before prices jump.

As Gregory learns more about the world of grasping men and scheming women, it becomes clear to the reader that Priestley through his protagonist is describing a rite of passage from one world-view to another, and that Gregory is conceived of as a symbolical figure. Gregory's initiation is into a world of suspicion and lovelessness, a world that puts emphasis on money and appearance, not on beauty or truth; a world that Dawson has in the present time of the novel unconsciously rejected, one which he can no longer even write for as a money-making script writer of money-making films.

The flashes into the past by which a time of sentiment and beauty is cinematically counterpointed with a career-struck and unlovely society anticipates the symbolical handling that distinguishes L. P. Hartley's novel of the same era, *The Go-Between* (1950). Both Priestley's novel and Hartley's strikingly resonate the theme of betrayal—of nation, of class, of self. The Proustian theme is spoken simply by Dawson. " 'One mistake we're apt to make . . . is to assume that we are just ourselves as we are now, whereas that's only the thin top slice of us. And whatever has happened to us in the past is still there, perhaps still working away at us.' "[12] It is his recognition of self in time that precedes his commitment to the future.

The time shifts, symbolically counterpointed, allow Priestley to throw into ever clearer focus the responsibilities of the present as the past is rediscovered. And most liberating of the discoveries of the past is the revelation made to Gregory by little Laura Bradshaw: she had witnessed the event that had signaled the end of the post-Victorian tribes of Alingtons—in a fit of jealous rage Joan had pushed her sister Eva to her death from a cliff. The cancer of destruction in the Alingtons had been implicit in the family itelf: the Nixeys had merely served as catalysts to bring about the inevitable. The knowledge of the brutal act sets Dawson free to live in the present and for the future. Laura's knowledge of the events of the past offer Dawson a bright day, and he decides to align himself with a young new breed of film workers who want more from motion pictures than quick and easy money.

It is difficult to fault *Bright Day*, for it is indeed the finest statement of Priestley's optimistic and romantic beliefs, held in firm check by the demands of the narrative and the subtle and uncompromising demands of characterization. For although Gregory Dawson may be in the final event the symbolical character of quester, he convinces because of his psychological validity. The rediscovery of his romantic self is the rediscovery of a moment of truth buried years before in the rich soil of youth. The enchantment may have dimmed with the years, is indeed almost destroyed by two wars, but it is recovered and found to be true. No character better illustrates the practical aspects of the romantic imagination than does Gregory Dawson. Although Priestley claims that he and Dawson are unlike in significant ways, they are compatible in their exercise of the imaginative faculty. The novels before *Bright Day* had largely described romance; *Bright Day* recreates its essence. Gregory Dawson is a far cry from the ingenuous Adam Stewart of *Adam in Moonshine.*

CHAPTER 6

Following the War

PRIESTLEY'S novels following World War II and extending into the 1960s represent various interests and concerns, a mixed bag as always; for Priestley has frequently stated that he is easily bored and moves from interest to interest as the spirit dictates. *Jenny Villiers, A Story of the Theatre*, appeared in 1947, followed in 1951 by the best novel of this group, *Festival at Farbridge*. *Low Notes on a High Level, A Frolic*, was published in 1954, and *The Magicians*, the least satisfying of this group of four, in 1954.

I Jenny Villiers

Jenny Villiers, the first full-scale indication of Priestley's interest in the time theories of Dunne and Ouspensky in his fiction, attempts to explain how time works dimensionally, in this instance in three dimensions: time present; time past; and through a continuum or tunnel, much like the one described in "The Town Major of Miraucourt." The tunnel is the means by which those of the present can communicate directly with those of the past through a mental effort induced in and by a sympathetic and mutually meaningful atmosphere. The life of the theater in general and the Green Room of the Theatre Royal of Barton Spa in particular offer the sympathetic background that allows a disenchanted dramatist-producer in 1946 to see, hear, and talk to Jenny Villiers, an actress who briefly performed in the Theatre Royal a hundred years before.

Martin Cheveril finds himself in 1946 with little will for life as he prepares to try out his latest play, symbolically called *The Glass Door*. After a desultory conversation with Pauline Seward, his leading lady and onetime mistress, during which he tells her that the play will be his last and that he will not alter its

depressing final act, Cheveril refuses to audition a young actress
who has asked for an interview. Taking four blood-pressure pills
instead of the two prescribed by his doctor, Cheveril awakens to
a dreamlike condition in the Green Room of 1846. He sees the
young provincial actress, Jenny Villiers, come into the Green
Room, watches her rehearse with the eccentric Victorian
company she has joined, sees her fall in love with the young
principal, Julian Napier, follows her through her first success,
and then witnesses the sad spectacle of her death after she has
been abandoned by Napier. Several times Cheveril and Jenny are
fully aware of one another as beings existing in different times,
and they communicate directly through the corridor that links
them to one another.

Of the many people Cheveril encounters in his return to the
theater of a hundred years ago, he is most in harmony with
Walter Kettle, the playwright in love with Jenny Villiers but
refused by her. From Kettle Cheveril learns that direction and
support given to those who give life to the theater is action never
to be lost, or, in terms of the time philosophy, it is time gained.
And from Jenny herself Cheveril learns to believe again in the
continuing life of the theater and to understand that the
experience of individuals in time is secondary to the more
fulfilling adventure of art. To Alfred Leathers, a character actor
in the present time, Cheveril says: " 'The Theatre's . . . always
been dying for the old hands. And it's always being born again for
the new ones. And that's not its weakness, that's its strength. It
lives—really lives and not merely exists, but lives as humanity
lives—just because it's forever dying and being born, because it's
always renewing its life.' "[1]

At the novel's end Cheveril finds himself promising to help the
young actress he had earlier refused to see. As he looks at her, he
feels that she is both familiar and strange to him. He asks her to
read Viola's lines from *Twelfth Night* and is both mystified and
delighted to discover that she stumbles over the identical
passage that Jenny had over a hundred years before. He gives
her the same direction that he had given Jenny in the past, and in
doing so he discovers in the girl Jenny's passion and dedication.
And to his even greater astonishment he discovers that the young
actress has married the reincarnation of Julian Napier, and that
her grandfather was the same Walter Kettle who had loved
Jenny in 1846. But most important of all to Cheveril is his

rediscovery of the value of experience in time, his knowledge that meaning depends on the intensity of dedication.

Unlike many of Priestley's novels, *Jenny Villiers* exhibits a full awareness of the dramatic form, emphasizing the unities of time, place, and action as elements of its theme. *Jenny Villiers* is more a narrated drama than it is a novel, and it was in fact originally intended as a play for the Bristol Theatre, whose general ambience and Green Room are largely suggested by the setting.[2] Indeed the work profits strangely from the fact that the lineaments of the dramatic form, of scene and act, can be constantly discerned beneath the action. Furthermore, *Jenny Villiers* pleases, much as do John L. Balderston's *Berkeley Square* (1929) and Barrie's *Dear Brutus* (1917) and *Mary Rose* (1920), because of its imaginative implementation of the Gothic impulse. Yet the use of time appears to be not so much the illustration of a theory as it is in his earlier play *Time and the Conways*, as an effective theatrical device to portray theme more immediately and more economically. Priestley had once suggested that the manipulation of time in *Berkeley Square* was a device to make the play work, and that the discovery of a second chance in *Dear Brutus* merely enabled Barrie to proceed with his main action.[3] Nonetheless, the plays are effective stage works, yet by no means dramatic masterpieces. In much the same manner, *Jenny Villiers* is an effective novel.

II   Festival at Farbridge

"I wanted to write a large-scale comic novel about post-war England. . . ," writes Priestley of *Festival at Farbridge*, "and, stupidly as I see now, I chose the 1951 Festival of Britain, which I welcomed and never sneered at, as a peg on which to hang the tale." After commenting on the disapproval leveled at the novel by the "intellectual reviewers" of the period, Priestley states his belief that the novel contains some of the funniest scenes he ever created, and that the work in fact is the only attempt in the language "at a comic wide panorama of post-war England."[4] A quarter of a century after its appearance, the novel appears more rightly as a dazzling comic symphony rather than a patronizing attempt to make a large audience feel smugly complacent. David Hughes aptly observes that despite "occasional fatigue in the writing, one or two inadequate scenes and the awkward burden of two of its characters [Ted and Laura]," the novel is far funnier than *The Good Companions*.[5]

Festival at Farbridge does celebrate Britain's festival year, but more importantly it celebrates the nation and its people. " 'Once you're outside London,' " says young Ted Jenks, articulating the novel's theme, " 'you seem to meet all kinds of people you never expect to meet, people you can't imagine meeting just from reading about England in the papers or most of the books. Not only odd characters, but people who seem to belong to other periods. You never imagine, when you live a long way off, that all the other Englands—Victorian and Edwardian, for instance— still survive in certain people.' "[6]

Second in length only to his novel of the 1960s, *The Image Men, Festival at Farbridge* is orchestrated rather than structured and in many ways suggests a symphony. Another novel similarly structured is Anthony Burgess's *Malayan Trilogy* (1956-59), which, in fact, is presented in three separate movements. The three large sections of *Festival at Farbridge* are preceded by a prelude, and an epilogue of sorts completes the plan. The prelude sets the tone, and the epilogue confirms it at the end.

The first movement brings together three individuals of differing temperaments and background into the common cause—the organization and production of a festival. Something of a confidence man, with the look of a character out of *Punch* circa 1919, Commodore Tribe, whose title is honorary and whose past is not exactly honorable, is immediately recognizable as a logical descendant of Baron Roland. He is the conductor—and behind him stands the composer, the author himself taking pleasure in his premiere production. Tribe is ready to conduct the orchestra and to present the program, but only after the orchestra has been tuned and readied by the lovers Laura Casey and Ted Jenks, who serve jointly as concertmaster. Romantic, headstrong, unreal, one of a long line of Priestley's romanticized maidens who refuse to languish on the vine, Laura has lost her job as secretary for Bulfoss and Sons, Estate Agents for the community. A good-natured blond giant with a trace of Chinese ancestry, Ted Jenks, a traveler from the West Indies touring the country before returning home, offers a more objective view of the domestic activities of festival planning. The three coincidentally come together in a tea room to collaborate on a plan to make the midlands city of Farbridge accept a festival and, incidentally, to give the Commodore and Laura employment.

The first section of the novel, the organization of the festival committee, brings the three into contention with the elements of town government and the pressures of the merchants of the community who want the festival but do not know how to marshal themselves against the Tory factions who have already decided against it. Seth Hull, proprietor of the White Hart, agrees to support the Commodore and his group, as does Joe Gisburn, who represents Labour. The Tory faction, represented by Alderman Tanhead, Colonel Whatmore, and Beverly Bulfoss, the local M.P.'s brother, stand opposed. The communists, represented by Ravenstreet, vacillate between the two larger factions. Moving into the environs, the Commodore and his assistants soon enlist the support of Lady Barth and her deaf secretary, Mrs. Wintle, Admiral Broadwater, Field Marshal Watton and his sister Beryl, Lord Barnleysale and his daughter Felicia, and numerous other remarkably vibrant and memorable types. Each encounter constitutes a richly satisfying comic vignette. The first section of the novel culminates in a farcical near-riot, the debate held in the Corn Exchange to decide whether or not the town government will reverse its decision and allow the festival to take place. " 'Liberal democracy. Expensive and elaborate, but best in the end,' " says retired drygoods merchant Jordan, confirming the wisdom of the town's decision to subsidize the festival (318).

The second movement of the novel, a jubilant scherzo following the andante of the first movement, the most imaginative and funniest of the three, concerns the engaging of the various groups and attractions that will draw the community and the environs to the festival. Music, dancing, poetry, drama, lectures, food, all are contracted for the two-week celebration. Best drawn of these groups is the Mossat Dramatic Society, briefly introduced into the first section through an acquaintance of Ted Jenks, engaged to perform in the Palace Theatre. And best drawn of the actors is the alcoholic leading man, Patrick Gorebarry, who, at one point, interrupts a lecture entitled "The Fierce Gay Anarchist," the funniest of many comic scenes. This section of the novel culminates in the first night performance of a modish but trashy verse play entitled "Why Should the Nightingale?" Drunken Gorebarry, playing an uncertain, lecherous Cardinal, speaks lines from Shakespeare instead of

Derek Boon's text, much to everyone's unknowing delight.

The third section, the performances and the problems they entail, an allegro, culminates in the spectacular fireworks display of the first weekend and the gala ball that concludes the festival, but not before all couples are suitably paired and sent on their happy way, including the Commodore, who sets up housekeeping with Grace Robinson, a mysterious middle-aged charmer who moves in and out of the action, mesmerizing Tribe and making him yearn to settle down to running a tight little pub.

To define the pattern is, however, to miss Priestley's intrinsic purpose: the presentation in broad comic fashion of a dazzling display of characters and events from all classes which represent the English spirit. Muleford and Archie Mobbs, Madge Bulfoss and her lover, Hatchet-Ferrers, the actresses Clare Chesbey and Philippa Hookwood, Dr. Barr and Group Captain Trevone—all are forcefully drawn and convincingly dramatized, occasioning delight in and of themselves. Mrs. Coote, Mr. Huntley, Johnny Jolly and his wife Alice, Mr. Atcham, the sleazy detective Smith, Sir Barclay Gishforth and his wife Daphne—all are instruments brilliantly orchestrated to present the nation to itself. A spirit of gaiety dominates the whole, and *Festival at Farbridge* becomes, as a result, one of Priestley's most satisfying works.

III   Low Notes on a High Level

If *Festival at Farbridge* can be compared to Frith's *Derby Day*, then *Low Notes on a High Level* suggests a vignette by Rowlandson. It is a satirical romp, a lighthearted frolic that mixes equal portions of romantic fantasy and good-natured farce to produce a lively and entertaining narrative. In *Low Notes on a High Level* the author returns to the world of broadcasting which he had explored earlier in *Good Night Children* (1942) and to his long-standing interest in the devices used to "popularize" culture. The novel is Priestley at his most genial, his most whimsical, his delightful best.

Alan Applerose, assistant musical director for the English Broadcasting Company, finds himself involved with the first production of the Tenth Symphony of Norroland's leading composer, a giant of a man named Stannsen, who happens to be the godfather of Inga Dobb, a lovely blonde child-woman who professes her undying love for Applerose the moment she sees him in the EBC studio. Her uncle, Roland Dobb, a onetime friend of Stannsen and eccentric inventor of the Dobbophone, a large and unwieldy instrument resembling a bass bassoon, decides not to pay his income taxes and to make a protest against government interference in his life. He decides to interrupt the normal schedule of television and radio broadcasts to point out to the nation the intolerable and restrictive activities of a bureaucratized government.

Stannsen has made it a condition of the EBC's premiere performance of his symphony that the Dobbophone be played, a condition which Dobb at first rejects but later agrees to when he learns that Stannsen himself and Dr. Bergenborg, the president of Norroland, both on a secret mission of good will, have come to England to settle earlier differences with him over a game of *Strunshka*, a card game of great significance in Norroland. The largely farcical situation involving the broadcast and the reconciliation of the old friends is resolved when the police apprehend the group making illegal broadcasts in the company of the Norroland dignitaries. Dobb, Alan, and Inga are exonerated on the grounds that they have brought the English sense of humor back into the arena of international politics: " 'Now, gentlemen,' " says the President of Norroland, " 'of the Great Powers, Britain is no longer the richest and strongest. But we still look to her for something that is very rare among the rich and powerful—for a spirit of humour, a spirit of tolerance. Very precious indeed in this iron world, gentlemen. There was much talk after the War of a Third Force, you will remember. But the real Third Force is this spirit of humour, of tolerance, of a liberal humanism that does not take itself too seriously.' "[7]

The tone and mood of *Low Notes on a High Level* are precise accommodations of extravagant farcical confrontations and broad comic characterization. Best of all is the introduction of four gigantic musicians, inventors of even larger instruments than the Dobbophone: Herr Grobemeir of the Great-German-Double-Bombardon; Signor Nicola Bertini, of the contra-fagotto; and the twin brothers, Louis and Alfred Sauvager, of the two-man fiddle.

The satire, leveled generally at the bureaucratic mismanagement of the EBC and the government, specifically at the infighting and in-breeding that characterizes mass media, aims well-placed barbs at those who stand against real enjoyment and pleasure. As inventor Dobb says to the Air Marshal, who runs the EBC, " 'You spend your time trying to please a lot of nitwits who haven't the sense to amuse themselves for an hour or two every night, who want to pay tuppence a week and have every idiotic prejudice considered and catered for, who can't even play their own parlor games any more' " (55). The tone and temper of *Low Notes on a High Level* are those of the *Spectator Papers;* the satire is kindly but no less effective for being so.

Alan Applerose is rewarded at the novel's end, both for his integrity and his willingness to enjoy a lark; he has not only the lovely Inga, but also Stannsen's franchise to conduct the new symphony for two years. Stannsen gives his reason for choosing Alan as his conductor, not that he likes the lad and wishes to give him and his goddaughter a leg up in the musical world, but that Alan has played his symphony correctly, after the original conductor, Sir Lancelot Telly, had fallen off the podium in Festival Hall, and not intruded himself upon the music.

IV   The Magicians

Like *Jenny Villiers, The Magicians* reiterates Priestley's fascination with time, and like the earlier novel *The Magicians* addresses itself to the possibility of recreation. The recapitulation of event in time occurs in this novel in an area of the time continuum deriving from his reading of Ouspensky and here called "time alive." Wayland, one of three ancient travelers befriended by the protagonist, Charles Ravenstreet, evaluates for Ravenstreet the significance of an event that occurred in the past, an event relived but understood in the present as it had not been understood twenty-five years earlier: " 'You were brought to recognise what exists. It is always there. It is really you—as you can't help being, and from which there's no escape, only certain possibilities of change, a new creation of one's life.' "[8]

General Manager of New Central Electric, a company he helped to make large and powerful, Ravenstreet, ousted by internal manipulation within the company, is asked to join a group of businessmen headed by Lord Mervil, a desiccated and sinister exponent of an elite power cult. Mervil and his associates are prepared to market a recently developed tranquillizer called Sepman Eighteen. Ravenstreet at first agrees to enter into negotiations with Mervil and his group. He is warned, however, about the evil Mervil will do with the chemical formula by three ancient wanderers he meets near his home. Wayland, Marot, and Perperek are the magicians of the title, and collectively they suggest the figure of the wandering Jew of the Gothic romances.

From the magicians Ravenstreet learns that it is possible for some men to relive the experiences of the past. He is taken back into a long-forgotten period of his life, when he was young and yet aware of dreams. He finds himself reliving his betrayal of his mistress Philippa, and he sees himself choose again Maureen, his employer's daughter, for with her comes her father's wealth and power. Ravenstreet relives his experience as it was, but understands in the present the enormity of his treachery in the past. He also finds that he can live partly in Philippa's past consciousness of time, and he realizes, as he had not in the past, her anguish and desolation.

Warned again by the magicians of the mysterious evil that Mervil represents, Ravenstreet hesitates before committing himself to the cartel, and he invites Mervil and his cohorts to his home to confront the magicians. There, through the occult power of the three ancient men, Mervil reveals himself as the representative of a sinister force that wants to enslave the earth, a force that the magicians are pledged to stand against—which occasions the major flaw in the novel. The forces that Perperek, Wayland, and Marot are to combat are never developed, neither through narrative nor dramatic interplay; nor is the possibility of a "new creation of one's life," the point cited in the quotation above. The reader is given instead a happy ending of sorts as Ravenstreet is united by Philippa with the son he never knew he had, secure in the knowledge that the magicians are abroad in the world, safeguarding it from the unspecified dangers of Mervil and his group.

But to what purpose? For the newspapers soon announce that a tranquillizer will appear on the market. And the reader can only recall the rhetoric of Mervil's statements concerning an elite who regard power as their chief reward: "'In all the progressive industrialized regions,'" he says, "'which alone count for anything, the great mass of people now will pay . . . for an easy painless life, without any real effort, responsibility, anxiety, fear, suffering. They want this all the more because they haven't the strength of mind to face their own despair. . . . If we all lived on this mindless mass level, with rapidly dwindling resources of courage, initiative, executive ability, creative thinking, in fifty years we shouldn't be able to feed, clothe, house ourselves'" (96-97). This statement in essence echoes that which Dobb makes to the Chief of the EBC, and reechoes the pessimism of the Doomsday men of Priestley's earlier fiction. But what all this means within the action of the novel remains mysterious, unassimilated.

Although *The Magicians* may be read as a partially successful quasi-Gothic novel, despite a certain listlessness of tone and characterization that neither convinces nor amuses, it is ultimately a failure as it fails to develop or dramatize the very point that is the burden of the theme: the possibility of a new beginning through a creative view of existence. If it is intended as either an explanation of Ouspensky's recurrence or Dunne's serial time, it is equally a failure, for the reader learns little. Indeed the story "The Town Major of Miraucourt" more easily explains Dunne than does the novel. For a fuller explanation of what Lord Mervil and the magicians represent, Priestley's reader will have to wait for the 1960s, for in his entertainments, *Saturn Over the Water* and *The Shapes of Sleep* (1962), lie the fuller dimensions of what *The Magicians* implies.

CHAPTER 7

Novels of the 1960s

BETWEEN 1961 and 1969 Priestley published nine novels. Two of these are thrillers, admired by Anthony Burgess, who describes them in *The Novel Now* as "admirable 'international conspiracy' thrillers."[1] They are *Saturn Over the Water* in 1961, and *The Shapes of Sleep* in 1962. These books are in the spirit of *The Doomsday Men,* and to them can be added *Salt is Leaving,* 1966, which, although set in England, reaches out to the world beyond. The 1960s also saw the publication of two lighthearted satires, or frolics, *The Thirty-First of June* in 1962, and *Sir Michael and Sir George* in 1964. Three more seriously conceived and executed novels also appeared: *Lost Empires* in 1965, *It's an Old Country* in 1967, and *The Image Men* in two volumes in 1968, and in one volume in 1969.

If one remembers that Priestley also published his *Literature and Western Man* in 1960, *The Prince of Pleasure and His Regency, 1811-1820* in 1969, and *The Edwardians* in 1970, the sheer bulk as well as the high level of his accomplishment during the decade appear staggering. At a time when most men are settling back into the comforts of their years, Priestley looked, as he has always done, to new horizons. The decade of the 1960s saw in effect the publication of some of his best works.

I   *Three Thrillers:* Saturn Over the Water,
The Shapes of Sleep, Salt is Leaving

In *The Doomsday Men,* his entertainment of 1938, Priestley had symbolized in the MacMichael brothers an enlightened pessimism born of despair. The chief purpose of the Doomsday men, if statements attributed to characters suffering from hubris, megalomania, and religious fanaticism can be at all believed, was to give the planet a new beginning. Their plan to destroy

87

appeared, ironically, as an act of disinterested generosity, for they planned nothing for themselves beyond the holocaust. Andrea and Malcolm's flowering love, supported by Hooker's scientific detachment and Edlin's warm humanity, implemented by Charlie Atwood's death wish, had managed to abort the detonation of the doomsday apparatus. The novel's ending, despite a certain wryness of narrative presentation, as a result appeared anticlimactic.

In *The Magicians*, Priestley had deployed an occult theme again through three symbolical figures, Wayland, Marot, and Perperek. They had maintained a hope for the future, nurtured by an ability to see into the tunnels of time; and their knowledge had come of an awareness of the possibility of recreation. The only indication that Lord Mervil represented something more than a power cult born of wealth had been dramatized in the brief sequence in which the magicians had exerted a power superior to his and returned him to a telling experience in "time alive." If love had been intended as the operative force behind the magicians, its power had been left unmotivated, for Ravenstreet's conversion from Mervil to the magicians remained largely arbitrary, and the happy ending of the novel, as a result, proved unconvincing. Both novels had, however, initiated themes demanding completion.

Saturn Over the Water and *The Shapes of Sleep* continue Priestley's interests in and preoccupation with the dimensions and responsibilities of power. Both novels are fantasies of science, both demonstrate Priestley's abiding interest in the patterns of time, both depend for their vitality on sharply etched characterizations, on briskly paced action implemented by means of flight and pursuit, elaborate paraphernalia and sensational events. Both are in fact successful thrillers and among the best books that Priestley has written. Both novels, furthermore, employ science metaphorically as a means of dramatizing the imminent possibility of fulfilling a universal death wish. The cult of power marshals all the inventions of science and its consequences to its ends: nuclear energy, will-suspending drugs, subliminal indoctrination, the effects of fallout on the Southern Hemisphere, mysterious hypnotic shapes that inhibit the will. Even governments are subdued by the power that seeks to enslave. Yet this cult of power can be opposed, can be countered by love, for love, as Priestley conceives it, embodies a challenge to time and is in itself a celebration of life and purpose. In both *Saturn Over the Water* and *The Shapes of Sleep*, the happy ending becomes an integral aspect of the loose allegories that contain the action and give resonance to the themes, as it was not in either *The Doomsday Men* or *The Magicians*. Love in *Saturn Over the Water* is supported by art, for art is the creation of beauty, of truth. And both the protagonists of *Saturn Over the Water* are artists.

Set within an encompassing framework—a writer sends Tim Bedford's first-person account of his adventure to a friend—*Saturn Over the Water* employs the entire globe as its setting. " 'A lot of space,' " says Rother, a scientist who suspects his employers of participation in an international conspiracy, " 'but all in such little time. I tell you, it is now a very small world. It is really smaller than Europe was two hundred years ago.' "[2] The action begins in England, moves to Chile and then Argentina, and culminates in Australia. In the Epilogue or Postscript, the reader is told that Tim Bedford and Rosalia Arnaldos, the grand-daughter of one of the inner circle of the cult, have obeyed the call of their masters and gone to Africa to challenge once more the threat of the Saturnians. There is no anticlimax at the conclusion of *Saturn Over the Water*, only another beginning, for the conspiracy that Tim and Rosalia have helped to abort in Australia continues throughout the world.

Honoring his dying cousin's wish to find her physicist-husband, who has gone to South America to work for the Arnaldos Institute, Tim Bedford becomes a catalyst in the war of power that the evil Saturnians wage against the earth. The conflict is explained to Tim and Rosalia by Pat Dailey, himself a magician who seems to possess the same credentials that Wayland, Marot, and Perperek had—an ability to see into "time alive." When asked who the Saturnians are and what their insignia, an 8 over wavy lines, represents, he says: " 'Saturn represents age, weight, authority, a cold exercise of power. So *Saturn Over the Water* means that the world begins again—only in the Southern Hemisphere at first, the Northern being uninhabitable mostly—under the absolute rule of a few, the master of millions of slaves. . . . It's all there in *Saturn Over the Water*. For water is also an ancient symbol of the unconscious. And if Saturn is *over* water, then the masters of this system will not only control men's conscious minds but also their unconscious. To a limited extent they're beginning to do it already . . . by increasing the hidden drives towards war. So Saturn, you might say, is already rising above the water' " (273–74).

Himself a Uranian, Dailey explains further that the cosmos is moving out of the age of Pisces into the age of Aquarius, that the Christian era is in fact in its final phases, and either the House of Saturn or the House of Uranus must dominate. Both camps draw their strength from powers in time yet beyond time, called the Masters. " 'Uranus,' " Dailey continues, " 'represents the feminine principle just as surely as Saturn represents the masculine. Its influences work through the sympathetic imagination. Most decent women and all true artists and all the people described by Saturnians as idle dreamers and crackpots' " are the challengers (274). As artists, Tim and Rosalia become proper champions of humanity.

Saturn Over the Water, in its ability to employ suspense and puzzle, and through its use of exotic locales and arcane manifestation, is indeed one of Priestley's finest fictions.

The Shapes of Sleep: A Topical Tale portrays much the same argument as *Saturn Over the Water.* The setting is here, however, restricted to England and Europe, but the action is still contained within the pattern of flight and pursuit, the standby of the thriller form. Instead of the artist as protagonist, *The Shapes of Sleep* employs a middle-aged journalist, Jake Sternberg, who writes articles-on-demand, usually on topical subjects, to eke out a living.

Sternberg is approached by a friend who works for an American tycoon named Julius to discover the whereabouts of a mysterious green sheet of paper that had disappeared from the desk of one of his colleagues. Needing the £50 promised him for the "detective" work, Sternberg, more at home in the grace and logic of the eighteenth century than in the corrupt world of twentieth-century London, embarks upon a mission of detection that takes him into sleazy walk-ups as well as into glossy London society, into Germany, where he becomes involved with Communist espionage activities, and finally to a group called "Antiants," an organization that believes that certain profiteers are making a determined effort to put an end to the free development of humanity. Antiants, like the Uranians, oppose " 'in many different ways . . . anything . . . creating dumb blind masses—.' "[3] The cult of power, in other words, operating much as it did in the earlier thriller, is opposed by those who have a belief in man.

The search for the "shapes of sleep"—that is, cut-out shapes that exert an hypnotic effect on the unguarded mind—leads Sternberg to an international intrigue where identities are doubtful, allegiances a matter of money, and affections without meaning. He does, however, meet Wanda, the niece of the Professor Voss who has discovered the mysterious shapes of sleep, and he falls in love with her. Ironically the love plot is identical to that of *Albert Goes Through*, the frolic of 1933 in which Priestley had ridiculed the Hollywood movies of the time. Wanda, Sternberg discovers, as had Albert Limpley of Felicity Storm, is not so much the mysterious and glamorous *femme fatale* as she is the ingenuous girl primarily interested in recovering the shapes of sleep to cover up her uncle's Communist affiliation. At the novel's end, once the puzzle is unraveled, Wanda's affection rescues Sternberg from his eighteenth-century nostalgia and returns him to the modern world and to some measure of faith in the future.

Exciting, ingenious, even as he parodies his earlier novel, employing calculated delay as his chief means of creating suspense, Priestley aims his devastating satire at journalistic adulterations, advertising practices, high-pressure campaigns designed to lull and thereby to cheat—in other words, he satirizes the very institutions he had previously attacked in *Wonder Hero* and *They Walk in the City*, except that here he is more successful since the attacks are integral to the activities of the thriller. The portrait of Julius, the ruthless American financier, more than likely a cohort of the Saturnians of the earlier novel (although the occult aspect of the earlier novel is not mounted in this book), is one of the novel's strongest and most convincing attractions. It is Sternberg's standing up to Julius's pressures—£200 for information about the shapes of sleep, £10,000 for the shapes themselves—that transforms him into an improbable although convincing hero.

Saturn Over the Water is perhaps the better of these two entertainments, for its display of scientific paraphernalia and its use of the occult are both witty and dazzling. The shapes of sleep are more subtly suggestive of the means that power uses to dominate the minds of the many, but in a thriller the spectacular is usually more acceptable than the subtle. Yet Sternberg is a stronger protagonist than was Tim Bedford, for he is more aware of the reality of corruption. He looks forward to Dr. Salt of Priestley's next thriller, which in some ways is the best of the three.

If *Saturn Over the Water* and *The Shapes of Sleep* suggest the thrillers of Ian Fleming and Len Deighton, respectively, *Salt is Leaving* suggests something of Agatha Christie, something of Conan Doyle. *Salt is Leaving* is quietly urbane compared to the other two thrillers, concentrating more on the puzzle than on a suspense generated and maintained by sensationalism, violence, and appealing gimmickry. Like Agatha Christie's Miss Marple books, *Salt is Leaving* is set in a comparatively small town, Birkden, and deals in its backgrounds with the felt but largely unacknowledged influences brought to bear on the moral life of the community. In some ways reminiscent of the wartime novel, *Black-Out in Gretley,* also a detective story of sorts, *Salt is Leaving* makes imaginative use of setting and politics to delineate an ambience appropriate to the intrigue. Suspense in the novel depends on characterization, and tone on a purposeful and convincing ambiguity.

Seven years a resident of Birkden, Dr. Salt, widowed, something of a specialist in kidney disorders, decides that, before he can leave the city for a more rewarding life in Malaya or some other faraway place, he must settle the whereabouts of Noreen Wilks, a patient missing for three weeks. Noreen suffers from nephritis which needs periodic attention, the chief reason of Salt's concern. He soon finds himself involved with Maggie Culworth, the daughter of a bookseller of nearby Hemton, who is searching for her father who disappeared the same day that Noreen vanished. Salt goes to the police, is rebuffed by them and by Sir Arthur Donnington, the head of the works that employs the majority of the town. Salt is sufficiently angered by these confrontations to pursue the search on his own. Using his knowledge of people and his professional ability to detect lies and evasions, Salt asks Maggie to combine forces to discover the truth of the two disappearances.

The search leads them first to Buzzy Duffield, perhaps the most amusing character of the book—his words end in "zz"s— proprietor of a sleazy dance-hall and fringe dealer in underworld activities. Buzzy puts them on to Derek Donnington, Noreen's lover, and the United Anglo-Belgian Fabrics Club, maintained by the firm that the town largely depends upon for its livelihood. Derek, Salt discovers, had committed suicide on the same day that Noreen and Mr. Culworth had disappeared.

Next they meet Jill Frinton, enamelled manageress of the Fabrics Social Club, where Noreen had last been seen. At Jill's apartment they confront Erica Donnington, Derek's sister, who professes a Lesbian attachment for Jill, which Salt immediately discounts.

Salt is certain that Noreen has been murdered; and he surmises that the body has been hidden in a deserted house adjacent to the club precincts. He soon locates Maggie's father in a nursing home, where he had been hidden by the factory bosses after receiving a nasty knock on the head while asking questions about Noreen. Maggie discovers that her father has felt responsible for Noreen because of a wartime romance with her mother.

The discovery of Noreen's body in the deserted house occasions the one false note in the ratiocinative process which is the novel's chief attraction. Priestley asks his reader to believe that the elder Donnington in protecting his daughter Erica, who had killed Noreen because of jealousy over her brother—with whom she had had an incestuous relationship—had hidden the body behind a quickly devised cardboard wall which he had then papered over. Where Donnington had found new paper to match the old in the bedroom of the derelict house is never explained, let alone how he managed to build the false wall.

But the puzzle, though inadequately explained, comes to matter little, for the entertainment's theme of ethical commitment dominates the novel. Salt is willing to keep the facts of the murder from the police, preferring his judgment to the law's, if Donnington will agree to have his daughter attended by competent psychiatrists and give up his stranglehold on the life of the community. " 'We English,' " says Salt to Maggie, who will shortly be his wife, " 'seem to have got stuck in a nasty place. It's possible to make a class system work with a certain amount of ease and dignity. But we've done with that. It's also possible to make a clean fresh start. But we daren't risk that. So we're bogged down in a morass of meaningless snobberies, sulkiness, anxiety, resentment; and for the time being I've had enough of it. . . .' "[4] Salt and Maggie will travel for a while and settle into a useful life somewhere outside England, thereby anticipating Tom Adamson of *It's an Old Country*.

Dr. Salt emerges as one of Priestley's strongest protagonists, despite a certain sanctimony of manner and speech. His determination to see a new measure of freedom brought to a community he has himself decided to leave portrays the enlightened altruism that many of Priestley's best-drawn characters demonstrate. And Salt's desire to leave England suggests that one of Priestley's longest and most constant love affairs— with his own country—has temporarily soured. What Priestley ultimately suggests through Salt is the responsibility that all sensitive and intelligent men must feel; the need of all men to understand themselves as free, to know that the work they do must liberate the spirit. United Anglo-Belgian Fabrics, under the guise of the paternalistic leadership of Donnington, who is in effect an exponent of the cult of power, had kept the free spirit in chains. And freedom of the spirit is here, as it is in all of his works, Priestley's most persuasive theme.

II   *Two Satires:* The Thirty-First of June
      and Sir Michael and Sir George

Subtitled *A Tale of True Love, Enterprise and Progress, in the Arthurian and Ad-Atomic Ages, The Thirty-First of June* is a lighthearted frolic in the tradition of *Albert Goes Through,* reminiscent of Alice's adventures in Wonderland and the Connecticut Yankee's in King Arthur's court. It lightly satirizes the art of creating illusion, whether it be practiced in medieval times by the sorcerers Marlagram and Malgrim, or in contemporary London by the advertising firm of Wallaby, Dimmock, Paly and Tooks.

Given a magic mirror by the magician Malgrim, the lovely Princess Melicent looks from the turreted medieval world of Perador into the high-rise modern world of Sam Penty, an artist for the advertising firm headed by Dimmock. Sam, in turn, has visualized Melicent as the maiden best suited to sell a product called Damosel stockings. Rival magicians representing youth and old age in Melicent's world, the younger magus shouldering the older one aside, Marlagram and Malgrim conspire to bring Melicent and Sam together, then to separate them, and finally to join them in marriage while yet permitting them to live in their respective times—and all to prove their powers. Both magicians are rewarded at the novel's end by Dimmock's offer that they join the advertising board as replacements for Paly and Took, shadowy members of the advertising firm who never appear.

The mode of fantasy allows Priestley to deal playfully, whimsically, with the time device of *Jenny Villiers* and *The Magicians.* There is even self-parody in the tale, a considerable aspect of its charm. The ability of Marlagram and Malgrim to allow Sam and Melicent to transcend time, by communicating through a tunnel that flows from the twelfth or thirteenth century to the twentieth, is off-handedly explained as a third sphere of "parallel times, diverging and converging times, and times spirally intertwined."[5] All that is necessary to enter into this mythical world is imagination, which is ultimately a meaningful view of reality.

The charm of the piece also is determined by the ingenuity of the satirical attacks made on the world of mass advertising, the theme to which Priestley will turn in earnest in *The Image Men.* The shoddy and the false remain the shoddy and the false whether they are found in Melicent's time or Sam's. The armor that Sam wears to do battle with the Red Knight, for example, is described as "utility trash once authorized by the Camelot Armour and Weapons Board" (116), and Crunchy Nut is thought to be a not very marketable product because of the sound of the words. Best of all are the individual scenes which transport the citizens of one time into the world of the other: Sam survives the attack of a giant knight (actually a flim-flam man he had met in London who has been refurbished by the magic of Malgrim), and the death-dealing fire-breaths of a giant dragon (a metamorphosed Dimmock) who insists on dictating letters to his secretary between blasts. The frolic ends as all fairy tales should, with a thoroughly happy ending: Sam and Melicent are married, each in his proper world, their wedding table stretching from Dimmock's office, where the food is prepackaged and very bad, to Melicent's palace, where the food is very good indeed. *The Thirty-First of June*, which begins on Lunaday and ends on either Tuesday or Wednesday, allows for a timely farce; and to insist on the satirical aspects of the whole is to miss its fancy and its delight.

Priestley's novel of 1964, *Sir Michael and Sir George*, subtitled *A Comedy of the New Elizabethans*, is written with the same tongue-in-cheek. It is a mock-heroic treatment of government agencies: of Cosma and Discus, the National Commission for

Scholarship and the Arts, and the Department of Information
and Cultural Services, respectively. The novel is written in the
same tone of exasperated good will that characterizes *Low Notes
on a High Level.*

Licensed by the government to further the arts in a space-age
society, Cosma and Discus are more inclined to rival each other,
while largely duplicating functions, mostly by refusing to
subsidize musicians and artists who lack talent. With no
knowledge of the humanities, Sir George Drake, head of Discus,
is more concerned with sound administration than with fur-
thering the cause of music or literature, despite the fact that
there is very little for him to administrate. His rival in the world
of mass culture, head of Cosma, is Sir Michael Stratherrick, a
pompous womanizer, who does possess some insight into the arts.
He is, however, completely preoccupied with his by no means
lonely bachelorhood.

The largely unmotivated manipulator within the mock-epic
framework of the piece is Tim Kemp, who has worked for both
Sir Michael and Sir George. A not-unfamiliar figure in Priestley's
fictional world, Tim is boozy, good-natured, largely tolerant of
hypocrites and buffoons, intuitive, aware of the marvelous
variety of people and language; in short he is the ringmaster or
master of ceremonies of Priestley's earlier books. But here he is
further characterized by a certain feyness of spirit, a restlessness
of mood, a purposeful malice, an ancient mischievousness. He is
in many ways closer to the trickster of legend and the fairy world
than some of Priestley's earlier organizers appear to be.

Tim decides to send young, pretty, empty-headed Shirley
Essex into the castled domain of Sir Michael, aware that the
attractive pawn will help to topple the kingdom of Cosma—
which in effect occurs. Sir Michael sees Shirley, recognizes her as
his soul's delight, and marries her, knowing full well that Tim had
sent her to him from Discus's typing pool simply to harass him. At
the end Tim tells Sir Michael that he is pleased that his plan to
use Shirley had misfired, for Sir Michael is no longer the man he
had schemed against.

Marred minimally by its attempt to round out and humanize
the two-dimensional characters, which briefly detracts from the
rapid farcical confrontations that the novel depends upon for its
effect, *Sir Michael and Sir George,* nevertheless, succeeds
largely because of its many scenes of gusto and imagination: the

evening in the Green Gong, during which Sir George and his wife are exposed to the antics of the mad artist Ned Greene; the scene in Sir George's office in which he confronts the O'Mores, a group of ebullient actors sent him by a drunken theater scout for an audition; the scene in which Sir Michael attends a provincial production of *Dummies*, a popular off-Broadway play of no merit whatsoever and destined for a long London run. There is no flagging of invention, no diminution of comic tone, from beginning to end. *Sir Michael and Sir George* is, perhaps, the most successful of all of Priestley's frolics and a novel deserving of admiration and applause.

III   Lost Empires

Published in 1965, *Lost Empires* is for Priestley a return to the past, employing the English music hall in its period of decline immediately preceding World War I. The novel profits from the same dual perspective that gave *The Good Companions* its nostalgic quality, the tender backward look to a time that was. And although the troupers in *Lost Empires* are in their way aware of their numbered days, they and their comic turns are not the chief artistic merits of the novel, as were the hi-jinks of the good companions on the road. *Lost Empires* makes use of the variety stage as a symbol that loosely allegorizes the politics of a world destined for war, as does Thomas Mann's "Mario and the Magician" (1929). The protagonist Dick Herncastle is contrasted to his uncle, Nick Ollanton, in much the same manner that Adam Stewart was contrasted to Baron Roland in Priestley's first novel, *Adam in Moonshine;* but here the contrast serves the structure in a way that the earlier presentation did not.

An illusionist in the halls whose appearance and tricks suggest the diabolical, as does Mann's Cipolla, as Ganga Dun Nick Ollanton and his fabricated magic allegorize the political activist and his propaganda techniques; he is in effect a mesmerizer who bends the will to his purpose. A time perspective on his influence is achieved by means of a deftly presented Prologue and Epilogue which encompass the action of the novel as well as the period of the war itself. The action proper ends with Dick Herncastle, Ganga Dun's assistant, enlisting "to take my chance, as so many others are doing,"[6] succumbing to the illusion of a better world brought about by war, and with Ollanton himself leaving the old country for the United States, revealing as he goes his bag of tricks as a private escape from the "bloody mincing machine" of global war (349). Dick's return from the war is briefly recounted in both the Prologue and the Epilogue. He marries the girl of his dreams, Nancy, herself a music-hall performer, and settles down to become a successful water-colorist, an illusionist of another sort.

The charm of *Lost Empires,* however, goes well beyond its symbolical structure; it lies in its descriptions of the variety theaters on the Empire Circuit, as it portrays the various "artistes" who perform there—Ricardo, the juggler; Tony Beamish, the comedian; Lily Farrish, the singer of sentimental ballads. The episodes are, however, fitted into the melodramatic plot which in itself echoes the activities of the times and fulfills the darker demands of the narrative. Ollanton and Herncastle collaborate to help Barney, a dwarf in their act who has murdered the tantalizing Nonie Colman, a relentless sexual tease, to escape the claws of Inspector Crabb of Scotland Yard, thus placing their own ethics, as had Dr. Salt of *Salt is Leaving,* over the law of the land. Their loyalty to Barney is determined by their understanding of the human situation they have witnessed. In helping the dwarf escape they also signal their end as performers. The motion pictures will soon make the halls obsolete, and wobbling banalities on an illuminated screen will replace the flesh-and-blood reality of the performers, as the world will accept the illusions of dictators and give over to the charade of war. Ollanton and Herncastle's challenge is a gallant but futile gesture to the inevitable.

And even Ollanton, one of Priestley's finest-drawn symbolical characters, will in his way succumb to the overwhelming compulsion of war, adding an unnerving ambiguity to the symbolical meaning of the tale: he will begin manufacturing machine-gun sights for airplanes, a fact recounted in the Epilogue. Dick, however, having given himself to the war, having suffered its realities, is able to put his relationship with his uncle and his experience as an illusionist into clearer focus. His becoming an artist is not so much a refuge from reality as it is a means of making moments of insight and feeling permanent, which is the novel's underlying theme. In *Adam in Moonshine* Adam Stewart was fully aware that the enchantment he found in his adventure was largely in himself; Dick Herncastle moves from enchantment through horror to art, a means of ordering experience and serving humanity. He suggests in many ways his author.

IV   It's an Old Country

Like *Lost Empires, It's an Old Country* is elaborately plotted and symbolically structured. Ostensibly Tom Adamson's search for the father from whom he was separated some thirty years before the narrative begins, the novel is in effect a search for the self and for allegiance in a world deprived of romance and largely given to despair born of deception. Indeed the motif of deception constitutes a coherent imagerial pattern that lends the work resonance and texture. *It's an Old Country,* set in contemporary England in the 1960's, is equal in craft and insight to *Bright Day* and *Angel Pavement,* revealing the artist in full command of his art.

Tom Adamson's search for his father (the name is symbolical) brings him from Australia, where he had been taken together with his sister by his mother after her seeming abandonment by her husband. An inheritance from a dour uncle makes it possible for him to return to England, the old country, to look for his roots and to uncover the cause of his mother's and his own unhappiness. His commitment to the search is at first half-hearted, an emotional response made to his mother as she lay dying. He is, however, intrigued by her change of attitude concerning the husband who had left her thirty years before, a change brought about as a result of a mysterious letter sent from the Old World.

The first person Tom finds in London is his cousin Chas, in whose reckless nature he senses certain aspects of self held in check by a wariness of purpose and a general sense of futility deriving both from his study of history—Tom is a teacher in an Australian university—and from the fact that he has been denied his birthright. The encounter with Chas initiates a series of doublings, which is resolved at the novel's end as Tom assumes full possession of his history and acknowledges the possibility of a meaningful future—in essence the same theme that had preoccupied Priestley in both *Bright Day* and, to a lesser degree, in *Lost Empires.* The recreation of the past presupposes renewal, as it does in many of Priestley's other books, most notably *Bright*

Day, Jenny Villiers, and *The Magicians.* It is the time theme fully
accommodating the demands of plot and characterization.

Through Chas Tom encounters a bewildering array of
caricatures and grotesques, reminding the reader of Dickens's
gallery of rogues. This aspect of the novel involves Priestley in
surrealized narration. Tom is, for example, taken to a large
country house, where he is told he must play the role of a foreign
dignitary in order to be admitted to the party which is being
given by an ancient woman who garlands herself with fantastic
garments and exquisite jewelry. There Tom encounters dilettantes and charlatans busily enacting their fantasies as clerics, as
officers, as diplomats, the entire sequence suggesting Genet's
The Balcony (1956). There he meets a seedy detective named
Crike to whom he guiltily entrusts the task of finding his father.

Tom also meets a mysterious and seductive woman, Countess
Helga, whom he immediately recognizes as the personification of
all his adolescent sexual fantasies. At the same time he meets
Judy Marston, a publisher's agent whom he idly dismisses as rude
and pert, thus continuing the doubling which characterizes the
novel's structure. Illusion and reality are constantly juxtaposed.
After an embarrassing interlude with Helga, Tom recognizes
Judy as the woman he has been looking for. And it is through
Judy that he finally finds his father. But not before he can accept
himself.

Chas also introduces Tom to Professor Firmius, a descendant
of Baron Roland, a charismatic figure who lives in a basement flat
while working on an enormously long and complicated book on
time and history. Firmius is paralleled within the symbolical
structure of the novel by Alison Oliver, a painter who specializes
in still life, "some flowers in a jug, a decanter and a couple of
glasses, some fruit and a plate or two. But all these things seemed
to glimmer in the dusk or shine in the sunlight of another
world."[7] Alison is the artist figure who, like Gregory Dawson of
Bright Day and Dick Herncastle of *Lost Empires,* can transcend
the forms of immediate reality and translate them into meaningful and lasting patterns. Through Firmius and Alison, both
seekers within the tunnels of time, Tom comes to understand
that everything is meant, that although things seem inside out
and upside down, there is a continuity behind the forms of matter
that exhibits itself at certain moments of insight as the eternal
return of experience.

To find his father, a failed actor and a second-rate painter, Tom must descend into himself, symbolized by the realization of his true motives in looking for his father in Firmius's basement apartment; he must enter into the search with his whole being. He must accept Crike's statement as true: that he at first did not intend to find his father; that he was not looking for the truth but for a way out of his promise. And this involves the tearing away of illusion, chiefly achieved through the motif of disguise and assumed identity.

After dismissing the seedy detective who has tried to pass off a hasbeen actor as Tom's father, Tom begins his recreation of his father's past. Portraying himself as a lawyer, Tom follows his father from the time he left Nelly Coping, the actress who had kept Tom's father's letters to and from his family. It is Nelly's servant who had sent the letter to Australia that had so affected Tom's mother. Tom traces his father through a prison sentence, a demeaning occupation as a salesman of tawdry novelties, a brief period as a ship's steward, and finally locates him, through Judy and her aunt when all paths seemed closed, waiting on tables at the Abbey Lodge, a job which is, ironically enough, the only one he has been able to hold onto through a life of gradually increasing despair. The disguise as lawyer that Tom had used in tracing his father has allowed him both to judge his feelings and to evaluate the meaning of his father's existence.

The search for father and self is paralleled in the novel by a quest for meaning in the world of the sixties, adding still another level of meaning to the whole. The once proud and haughty England, once Priestley's greatest love, is described in this novel as suffering from stasis, a country "trying to move and to stand still at the same time, which takes a bit of doing" (176). The only hope, Tom discovers, lies with the young, the "beatniks" who have "done more in ten years to destroy the power of social position and money than the rest of us have done in the last hundred years"—youngsters who have, in fact, made "a new kind of revolution" (194). Tom finds his cousin Leonora's son's rejection of class and responsibility a healthy admonition to a country "filled with noisy lunatics, the daftest of them at the wheel, men who could hardly have been more dangerous if they had been given machine-guns and hand grenades. . . . Perhaps in another twenty years, machine-guns and hand grenades would be allowed on Saturday nights, just to add a once-a-week spice to the lives of London's twenty million citizens" (186) in a world not too far removed from that which Anthony Burgess imagines in his nightmare vision that dates from the same period, *A Clockwork Orange* (1962).

At the novel's conclusion, Tom first makes a future for his father possible, then decides to give up his position in his Australian university to devote himself to a larger cause, one that offers a glimmer of hope for a future that he can believe in. Having had intimations of a "Third Time," one in which he and Judy can live "with what we have imagined. . .our own Heaven, our own Hell" (198), Tom moves into the future. From Firmius, as well as from the others who touched him in his search, Tom has learned that time is much more than a "conveyor-belt to the grave and oblivion" (198). Such knowledge forces him to "live and work for the world, for the whole bedevilled human race, for a global civilization" (228), which is indeed the fulfillment of the romantic dream.

It's an Old Country is very much the usual mix of adventure and intrigue, of love discovered and time transcended, but in this novel, as is not always the case in the other novels that mix these ingredients, there is a successful marriage of theme, action, and character, largely achieved by the dexterous handling of symbol and imagery. The time theories in *It's an Old Country* serve the dimensions of the fiction by quietly amplifying the individual's search for meaning in a world which seems largely gone to ruin. And yet there is optimism for a future which depends on love and forgiveness of the past. In *It's an Old Country* the happy end seems justified by the whole, not so much a convenient means of ending the fiction.

V   The Image Men

J. B. Priestley's most ambitious undertaking of the 1960s is his longest novel, *The Image Men*, in two volumes entitled *Out of Town* and *London End*, both published in 1968. *Out of Town* is largely a portrayal of academic institutions; *London End*, of the world of politics, advertising, and mass media. A mixture of broad farce and seriously intended satire, *The Image Men* is distinguished by a genial and leisurely narrative style, a large cast of convincingly drawn and well-dramatized minor characters, and by its two protagonists, Cosmo Saltana and Owen Tuby, both failed academics who can easily be identified as logical descendants of Baron Roland and Adam Stewart of *Adam in Moonshine*. Both Saltana and Tuby are romantics, both are aware of the self-seeking opportunism that characterizes the post-World War II temper, and both are fully aware of themselves as intelligent and humane beings for whom the modern world has little respect, and to whom it offers no employment. Priestley himself describes his intentions concerning the novel and his middle-aged adventurers:

Now clearly it represents an attempt to bring into contemporary writing the old leisurely *picaresque* tale that has always fascinated me. This does not mean that it is out of date. In fact it was—and still is, as I write this—very much up to date, if only because it satirizes so much that belongs to our age—notably academic life and especially its social sciences, the mass media, big business and our present style of politics. . . . My two central characters, Saltana and Tuby, are introduced as if they were failed academics turning themselves into cynical con men. But they develop into . . . true heroes, able to swing the narrative over from the fashionable negative into the positive. . . . Saltana and Tuby may be regarded to some extent as comic characters; but they are heroes, not anti-heroes. And the positive values and qualities they come to embody . . . are not brought in to please the idle-minded reader: they are the values and qualities I cling to in my own life.[8]

In her study of Priestley's works Susan Cooper argues that Priestley is not really a satirist: "When he uses fiction as a weapon of social criticism," she writes, "he ridicules rather than savages, and his prime weapon is an amiable mockery rather than an avenging sword"[9]—which is to say that Priestley's satire belongs to the tradition of Addison and Steele's *Spectator Papers* rather than to that of Swift's "A Modest Proposal" or his *Gulliver's Travels*. Iris Murdoch, with whom Priestley collaborated in the dramatization of her *A Severed Head* (1961), thinks the novel very clever indeed,[10] and Anthony Burgess has marveled at its energy and ingenuity.[11]

   The Image Men belongs, as Priestley points out, to the picaresque tradition of *The Good Companions*, but its satirical temper more nearly approximates that of *Sir Michael and Sir George*, a fantasy that makes characters and events acceptable primarily through distortion and exaggeration. There is,

however, surprisingly little distortion, little exaggeration, and a
minimum of the fantastic in *The Image Men*. The novel, in fact,
demonstrates Priestley's craft at its most convincing, despite a
certain pompousness in both the style and the presentation of his
two protagonists. The world of academe and mass hype are, in
effect, presented not so much as exaggerations of reality as
reality itself, and the fantasy that both areas purvey needs only
to be truthfully recorded; academe and advertising's self-
generated myths being in effect self-satire, so much so that
Priestley needs only to point out the obvious by means of his
sensible yet by no means unromantic principal characters.

The Image Men deals with a post–World War II mentality that
sees and insists on appearance as reality. It introduces two
middle-aged characters, Cosmo Saltana, Professor of Philosophy,
lately returned to England after a number of years as a teacher in
South America, and Owen Tuby, honorary doctor, English
teacher in various Eastern and Near Eastern universities. Saltana
is tall, slightly sinister, and very attractive to liberated middle-
aged women. He is immediately recognizable as a seedy
descendant of both Baron Roland and Golspie of *Angel
Pavement*. Owen Tuby is rotund and jolly by comparison, and
irresistible to frustrated middle-aged women who want to
mother him. They become confidence men, not by choice but of
necessity, yet they have about them an innocence of demeanor,
an integrity of manner, which they are always quick to point out
to any and all they encounter. What in fact they purvey is their
intelligence, their humanity, their self-knowledge, their wit, and
their sexuality.

Again the common cause figures as the principal plot device as
Saltana and Tuby attach themselves to Elfreda Drake, the recent
widow of an American millionaire, in England to spend her
inheritance on something having to do with sociology, her
husband's great passion before he died. Needing work, down to
their last pounds, Saltana and Tuby dream up the Institute of
Social Imagistics, "the selection, creation, and projection of
suitable and helpful public images."[12] Saltana and Tuby are
drawn to Elfreda by her mournful vulnerability, but the reader
soon learns that they have no intention of taking advantage of
her; they will simply use her to help themselves get a leg up in
the dishonest and career-struck world of the 1960s. They will

succeed by virtue of their honest hearts and superior minds. That they have not succeeded in their original careers is simply explained by the fact that, like Professor Linden of *The Linden Tree* (1947), they had played fair with others and had, consequently, failed to find security in their middle years.

Realizing that their Institute of Social Imagistics has little chance of getting off the ground unless it secures an institutional attachment, the image men decide to attack a new red-brick university called Brockshire, formerly a CAT, that is, a College of Advanced Technology. The arrival of Saltana, Tuby, and Elfreda Drake into provincial Tarbury and the red-brick precincts of Brockshire allows Priestley the opportunity to satirize the parvenus, the deceivers, the bullies, and the racketeers of the academic world. The reader in effect finds himself in the milieu of Kingsley Amis's *Lucky Jim* (1953).

Chief among the university bigwigs is Jayjay Lapford, Vice Chancellor, whose wife, Isabel, immediately develops an attachment for Tuby; Professor Brigham, head of the English Department, who seems to know nothing about literature; Ted Jenks, artist-in-residence who has written a play called *Stuff It, Chum;* Dr. Lois Terry, who is slowly recovering from a painful love affair with a married man and to whom Tuby is immediately attracted; and Primrose East, former model with a passion for sociology and a fixation on Saltana. Needless to say, among such crows Saltana and Tuby are wild swans of intellectual integrity.

While attempting to bribe or coerce Lapford (who is afraid of his wife) to accept the Institute of Social Imagistics into the university, Saltana and Tuby are forced first to define and then to publicize their function, which they do in jargon of the most outlandish kind. Social Imagistics reduces to an ability to combine the practices of public relations with those of advertising, employing as much as possible ordinary common sense and honest criticism. For example, when asked by Jimmy Kilburn, a newly made cockney millionaire, for an image to please his new and socially conscious wife, Saltana advises against one that would portray Jimmy as a duplicate of several other philanthropist-millionaires, but in favor of the cultivation of his essential persona. Instead of playing the role of a generous millionaire, Kilburn would play that of a skinflint, a penny-pincher most of the time who, on suitable and well-publicized

occasions, gives large sums of money away for no apparent
reason. Jimmy, Saltana advises him, will become a "character"
first, and then a legend.

Balked by both the university administration and the
American branch of Elfreda's husband's family, the Institute of
Social Imagistics is forced to hand over its university affiliation to
sociologist Dr. Hazel Honeychurch and to move to London in
order to come into being as a viable business enterprise.
Realizing the power and value of their projected images, Saltana
and Tuby, Elfreda and Primrose leave Tarbury and Brockshire
for the world of London, for its advertising agencies, its
newspaper and periodical offices, for glamour, success, and
wealth.

A brief outline of the events of the narrative does little more
than imply the satirical purpose—to comment tellingly on a
civilization that depends on manufactured illusions while re-
jecting the homely beauties of personality, morality, and language. If *Out of Town,* the provincial half of *The Image Men,*
succeeds at all, it is largely on the grounds of the truths of
character somewhat belligerently portrayed by Saltana and
Tuby. The chief difficulty of the characterizations, however, is
that the two rascals largely condescend and patronize, despite
the fact that they know they are as involved in fraud and deceit
as those they defraud. They keep insisting on the knowledge of
their motives, of necessary self-interest; but the reader would
rather gain an understanding of the characters for himself than
have them repeatedly explain themselves to him.

A number of set scenes, however, are in themselves rewarding
and reveal Priestley's craft: Tuby easily proving his superiority
to his interlocutor during a radio broadcast; Saltana turning his
television talk-show host into a buffoon; Tuby, Saltana, and
Elfreda disguised as an Indian educator, a Spanish grandee, and
an American housewife, respectively, crashing Isabel Lapford's
party for Ted Jenks, author of the play about an incestuous
window washer; the antics of Primrose as she valiantly attempts
to seduce Saltana.

London End, the second volume of *The Image Men,* is set
chiefly in the capital and concerns itself with the establishment,
publicizing, and selling of the wares of the Institute of Social
Imagistics. Brockshire behind them, the university branch of the
institute in the hands of the American controllers of Elfreda's

money, Saltana and Tuby, together with Primrose and Elfreda, joined by Eden Mere, frightening wife of public-relations man O. V. Mere, begin to sell their illusions to whoever will pay most for them.

In *Journey Down a Rainbow* (1955), an exchange of observations between himself and his wife, Jacquetta Hawkes, Priestley writes of a word that he had recently coined that, to him, describes a pattern of values that eschews ethics and sets up material advantages as the measure of a man's human worth:

Admass. This is my name for the whole system of an increasing productivity, plus inflation, plus a rising standard of material living, plus high-pressure advertising and salesmanship, plus mass communications, plus cultural democracy and the creation of the mass mind, the mass man. (Behind the Iron Curtain they have *Propmass*, official propaganda taking the place of advertising, but all with the same aims and objects.) The people firmly fixed in *Admass* are *Admassians*. Most Americans (though not all; they have some fine rebels) have been *Admassians* for the last thirty years; the English, and probably most West Europeans, only since the War. It is better to live in *Admass* than have no job, no prospect of one, and see your wife and children getting hungrier and hungrier. But that is about all that can be said in favour of it. All the rest is a swindle. You think everything is opening out when in fact it is narrowing and closing in on you. Finally you have to be half-witted or half-drunk all the time to endure it. So much for *Admass*.[13]

London End is Saltana and Tuby's invasion of the world of Admass, their triumph over it, and their subsequent withdrawal from it.

Largely episodic, as is the first volume, *London End* permits Priestley to satirize leisurely various aspects of a media-controlled culture which he finds most reprehensible—the worlds of industry, entertainment, and high politics; and in the background of the novel is to be discerned an unspoken condemnation of Marshall McLuhan and his media theories. Playing the game of public-relations and high-finance advertisers, Saltana and Tuby manage while selling themselves to somehow bed down nearly every woman over the age of consent, never intending less than to take all the money the traffic will bear from those who have it to squander, anyone from wool merchant to Prime Minister. Their "images" are little more than spiced-up common sense, described in such jargonish terms as "frayed" images, "reverse" images, "emergent" images, "warm" and "counter" images.

Among the customers who employ the Institute are Lon Bracton, stage comedian, who is counseled to exaggerate the nervous tendencies already in his nature; Meldy Glebe, Hollywood actress, infatuated with Tuby, who is unhappy in her role of sex-goddess. Tuby constructs for her a new image which transforms her into a 1960s version of the career girls played in the 1930s by Katharine Hepburn and Rosalind Russell—less slap and tickle, more brain and grit. For Alan Axwick, a dull and witless M. P., the image men construct a romantic persona that keeps the politician on the run between Grenoble and London. Enchantment is what his image sorely needs: a concocted, mysterious, nonexistent love affair in France soon brings him to the notice of the government, and he is appropriately given a post as Secretary to the Shadow Minister of Transport.

Saltana and Tuby's most significant achievement in the barter of images for large sums of money, however, is one that involves them in a mock break-up of their friendship and their institute so that each may help rival politicians develop winning images for the upcoming general election. Saltana works with Prime Minister Ernest Itterby, convincing him to change his dull solicitor look for that of a concerned and aggressive champion of the people. At the same time Tuby works with Sir Henry Flinch-Epworth, Itterby's opponent, convincing him to change his image as a musty landowner into that of a concerned and aggressive champion of the people. Indeed the same image is sold both politicians, the electorate consequently given little or nothing to choose between, as the medium becomes the message, and each collects £5000 as his fee.

At the novel's conclusion the institute is sold to an aggressive American firm, and Saltana and Tuby, richer by about £50,000 each, decide to marry their steadfast and truest admirers, Elfreda Drake and Lois Terry, the mournful little English teacher from Brockshire. With the money they will found a university on the Isle of Man, where taxes are lower and rates are cheaper, to cater to men and women over forty who have forgotten the joys of culture and the life of the mind—jaded businessmen, tired industrialists, disappointed politicians; there will even be money for a scholarship holder or two once the enterprise is fully underway. Meanwhile Elfreda and Lois confess to each other, several times, much to the reader's dismay, that they would follow their overaged Romeos anywhere, anytime. For such is the stuff of happy endings!

Along with *The Good Companions* and *Festival at Farbridge, The Image Men* is one of Priestley's largest canvases, and like the earlier novels it achieves its aims through energy and verve. The presentation of two somewhat scoundrelly Englishmen in their fifties to an England that they have been absent from for a generation affords Priestley sufficient latitude to examine keenly and wittily a contemporary world whose values have gone askew. A fresh eye, a good head, a keen understanding of other cultures their chief assets, Saltana and Tuby are workable devices for a pervasive and meaningful satirical investigation of a culture drunk on appearances, in fact the same symptoms of social disease that Priestley had satirized in *Wonder Hero* and *They Walk in the City;* but here the mixture of social commentary and fairy tale produces a more convincing novel. Finally, *The Image Men* succeeds despite its protagonists. Intended as witty and honest men, with enough mischievousness and eccentricity to make them memorable, Saltana and Tuby are too often platitudinous, sententious gasbags. Their presence occasionally even inhibits scenes of otherwise comic vitality, for in insisting through narration on the charm of his protagonists, Priestley fails to accomplish what he succeeds in doing almost effortlessly in the majority of his novels—to dramatize events so that the reader can appreciate character for himself. The novel also suffers from a sentimental view of women that the cause of women's liberation might rightly take exception to. *The Image Men* lacks the buoyancy of Amis's *Lucky Jim,* the ruthlessness of John Braine's *Room at the Top* (1957), the rage of John Osborne's *Look Back in Anger* (1955). But it makes up for these deficiencies because of its energy, its thoroughly captivating secondary characters, its pungent satirical thrusts at pedantry, callousness, and stupidity of all sorts. It is, in fact, a remarkably vital work, one that speaks to our times in eloquent and cautionary fashion. It is Priestley's most enterprising novel, written at a time of life when most writers are content to rest on their laurels.

CHAPTER 8

Miscellaneous Pieces

I   Snoggle *and* Found, Lost, Found

PUBLISHED in 1971, *Snoggle*, subtitled *A Story for Anybody Between 9 and 90*, is a science-fiction fantasy intended chiefly for children. The three precocious youngsters, Peg, James, and Robin, are reminiscent of Wendy, John, and Michael of *Peter Pan* (1904), not only in their imaginative flights, but also in the warmth of their convictions. In befriending Snoggle and his cohort Snaggle, the pets of the superior beings who land their invisible spacecraft near their country home, the children, together with Grandfather Hooper, band together to save the fugitive invaders from the reactionaries of the community, Mrs. Bing-Birchall, Major Rodpath, and Inspector Crope. Pat and James are rewarded for their kindness to Snoggle with a thought-picture-message sent from the spaceship on its voyage away from earth. The moral of the simple tale is spoken by Grandfather Hooper: " 'I've sometimes thought there might be a plan for everybody and everything in the universe. If there isn't, then the whole thing's idiotic—even more idiotic than we humans are, because at least we can sit here quietly and talk about a plan. But then our idea of a divine purpose behind the razzle-dazzle of atoms and molecules would itself be part of the universe, wouldn't it?' "[1] If Grandfather Hooper portrays the author, as indeed he must, then the statement itself indicates an undiminished optimism in the adventure of life, and represents, even in the guise of the children's tale, a continuation of the romantic attitudes that characterize the bulk of Priestley's writing.

More substantial, though no less winning a tale, is the frolic of 1976 entitled *Found, Lost, Found, or The English Way of Life*. Written in the same spirit as *Low Notes on a High Level*, and

110

perhaps in part intended as a spoof of an earlier novel of love found and lost and found again, *They Walk in the City, Found, Lost, Found* recounts the adventures of Tom Dekker, Chief Establishment Officer of the Ministry of Export Development. Tom meets his beloved, Kate Rapley, but loses her when she decides to disappear from London. He finds her again, and incidentally finds himself while doing so. The tale of love recovered is itself a simple frame, however, to allow Priestley to satirize in a kindly yet meaningful manner the buffoons who pass for leaders of government, the pretenders who pass for actors, and the functionaries who under the guise of goodwill display only petty malice. The adventures that Tom encounters finding Kate are comic hi-jinks, escapes from the world of too much getting and spending. Tom explains to Kate's aunt that he drinks because life in the contemporary city is boring: " 'Life in the Civil Service, life in London, and the general English way of life. I've simply had to keep floating through them. But Kate, if she's really involved, might put an end to the boredom and irritation. Together . . . with a reasonable allowance of gin.' "[2] The answer to Tom's problem is the same one that Charlie Habble and Ida Chatwick of *Wonder Hero*, as well as others of Priestley's heroes and heroines discovered in the 1930's: goodness and love exist. Yet the ease of presentation, the whimsy, and the wit gratefully serve the satirical purpose as they did not always do in the earlier pieces. There is no curtailment of fancy, no lack of invention. The frolic is akin to the delightful line drawings that Picasso threw off in his last years, the still potent flowerings of an unquenchably creative spirit. *Found, Lost, Found* is further evidence of a faith in man that is life-enhancing and endurable.

II   Short Stories

J. B. Priestley has published three collections of short stories, *Going Up* in 1950, *The Other Place and Other Stories of the Same Sort* in 1953, and *The Carfitt Crisis and Two Other Stories* in 1974. Of the three, the latter two are the more interesting thematically. *The Other Place* comprises nine tales of the supernatural, and *The Carfitt Crisis* three tales that make use of god-figures as well as supernatural devices. All the stories in one way or another comment on time and its transcendence, giving further evidence of Priestley's preoccupation with that subject.

The title piece of the second collection records the travels of Harvey Lindfield, an engineer from Toronto, who is given access into a space that is just " 'round—a different kind of corner . . .' "[3] by Sir Alaric Foden, a desiccated and mysterious creature reminiscent of the three magicians of Priestley's novel of the same period. In the other space, a place "out of this world all right, but it oughtn't to have been" (17), Lindfield sees the same people he grudgingly works with in the gloomy town of Blackley, but in the other place they are happy and carefree, alive and full of goodness. Lindfield, for no apparent reason, disobeys the simple instructions given him by Paula, the woman his romantic imagination has always portrayed for him, and is returned to the dreary world of reality, to search for that other place, which he fails to understand lies within himself.

Two of the best stories in the collection insomuch as they combine the Gothic element with effective satire of a contemporary world are "The Grey Ones" and "Uncle Phil on TV." "The Grey Ones" addresses itself to a world that takes no pleasure in anything creative, original, counter, or spare. Mr. Patson tells his psychiatrist that he thinks society is being taken over by semitransparent, toadlike monsters with " 'no centre, no feeling, no motives' " (54), with nothing " 'but a sort of cold determination to keep on moving up' " (55), only to discover that Dr. Smith is himself one of "the grey ones." "Uncle Phil on TV" satirizes in robust comic fashion the lower middle class through the malignant Uncle Phil, recently dead because one of the members of his family put his heart medicine just out of his reach. The Grigsons decide to use Uncle Phil's insurance money to buy a new telly that the whole family will be able to enjoy. " 'Now listen, listen!' " says the Grigson son-in-law, George Fleming. " 'We've got TV here in Smallbridge at last, and comes over good too. . . . Gives you everything. Sport for me and Dad and Steve. Plays and games and all that for you women. Dancing and fashion shows too. Variety turns we'd all like. Serious stuff for Ernest. Ask your friends in to enjoy it' " (74). But Uncle Phil uses the medium to convey outrage at having been sent off before his time. He keeps appearing on all the shows, and even addresses the Grigsons, accusing them of " 'a kind of murder' " (102). Finally, in despair, daughter Joyce, who had misplaced the heart medicine, throws a stool at the screen.

Less successful are the stories "Guest of Honor" and "Look After the Strange Girl." The former records Sir Bernard Clipter's unprepared-for but ultimately meaningful awareness of mortality, while the latter recounts an event wherein two young people are transported to a time fifty years before that in which they live. They meet in the past but understand one another's yearnings in the present.

"The Statues" and "Mr. Strenberry's Tale" are science-fiction fantasy rather than tales of teleportation or space and time transcendence. In the former, Walter Voley, reporter for the *Daily Record,* sees into the future. He envisages a London dominated by gigantic statues. In the latter tale Mr. Strenberry tells a sympathetic writer of an occult experience on Opperton Heath. A voyager from the future, attempting to escape the holocaust of his own time, attempts to reach Strenberry's time, but he is drawn back into his own era by " 'something black . . . one of those things, getting hold of him—the last man left' " (208). "The Leadington Incident" records Sir George Cobthorn's growing awareness that most people are either living a death in life or are profoundly asleep, himself included.

The concluding story of the group, entitled "Night Sequence," the longest of the stories, portrays, as does Barrie's *Mary Rose* and Priestley's own *Jenny Villiers,* the existence of another dimension wherein the life of the present can mingle feelingly with the life of the past. Two jaded and cynical young people, Betty and Luke Gosforth, take refuge in an old Georgian house during a torrential rainstorm, are courteously entertained by Sir Edward Periton and his niece Julia. They discover in their eighteenth-century host and hostess those elements in themselves which they have denied. In the morning, they understand that their adventure of the night can inform the quality of their lives in the present. They come to understand that in the process of making a living, of getting on, they had denied their lives " 'style, ceremony, admiration, deep feeling, and the enchantment of long vistas' " (239). " 'You wanted us, I think, and here we are,' " says the lovely Julia to Luke before she recedes into her own time. (234).

Published in 1975, *The Carfitt Crisis and Two Other Stories* contains two novellas originally written in dramatic form, and a short story entitled "Underground," which first appeared in the *Illustrated London News* in 1974. In recasting *The Carfitt Crisis* and *The Pavilion of Masks* in novella form, Priestley adapted dramatic structure to his narrative ends; that is, both works exhibit economy of time, place, and action, and avoid all but essential description and comments on character, feeling, and motive.[4] In this respect they are like Priestley's earlier novel, also an adaptation of the dramatic form, *Jenny Villiers*.

In *The Carfitt Crisis*, an engaging and enterprising character called Engram moves into Sir Brian Carfitt's household as a temporary cook-butler to stave off impending disaster. He is, in effect, the organizer or master of ceremonies of many of the earlier works, except that in *The Carfitt Crisis* he is presented as a member of a group of charismatic seers who dedicate themselves to bringing about right action. He is closer, consequently, to Dr. Görtler of *I Have Been Here Before*, in which Ouspensky's theory of recurrence gives resonance to the gothic theme, than he is to the organizer of *Festival*. Engram has precognitive powers as well as the ability to cloud the minds and feelings of those under his aegis. His presence in the Carfitt household prevents a shooting, a suicide, and, most importantly, the defrauding of thousands of subscribers to the Fallowfield Trust, Sir Brian's business in imminent danger of bankruptcy. He reconciles Marion, Sir Brian's wife, to her place in society and inculcates in Sir Brian the idea of service to others. The chief difficulty with the novella lies with the characters: the reader cannot help but wonder whether they are worth the attention that the author pays to them. And Engram's function as catalyst seems little more than plot convenience.

In "Underground," a tale marred by its sentimental ending, Ray Aggarstone, a rascal about to depart from England with his wife and mother's savings for a selfish life as an adventurer in South America, is travelling for the last time to his family's home by way of the Underground. Given several opportunities to change his mind by mysterious passengers on the train, he suffers a heart attack and is doomed for all time to ride deeper and deeper into the Northern Line. A god-figure arbitrarily takes pity on Ray's family by obliterating the evidence of his contemplated betrayal.

The most successful of the tales in *The Carfitt Crisis* is "The Pavilion of Masks." Preceded by a Prologue set in the present time, in which a musty academician reluctantly entrusts his family history to the author to have it set into suitable form, and concluded by an Epilogue, in which the academician voices strong disapproval over the finished version, the novella is a delightful romp in the vein of Anthony Hope's Ruritanian caprice.

The adventure of Nicolo Novelda, dismissed from the staffs of three European universities and presently official astrologer, majordomo, and stage manager to Cleo Torres, an emancipated woman of self-proclaimed passion and genius, is set in Cleo's residence, an elaborate pavilion decorated with the masks of comedy and tragedy, in the mythical principality of Mexe-Dorberg in the 1830s. About to be cast off by her lover, Prince Karl, the flamboyant Cleo schemes for a better future with the romantic poseur-poet Victor Vatannes. Victor, who, as Novelda informs the reader, " 'in private is impotent,' " and Cleo, " 'who's frigid except in public' " (181), will elope from Mexe-Dorberg, wasting not a moment in each other's arms, instead working out the percentages of a mutual exploitation of a credulous public. Victor and Cleo belong in effect to the future, an age of the cheap press, of type-casting machines, and the electric telegraph, " 'an age when appearance will defeat reality, when what is said is more important than what is done, when the shadow will be accepted for the substance, and more and more people will stop living their own lives to dream of living somebody else's life' " (180).

Through polite blackmail and elaborate stage management Nicolo makes such a future possible for Victor and Cleo; but for himself, and the woman he has loved in a darkened hunting lodge, he chooses a life of purpose in South America. " 'Nobody punishes us for being happy, Louise,' " Nicolo says to his mistress. " 'We Latins know that. If God exists—and ever thinks about us—then it must be our determined unhappiness that annoys him' " (190), voicing the novella's central theme—and perhaps Priestley's own.

CHAPTER 9

The Plays: Influences and Motifs

THE achievement of J. B. Priestley the dramatist is greater than that of J. B. Priestley the novelist. Whereas Priestley the novelist can be seen within the mainstream of British fiction of the first half of the twentieth century, Priestley the dramatist is a unique figure. The relative merits of the two genres in the first fifty years of the century are responsible for his position. As a novelist, he is a minor figure among giants performing miracles; as dramatist, he stands alone. From Bernard Shaw to John Osborne British drama is a waste land. It is Priestley, the solitary Englishman, who bridges the gap, along with Sean O'Casey the Irishman and James Bridie the Scot. In the 1930s and 1940s only these three could be named in one breath as dramatists of distinction and serious intent actively engaged in expanding the theater's horizons, with Priestley by far the most prolific. The plays of John Galsworthy and James Barrie had already dated, with the exception of the latter's *Peter Pan*, with its character who refuses to grow up in a fantasy which will never die. And the verse drama of T. S. Eliot would prove a literary curiosity.

With the emergence of the angry young men the 1950s and 1960s witnessed a diminishment of Priestley's reputation as a dramatist, along with the total eclipse of Bridie's (aside from one major revival of *Mr. Bolfry* in 1956). Priestley's reputation barely survived the period; O'Casey's, however, continued strong, while Christopher Fry took up the mantle of poetic drama, with no more lasting success than Eliot.

In the 1970s, a time in which O'Casey's work would seem especially timely, Priestley, no longer writing for the theater, was rediscovered. The National Theatre's observance of his eightieth birthday in 1974 with a revival of *Eden End* (1935), later broadcast by the BBC, was in part responsible for the refocusing of attention on his drama. But the Mermaid Theatre's

116

1973 revival of *An Inspector Calls* (1945) in fact preceded the National's tribute to Priestley, and before the decade ended *When We Are Married* (1938) and *Laburnum Grove* (1933) successfully returned to the West End and *The Good Companions* saw life anew as a musical comedy (1974). Yet even before the 1970s, while Priestley's plays may have been neglected in London, they were constantly before an appreciative public's eye in repertory productions throughout the country, as even a cursory glance at newspaper listings quickly reveals.

While Priestley's drama which celebrates England and the English has never captured the fancy of the American public, with the exception of the frequently performed *Dangerous Corner* (1932), or the American critics, who do not consider him the equal of Eugene O'Neill, Tennessee Williams, or Arthur Miller, his reputation in the Iron Curtain countries soared after World War II.[1] A clear-eyed view of his countrymen's faults, along with a forthright honesty in plays and novels concerning his nation's failure to cope with the postwar world, blunted the enormous popularity at home which his wartime broadcasts had won him. This may have caused a critical downgrading of his work at home at a time when, growing older, his interest in the theater was waning. Yet his criticism of and growing disenchantment with Britain, despite an unquenchable love for the land and its common people, were the very elements in his drama, most prominent in *An Inspector Calls* and *The Linden Tree*, which revitalized the communist world's interest in his work.

That same honesty, at times overwhelmed by a romantic optimism, is, however, present throughout his career as a dramatist. It is a serious concern for the middle classes, those sharing his own background and interests, that led him into an exploration of vital themes and experimental theatrical forms, that forced him to part company with mainstream English playwrights like Somerset Maugham, Frederick Lonsdale, and Noel Coward, who often trivialized the English theater by neglecting the essential English character. The others carried on the British tradition of high comedy, forgetting the seriousness, the critical purpose of the comedy of manners at its best, as exemplified by the incisive wit of Bernard Shaw. Early on Priestley tried his hand at the genre, imitating Maugham and Coward in *The Roundabout* (1933) and *Duet in Floodlight* (1935). Although he could not quite match the masters of the form, the pointlessness of such exercises rather than a lack of wit on his own part eventually discouraged him from pursuing such sophisticated ends. Yet later on he would twice return to the form, in the gratifying *Ever Since Paradise* (1946) and the again unsatisfying, therefore unpublished, *The White Countess* (1954).

Once an habitué of the fourpenny balcony of the Bradford Empire, Priestley has always believed that the theater is a place for enchantment and for entertainment. An audience, however, can be enchanted as its experience is widened, as it enters a new dimension whose presence has only vaguely been imagined in dreams. And an audience can be entertained even while its attention is focused on the problems of a contemporary world enmeshed in a depression, decimated by war. Even as didactic a writer as Bertolt Brecht, a dramatist with whom Priestley would not care to be allied, understood the power of entertainment. In the theater Priestley had to be, like Shaw, an entertainer with a purpose. His focus had to be, as in his novels, on the common man in a common cause. After Shaw, an Irishman at home in England, until the coming of John Osborne, Arnold Wesker, and Harold Pinter, there would be no English dramatist to stand beside him. For years he held the stage of a committed English drama alone.

Aside from a seriousness of intent, there is little direct influence of Shaw upon his work. In a way both are romantics. Shaw's notion of man evolving into superman is as romantic as Priestley's unshakable belief in the perfectibility of man. But Priestley would even deny Shaw his commitment. He writes of the older dramatist, "He held many beliefs but he did not hold them as most of us do. He never appeared to be emotionally committed to them. He could advance or defend them without anger."[2] And he continues: "Because he could hold his beliefs in his own peculiar fashion, keeping them free of negative emotions, he was able to create his own kind of comedy, good enough to put him among the world's great dramatists. This comedy of his has light without heat. The superbly theatrical wit crackles and dazzles and strikes without wounding. Behind the cut-and-thrust of the talk, like some smiling landscape behind a battle scene, is a vast golden good humour. The master quite early of a magnificent debating style, he heightened it and orchestrated it to provide us with this comedy of argument, the Mozartian opera of witty debate" (TW, 184–85). Late in his career, Priestley, with his wife and collaborator Jaquetta

Hawkes, fashioned an experimental drama of debate, but *Dragon's Mouth* (1952) is more Jungian than Mozartian. Only once would Priestley's characters engage in Shavian debate, in the elegantly witty *Ever Since Paradise*, his only dramatic work devoted to the battle of the sexes.

Shaw, the brilliant music critic, once told Priestley that he nearly always began his plays "without any ground-plan of action, hearing and not seeing his characters, trying a duet, then a trio, then perhaps a full ensemble" (TW, 185). If this is not Priestley's method (except in his 1949 opera libretto, *The Olympians*), Priestley is as knowledgeable as Shaw about music and frequently employs it to enhance a mood or enrich a scene. A music-box is the key prop in *Dangerous Corner*, its tinkling sound dividing time, just as the string quartet of the novel *Bright Day* is a Proustian device carrying the protagonist back and forth in time. In *Time and the Conways*, too, music accompanies Kay's movement from one time dimension to an awareness of another, and the play's songs are carefully chosen: the lyrics of Brahms's "Wiegenlied" and Schumann's "Der Nussbaum" comment on the play's dramatic situation and underscore its theme. In *The Linden Tree* the Elgar Cello Concerto hauntingly evokes the mood of a lost era. Music also figures prominently in Priestley's experimental plays: Benjamin Britten composed an integral score for *Johnson Over Jordan* (1939), and just as some of the novels loosely take on a symphonic shape, *Music at Night* (1938) is carefully structured as a violin concerto in three movements or acts. No bolder experiment in integrating music and drama would be attempted in England until Tom Stoppard's partially success-ful one-act play for six actors and full symphony orchestra, *Every Good Boy Deserves Favour*, in 1977.

In one other respect Priestley is like Shaw, if not influenced by him. Priestley writes of Shaw, "As for his assorted kittens, from Cleopatra to Orinthia, they are hygienic toys with never a gland in working order between them. No wonder that his greatest part for an actress is Joan of Arc" (TW, 184). Priestley himself, like Shaw, is generally less successful with his female characters than with his male characters. The plays, like the novels, have a full complement of women without glands: pert young maidens (Carol of *Time and the Conways*, Dinah of *The Linden Tree*); dazed retainers (Sarah of *Eden End*, Mrs. Cotton of *The Linden Tree*); forthright chars (Mrs. Northrop of *When We Are Married*,

Mrs. Batley of *They Came to a City*). Mrs. Radfern of *Laburnum Grove* and Mrs. Linden of *The Linden Tree* are contrived character sketches whereas both their husbands are fully realized, often contradictory, but wholly credible human beings. Nonetheless, the women of the plays are finally better drawn than their counterparts in the novels for a significant reason: in his drama Priestley eschews the sexual encounter often clumsily handled in his fiction, a gratuitous element there. Only in *Ever Since Paradise* does the sexual battle rage, and there it is all tongue-in-cheek, with lively banter and engaging repartee. Generally the women's roles are more central to the dramatic structure of the plays. In *Time and the Conways,* for example, Priestley effectively mines the special sensibility of the female. It is Kay, rather than Alan, who is convincingly aware of a life beyond the present tense.

Only three Priestley plays reveal direct Shakespearean influence. A structural pattern of order-disorder-return-to-order is gratuitously grafted onto the frail comedy *Spring Tide* (1936) after being suggested in the ending of *Dangerous Corner*. More significantly Shakespeare is directly quoted in *Summer Day's Dream* (1949) in which Stephen Dawlish becomes, like Prospero, a master of ceremonies or master of the revels. Dawlish, like many characters in the novels, becomes the god-figure, a life-enhancer, and old Linden too orders and defines the quality of life around him as does Mr. O'Hara in *Spring Tide*. As in the novels the ordering figure is sometimes touched with the sinister, but in the plays as in the fiction good is more often than not triumphant. Here too Priestley is more convincing as he plumbs the basic goodness in man, less so as he portrays the evil which would ensnare him. Dr. Görtler seems at first a sinister devil-figure in *I Have Been Here Before,* but eventually the others come to look upon him as a celebrant of life, teaching them to live to the fullest, to avoid life's pitfalls. In *The Golden Fleece* Will Lotless turns sinister as he uses money to wield power, but before the end he is replaced at the play's center by a life-celebrant in the guise of a chambermaid, Molly Cudden, who rescues him from the very evil whose slave he has become.

Other British dramatists have had no more effect upon Priestley's work than the token influence of Shakespeare and Shaw. Although Barrie, a friend and godfather to his son Thomas, was consulted during the writing of his time plays, Priestley avoided the sometimes cloying feyness of works such as *Dear Brutus* and *Mary Rose*. Even more time obsessed than his colleague, who seems, like Peter Pan, to have tried to make time stand still, Priestley is a fervent explorer along a fourth dimension. And Gareth Lloyd Evans has suggested the influence of Galsworthy on Priestley's drama in that "the effect of *Cornelius* is that of a Galsworthy novel,"[3] but a mercantile ambience had already served Priestley well in *Angel Pavement*. A clerk for a wool firm in Bradford in his youth, Priestley had no need of books for an understanding of a commercial world. He had lived there himself.

More so than British drama, continental drama has influenced Priestley's development, with Ibsen as strong a factor in his work as in Shaw's. With Priestley, however, it is the structure rather than the content which is of primary importance; he writes of Ibsen, "He was like an engineer who by simplifying and strengthening the boiler was able to increase the steam pressure."[4] Priestley learned his craft, and a master craftsman he was to become, from such tightly coiled plays as *A Doll's House* (1879) and *Ghosts* (1881). Along with the craft came a strong sense of the coexistence of past and present. *Dangerous Corner*, like *Ghosts*, depends so completely upon its characters' past actions that past and present are as inextricably one for them as for Mrs. Alving and her son. And in that past and present, the future coexists. Priestley's view of the nature of time would probably have held few surprises for Ibsen, who seemed himself to have rejected the limited life of the present tense.

A lost past and an anticipated future fill the no man's land of the present in the plays of Anton Chekhov, whose spirit, more than any other writer's, pervades all of Priestley's drama. The characters of both dramatists are fools who have lost their way and wander through a limbo which they do not fully comprehend. Both writers love the people they create, but neither one is blind to their faults, their own responsibility for their suffering. A gentle irony informs their work, and pathos frequently gives way to genuine laughter. Priestley borrows characters as well as situations from Chekhov, but, most significantly, he learned from his Russian mentor how to create and sustain mood. He writes of him, "Chekhov's object . . . was to enlarge and, so to speak, orchestrate . . . certain effects that were reasonably realistic but were primarily intended to create atmosphere, to heighten the emotion of a scene. When, for example, in Act Four of *The Three Sisters* [1901], we hear the regimental band in the distance, it is not there because regiments must have bands to play them out of a town and this is realism; it is there because the distant fading marching music at once widens and deepens the emptiness and desolation of the sisters' garden."[5] In such realistic plays as *Eden End, Cornelius,* and *The Linden Tree,* Priestley evokes a sense of loss more subtly than any dramatist since Chekhov. Even his experimental plays, *Johnson Over Jordan* and *Music at Night,* are textured by a poetic sensibility that can be regarded as Chekhovian.

Priestley's few attempts at actual poetry within his experimental plays do not always come off well. Early on he realized that poetry was the one literary genre he could not master, yet his plays share with Chekhov's what he calls the "poetry of the Theatre":

The closely ordered modern prose drama, tied to probability and realistic behaviour, cannot achieve the wild and startling beauty of great poetic drama, but its very construction, to an alert mind, can bring intellectual delight. And it can have poetry, its own poetry. . . . Read *The Cherry Orchard* [1904] and it seems a mere jumble of odd speeches, but see it lovingly produced and its poetry of the Theatre enchants the mind and melts the heart. In one good modern play after another there are at least moments of this poetry of the Theatre, often all the more moving because, like fruit that has fought for its juices against frost and rain, they have been wrung out of our harshly prosaic circumstances. (AD, 28)

Even Priestley's naturalistic plays are no more so than Chekhov's; and like Chekhov's, they refuse to submit to any strict labeling. But an English dramatist who eschews actual verse has a special burden. According to Priestley, "The realistic prose dramatist finds it hard to express the great emotional moments— and if he is English he will find it harder still because the English prefer to say nothing and not make a scene—which is precisely what the dramatist *has* to make" (AD, 26). He reveals how he overcame the problem in *The Linden Tree:* "In this play—as in several others of mine—I open with absolutely realistic flat dialogue of the kind that any English audience knows only too well, and then gradually I begin to move away from complete naturalism in speech, so that in the last half-hour the characters are using a far richer and warmer idiom, often making speeches that would be impossible to them in real life" (AD, 76-77). By the end of the play Priestley's poetic sensibility has extended the range of the Lindens' voices. Occasionally the range from naturalism to poetry occurs within a single speech, as in Christopher's emotional outburst in *Summer Day's Dream:*

I beg your pardon, Madame Shestova. I realise I am behaving very badly to a guest. Please forgive me. I'm not quite myself. I was up early this morning and worked very hard, because we were haymaking. So I'm tired. I'm also bewildered, baffled, and light in the head. Sorry! *(He turns away, making for door out, but then suddenly wheels round, staring at her and speaking with an exasperated warmth.)* You are the most beautiful woman I have ever seen—and yet nothing I do or say touches you at all. As if a man tried to pluck the flower of the world and found it was made of steel and ice. It's blue midsummer here, and yet you stare at me out of a Siberian winter.[6]

Priestley's fascination with time and his own time plays led him quite logically to the experiments of *Johnson Over Jordan* and *Music at Night:* "What I wanted them to suggest was life outside Time as we usually know it, the kind of freedom of the fourth dimension that comes to us in a fragmentary fashion in dreams, events out of chronological order, childhood and adult life interrupting each other, all of which can bring a piercing sweetness, a queer poignancy, and, again, dramatic experience a little different from what one has known before" (AD, 52). That different dramatic experience can be viewed as Priestley's kinship with still other continental dramatists, the expressionists. Although Priestley denies this element in his work, or at any rate the label, he does share their subjectification of experience, their distortion of surface reality, their fluidity of movement in time and space. Perhaps Priestley's personal view of time, that man is at all times beyond mere chronological time, leads him to deny that any "distortion" takes place, to see these works in another light. Yet even another offshoot of expressionism, the epic theater of Bertolt Brecht, shares certain elements with at least one Priestley play, *Ever Since Paradise.* The gulf between Brecht and Priestley, however, is so wide that similarities here are probably coincidental. What may seem Brechtian in Priestley's work could conceivably have found its way there via the plays of Thornton Wilder, the one American dramatist for whom the English writer has voiced considerable admiration.

When the angry young men ushered in a new era of British drama in 1956, Priestley, alone among English playwrights, had paved the way toward that revolution; yet his contribution was entirely overlooked. Ironically, in *Look Back in Anger* John Osborne's angry protagonist, Jimmy Porter, refers to Priestley the journalist-essayist, not the man of the theater. He describes a Priestley piece he has just read in the Sunday papers: "He's like Daddy—still casting well-fed glances back to the Edwardian twilight from his comfortable, disenfranchised wilderness," and the line is echoed when Daddy, a bewildered, retired Colonel Blimp, is told by his daughter what his son-in-law thinks of him: " 'Poor old Daddy—just one of those sturdy old plants left over from the Edwardian Wilderness that can't understand why the sun isn't shining any more.' "[7] For Osborne then, at any rate for Jimmy Porter, Priestley is the symbol of the ineffectual dreamer rather than the man of action doing what he can to rebuild a shattered world.

After commenting not on Osborne's anger but on his "Barri-esque gooey sentimentality, which already can see husbands as bears and wives as teeny-weeny squirrels," Priestley good-humoredly responds to Jimmy Porter's reaction to his article: "A bit much . . . seeing that most of my contributions to this paper have been attempts to take a genuine look at our present time—discovering, for example, political apathy about two years before the politicians and leaderwriters found it out" (TW, 175). Evans astutely compares Ormund's description of his mother's death in *I Have Been Here Before*, written twenty years earlier, with Porter's recounting of his father's death in *Look Back in Anger* and puts his finger on the later play's major weakness: Porter's "anguish is totally self-indulgent; there is no relationship made between the experience of another man's death and any conception of what life is, or is not. Porter is an emotional hedonist, Ormund a sardonic philosopher. . . . Ormund, the angry old man, not only has a personal sense of futility, but an ability to relate personal experience to what he takes to be the general nature of life itself."[8]

Priestley's own angry young man, Bob Elrick, the works superintendent well motivated in his anger in the novel *Daylight on Saturday,* precedes Osborne's by thirteen years, but nearly all of Priestley's protagonists in novels and plays from the 1920s to the 1970s share Jimmy Porter's concerns. Priestley's characters, as do Osborne's, wish to see life enriched, enthusiasm rekindled, mankind free to work, to build, to love; but Jimmy Porter is himself a life-denier, striking out at those who love him. For Priestley, on the other hand, there is only futility in anger. He and his characters are life-enhancers, like the gentle, loving, yet rebellious George Kettle of *Mr. Kettle and Mrs. Moon* (1955), which opened in London only eight months before *Look Back in Anger* in a production directed by Tony Richardson, whose next endeavor was the Osborne drama, a work now significant for its historical moment rather than its artistic merit. Osborne's estimate of Priestley may reflect the critical attitude of the 1950s, but a letter to the author from Barrie on the publication of the novel *They Walk in the City,* in an incisive rather than sentimental mood, more accurately reflects the optimistic view of man which Priestley's works generally portray: "You face the woes of life without any flinching and some others can do that but not I think with your sanity and your great saving grace of seeing the good and giving it a dwelling-place in your pages and so being a heartening writer because you are a heartening being."[9]

As he grows older Priestley becomes the disillusioned optimist, yet one who never loses sight of man's goodness. His vision is based on a Jungian concept of the oneness of all men, best expressed in the experimental plays, *Johnson Over Jordan, Music at Night,* and *Dragon's Mouth.* That oneness leads him to concentrate on man as a member of a charmed or magic circle. As his career as dramatist progresses, the circle widens. At first Priestley explores the circle of the family (*Laburnum Grove, Eden End*). Eventually his lens widens to focus on the nation as family (*They Came to a City, How Are They at Home?* 1944), and later still on the world as family (*Home Is Tomorrow,* 1948; *Summer Day's Dream,* 1949). He is realist enough to note that the circle is continually broken, but the romanticist in him never wavers from the belief that the circle will one day be mended.

CHAPTER 10

Celebrated Apprenticeship

A SKED the question, "If there was a theme that affected you profoundly, one that you felt it all-important to record before you died, what medium would you choose to express it?" Priestley once responded to an interviewer, "If I wanted to make people *feel* deeply I should use the drama. You can create a quality of emotion in the theatre beyond any you can achieve in another medium."[1] "Twice, and only twice," he has written, "has a play of mine so wrung me I could no longer see."[2] The first occasion was the last night of the disappointing run of *Johnson Over Jordan*. The second was in 1946 in Vienna, where *Time and the Conways* was performed by a very young company in a translation that had been hidden for years while the Nazis had banned all his work. For Priestley the play, especially Act III, seemed "stronger, more poignant, than ever before. And to this must be added the whole circumstances of the production, the enchanting old playhouse, Vienna itself dark and ravaged; and then again, for me, flashing memories of where and how I had written this scene or that, years before in another time and place, almost another world. The total effect was overwhelming. Perhaps it is more sensible to write books and not plays, but it is not out of books such moments arrive, beautiful and terrible" (MR, 211).

Inevitably the stage-struck Bradford youth would one day write for the theater. But the mature writer wisely bided his time. Priestley understood the theater's conditions, its hit or miss chanciness, its "gaming-house atmosphere" of "dazzling successes and shameful flops." He was suspicious of its glamour and disliked the thought of giving up control of his work to others. "What happens after the writing is done" is what discouraged him: "It is as if an author of books had to find not only the right publisher but also the right paper-maker, the right compositors and machinists, the right binders, the right salesmen" (MR, 199–200). The extraordinary success of the novel *The Good Companions,* however, changed his mind. Once he was established as a writer and knew that his "children's food and clothing could be paid for" (MR, 201) after the difficult years of his first wife's illness, Priestley was ready for the fray, but to insure that control he coveted, which few aspiring playwrights ever achieve, he formed his own production company, contrary to the advice of Bernard Shaw.

Fourteen years after James Agate's favorable review of *Dangerous Corner* appeared in the *Sunday Times,* the most influential drama critic of the 1930s quoted his praise of Priestley's first play as a rebuttal to an attack by Sean O'Casey that the critics never fought for a hearing for any novice playwright from home or abroad.[3] It would seem that by 1946 Agate had forgotten that Priestley in 1932 was by no means unknown. Once the popular author of *The Good Companions* decided to write a play by himself, the result of his endeavor was eagerly anticipated, with the cities of Bradford, Leeds, and Glasgow (the eventual winner) vying for the honor of hosting the play's one-week tune-up prior to the West End.

The first night of *Dangerous Corner* in London in May 1932 was hardly the unheralded opening of a novice writer. Priestley was over forty years old at the time and a celebrity. Society editors covered the event and reported that " 'Lady Cloefax [*sic*] was responsible for the loveliest frock worn in the first-night audience.' "[4] Following the performance, a large supper party at Quaglino's included Somerset Maugham, Hugh Walpole, Noel Coward, G. B. Stern, and Margaret Kennedy. Priestley's first opening night was exactly the "occasion" he would seek to avoid for the rest of his theatrical career.

I   The Good Companions *(Adaptation)*

The doors to the world of the theater were actually opened to Priestley by the obvious theatrical possibilities of *The Good Companions.* With Edward Knoblock, an undistinguished writer with a flair for craftsmanship, a "play doctor," as Priestley calls him, he undertook the novel's adaptation for a production at London's Haymarket Theatre in May 1931, a year before writing *Dangerous Corner.*[5] Until then, aside from a few brief sketches, his only attempt at playwriting had been an abandoned adaptation of Thomas Love Peacock's *Nightmare Abbey,* the atmosphere of which worked better for him in the novel *Benighted.* Priestley acknowledges that *The Good Companions* collaboration helped him to hone his dramatic technique, "to delay an entrance here, to hurry an exit there," but even more significantly it provided the confidence Priestley needed to set out on his own. The final scene of the adaptation, which precipitated a disagreement with his collaborator, proved to the fledgling playwright that his theatrical instincts, that his own intuitions, ought to be trusted. When Priestley suggested that the play end with Oakroyd boarding a liner for Canada, Knoblock asked him to write some dialogue for the scene. He refused. If the adaptation was successful to that point, no dialogue would be necessary, he thought, could even be heard. With the hooting of the liner, the cheering from the audience, and the music from the orchestra, the scene would carry itself. The director was prevailed upon to try it Priestley's way, and the audience's noisy reaction told them all that the "novice" had been right from the start.

II Dangerous Corner

Shortly afterwards Priestley wrote *Dangerous Corner.* Initial reaction to the play was unfavorable. Knoblock saw him during one of the first performances at the Lyric Theatre and let his ex-collaborator know that he found it a confused work lacking the skill and knowledge of the drama that the more experienced playwright might have brought to it. The critics of the daily newspapers seemed to agree. Had it not been for Priestley's tenacity, the play would have closed after five performances, and the British theater might have lost one of its most energetic, most innovative dramatists. Before he would allow the play's closing, however, the author insisted on learning the verdict of the critics of the Sunday papers and took over the management of the production. The natural stubbornness of the Yorkshireman averted disaster. From "This is Mr Priestley's first play and we don't mind if it is also his last" (MR, 198), the tone changed. James Agate wrote in the *Sunday Times:* "If this play does not take the town it will be the town's fault. In Mr Priestley we have an obvious first-class playwright in the making. If adequate encouragement is not forthcoming and Mr Priestley should decide not to go on with the job, the public will have only itself to blame."[6]

Dangerous Corner, although not among the author's own favorite works, has been one of his most popular successes. It has played all over the world and is still occasionally performed by provincial reportory companies in Britain as well as community theaters in the United States. Even if it is badly cast or faultily produced, Priestley asserts, it is effective "in creating its own atmosphere and imposing itself upon all manner of audiences."[7] Written to prove that he "could think and create like a dramatist and not necessarily like a novelist,"[8] *Dangerous Corner* is a remarkable first effort—taut, suspenseful, and economical. Nonetheless, despite the play's borrowings of theme and technique from Ibsen, Strindberg, and even Sophocles and Shakespeare, it fails as literature but succeeds as theater. In the introduction to the first volume of his collected plays, Priestley makes a convincing claim that the theatrical work need not stand the literary test; that it must be judged by another standard:

Although the dramatist may also be a man of letters, capable of producing novels, poems, essays, criticism, I believe that drama is not simply a branch of literature but a separate little art, with its own peculiar values and technicalities. . . . I hope that the[se] plays . . . can be enjoyed by a reader, but I must stress the fact that they were not written to be read but to be played in theatres, where if properly produced and acted they come alive. A play that has never found a theatre, actors, audiences, is not really a play at all. A dramatist is a writer who works in and for the Theatre.[9]

In the theater, where it belongs, *Dangerous Corner* survives Priestley's test.

A three-act play which takes place during the course of an evening in the drawing-room of a country house, *Dangerous Corner*, like the works of Ibsen, investigates the necessity of illusions, the folly in the revelation of the half-truth, the impossibility of knowing the whole truth. The play opens dramatically, almost too much so as the apprentice playwright eagerly reveals a command of his craft, with the stage in darkness and the sound of a revolver shot. The lights come up on four women listening to the conclusion of a radio play, *The Sleeping Dog*, about a man who forced a painful truth from his

friends, then shot himself in despair. The truth as sleeping dog
becomes the subject of discussion as the women are joined by
four men who have been smoking their cigars in another room.

A dinner party is in progress in the home of Robert and Freda
Caplan. Among the guests are Robert's partners in a publishing
firm, Freda's brother Gordon Whitehouse and his wife Betty, and
Charles Stanton. The others are Olwen Peel, an associate in the
firm, and the visiting novelist whom they publish, Maud
Mockridge, the nosey catalyst who, like Gregers Werle in *The
Wild Duck* (1884), insists on pursuing the subject of truth.
Robert, the host, who is unknowingly about to force some
disturbing confessions from the others, thinks the truth is always
healthy, but his cynical partner Stanton disagrees. "I think telling
the truth is about as healthy as skidding round a corner at sixty."
"And life's got a lot of dangerous corners," Freda adds.[10] Olwen,
obviously Priestley's *raisonneur*, responds with a statement of
the play's theme: "Well—the real truth . . . wouldn't be
dangerous. . . . But what most people mean by truth, what that
man meant in the wireless play, is only half the real truth. It
doesn't tell you all that went on inside everybody. It simply gives
you a lot of facts that happened to have been hidden away, and
were perhaps a lot better hidden away. It's rather treacherous
stuff" (5).

As Miss Mockridge sees them, the Caplans and the
Whitehouses have perfect marriages. She urges Stanton and
Olwen to marry in order to complete the charmed circle of well-
matched, handsome and witty couples. But perhaps the fawning
novelist senses a smugness in the camaraderie of the highly
successful, seemingly happy sextet. Embarrassingly, she disturbs
their lighthearted calm by raising the subject of the suicide a
year earlier of Robert's brother Martin, another member of the
firm.

A further discordant note is sounded when Olwen recognizes a
musical cigarette box, which ironically plays "The Wedding
March," as having belonged to Martin. Freda is disturbed, for she
had given it to Martin the day he died; Olwen, therefore, could
not have seen it before. Gordon abandons his effort to get some
dance music on the wireless as talk about Martin continues, and
Miss Mockridge calls for more information about the cigarette
box. Gordon, believing himself the last person to have seen
Martin alive, or so he had testified at the inquest, now learns that

his sister had been to Martin's cottage to give him the box late that afternoon, and Olwen had noticed it there when she had gone to Martin's home even later that night to clear up the matter of a check for £500 missing from the firm.

Once Miss Mockridge, who is of no further use to the playwright, takes her leave, the party breaks up, with Olwen remaining with the Caplans. The three continue to discuss the suicide, eventually revealing that the Caplan marriage is far from perfect, that Olwen is in love with Robert, that Stanton had played the brothers off against each other by telling each that the other had stolen the money. Once they suspect that Stanton himself may be the thief, Robert determines to uncover the whole truth. He telephones his partners and insists that they return at once, as the first act ends.

The action of the second act is continuous as more sordid truths come to light, that Stanton in fact stole the check, that both Freda and her brother were in love with Martin. In attempting in *Dangerous Corner* to follow the structural pattern of Ibsen's *Ghosts* or Sophocles's *Oedipus*, where one revelation follows fast upon another, as veils are lifted from an inescapable past, Priestley actually takes himself perilously close to the standard formula of the who-done-it. If Martin was no embezzler, why did he kill himself? Or did he kill himself? The act even ends with the conventional momentary shock of countless murder mysteries. Olwen stuns the others with a revelation: "Martin didn't shoot himself" (38).

Act III carries on the action without pause. Olwen admits that she shot Martin. She describes her late visit to his cottage. Seeking the truth concerning the money, she had gone to question Martin, who had told her that Robert was the guilty one. Martin, who fancied himself irresistible to all women, even to men, had been maliciously amused by Olwen's concern for the man she secretly loved, Martin's staid brother Robert. Under the influence of drugs, Martin had baited Olwen, then attempted to seduce her. After some pornographic drawings had disgusted rather than aroused her, he had threatened her with a gun. In their struggle the gun had gone off. Thinking that Stanton was the one person she could confide in, she had gone to his house but could see through the window that he was not alone, that he was with his mistress—Betty. Living with the horror of what had occurred, Olwen had told no one.

As the complexities of the group's Strindbergian entanglements are revealed (entanglements which the author feared
might lead some waggish critic to call the play *The Bad
Companions*),[11] each character accuses the others of responsibility for Martin's death. Olwen, loving Robert, had gone to
Martin about the theft, which had only taken place because
Stanton needed money to keep his mistress, and Betty, in
desperation, had gone to him only to be assured of her attractions
as a woman after her rejection by her husband, who perversely
preferred the charms of Martin. Tensions build like the springs in
the cigarette box which had provided the impetus for the search
for truth. The charmed circle is broken, the firm is shattered,
and friendships die.

For Robert the final revelation is too much to bear. He had
never known the truth about his decadent brother, had been
unaware of his wife's affair with him, his brother-in-law's
perverse relationship. But even worse for him is the knowledge
that his romantic view of the purity of one member of their
intimate group is yet another lie, for Robert has long been in love
with Betty, or at least with his image of her as an untainted, vital,
perfect being. He understands now that he has lived among
illusions, and he cannot go on without them: "They've given me
hope and courage. They've helped me to live. I suppose we
ought to get all that from faith in life. But I haven't got any. No
religion or anything. Just this damned farmyard to live in. That's
all. And just a few bloody glands and secretions and nerves to do
it with. But it didn't look too bad. I'd my illusions, you see" (51).
He rushes from the room, and there is the sound of a revolver
shot. The lights fade. In the darkness Olwen's voice is heard
"with great emphasis but with a certain hysterical quality: It
can't happen. It *shan't* happen" (52).

The lights come up again on the identical scene with which the
play began. Freda, Olwen, Betty, and Miss Mockridge are
listening to the wireless. A play has just concluded with a shot.
Once again they are joined by the men. Once again Gordon
fiddles with the wireless. But as Olwen once again recalls having
seen the cigarette box before, its tinkling rendition of "The
Wedding March" signals a split in time as the characters' lives
take a new direction. Gordon suddenly interrupts, "Wait a
minute. Listen to this" (54). The music from the wireless comes
in clearly. Ironically the song is "Can't we talk it over," exactly

what the friends have been doing disastrously for three acts. The play, like the circuitous route its horrible revelations have taken, has turned back on itself and begun again. This time, however, the young people pair off two by two. *Dangerous Corner's* new beginning suggests the harmony of the dance, an effect with which Shakespeare frequently ended comic misadventures inspired by the disparity between illusion and reality. Yet where Shakespeare suggests a return to world order, Priestley suggests a hypocritical society masking destructive passions.

The return to the beginning and a second chance for his characters in *Dangerous Corner* is the first of Priestley's several attempts to juggle the conventional time sequence of otherwise naturalistically styled drama. Later, time itself would become an important theme in his work, but the ending of *Dangerous Corner*, while providing a jolting surprise for an audience, is not an integral part of the work itself. Although Priestley prepares for it early on with dialogue about maneuvering life's twists and turns, it remains a contrivance, a theatrical gimmick, revealing finally that the play has little substance. If Priestley expects an audience to understand its second beginning as willed into being by Olwen's inner strength, he has not found a way to make this clear in the momentary darkness before the lights come on again. That the group is granted a second chance seems rather an arbitrary whim on the part of the dramatist. Priestley himself, in his preface to the novelization of the play by Ruth Holland, explains the ending: "All that happens between the two blackouts in the play and between the Prologue and Epilogue in this novel is neither an actual happening nor yet somebody's dream, but a What-Might-Have-Been, a sudden excursion for all the people concerned into some other kind of time. You must suppose that Olwen alone, in a moment of agony, guessed this. You can even assume . . . that by a grand effort of will, she pulled them all back into our own world and time again."[12] Holland's novel, for the general form of which Priestley accepts responsibility, is inferior to the play since the confrontations, as the original author realized, lend themselves better to dramatic rather than narrative treatment, but the "time-twist" (as Gareth Lloyd Evans terms the ending)[13] is handled more successfully there: voices swim in Robert's mind, and Olwen's line is "It *can't* happen! . . . I won't *let* it happen!" (260).

Tyrone Guthrie, who directed the first production of *Dan-*

gerous Corner, cites it as the one play he had more than ample time to prepare. His cast mastered it after only a short rehearsal period, and Guthrie understood why: "It is a highly ingenious piece of construction but has not very much content. Like the musical cigarette box . . . it was a beautiful but perhaps rather trivial mechanism. . . . In two weeks we all felt we had explored the play's rather narrow limits of characterization and philosophy."[14] The play flirts with serious themes, only to skirt them, yet Evans recognizes in *Dangerous Corner* an important Priestley element in embryo: "Thinly, the theme of the responsibility of the individual as a component part of a group, has its first airing in a Priestley play. 'No man is an island' is its motto."[15] But the idea is undeveloped here despite a contemporary reference to the play as "a study in satirical vein of the postwar generation."[16] A highly melodramatic rendering of a group of gifted but irresponsible young people, *Dangerous Corner* is all glittering effect, a triumph of technique.

In language, form, and subject matter, however, it remains an impressive first play. If the characters of *Dangerous Corner* are the stock figures to be found in English country houses, they are credibly individualized and speak serviceable dialogue. At one point Stanton says to Robert, "Don't talk like a man in a melodrama" (29), but Robert and the rest *are* melodramatic characters, and Priestley need not have offered a coy apology for their manner of speech. Also contributing to the work's cumulative effect is the author's taut handling of the unities of time and place, revealing him as a fast-maturing craftsman.

Just as sure is Priestley's controlled handling of a then taboo subject on the English stage, Gordon's latent homosexuality. Avoiding anything that might offend his thirties' audience or indeed the Lord Chamberlain who acted as censor, Priestley still makes clear what has gone awry in the relationship between Gordon and Betty, and Robert's angry description of Betty as "a greedy little cat on the tiles" (51) suggests *Dangerous Corner* as a possible source of a later play which deals more openly with homosexuality as the rift between husband and wife, Tennessee Williams's *Cat on a Hot Tin Roof* (1955). This element of the play, along with Robert's strongly stated recognition of life's darker currents, which most commercial playwrights studiously avoided in the 1930s, reveal in Priestley a dramatist who would bring fresh material into the theater and deal with it with skill and honesty. Not the least of Priestley's accomplishments in *Dangerous Corner* is that he had accurately gauged his audience and found them ready to be dared.

CHAPTER 11

Early Comedies

O N the whole," Priestley writes, "I think I find it easier to plan
and then to write a serious play than I do a comedy. . . .
There is about a serious play that is properly constructed a
natural sweep forward, an inevitable progress, that makes it
easier to write, so that often a big scene of considerable technical
intricacy will almost write itself."[1] The cleverly crafted, clearly
focused *Dangerous Corner,* which took little more than a week
to write, unwinds with inexorable force. His early comedies, on
the other hand, are sometimes sprawling, often clumsily
constructed. The obligatory scene of *The Roundabout,* for
example, oddly enough takes place offstage. With the exception
of the popular *Laburnum Grove,* Priestley's six comedies written
in five years, from 1933 to 1937, seem more labored than labors
of love, suggesting that the dramatist had not yet found the
proper form for comic plays exploring serious ideas. The social
satire of *The Roundabout* and *Duet in Floodlight* is slight,
strained, and artificial, and their occasional political jokes miss
the mark; yet the more serious political implications of *Bees on
the Boat Deck* overwhelm what might have been an entertaining
if mindless frolic. Priestley has written, "There is no real humor
without empathy, a liberal imagination, tolerance, some measure
of affection."[2] Only *Laburnum Grove* displays these essential
elements, and, significantly, it is the only play of the group to find
its audience. Two of the others, *The Roundabout* and *The Bad
Samaritan,* never reached the West End. Priestley would
eventually find his comic voice, but not in plays frankly imitative
of wittier playwrights.

I   The Roundabout

Obviously   patterned   on   Somerset   Maugham's   *The   Circle*

(1921), as even its title suggests, *The Roundabout*, Priestley's first comedy of manners, written in 1933, observes the unities of time and place, but lacks a central action to give point to random observations on the life of the titled class. Priestley, a middle-class Yorkshireman, is clearly ill at ease in the country home of a British lord.

Pamela Kettlewell has not seen her father, Lord Kettlewell, since her parents separated ten years before. Paying him an unexpected visit on her return from an extended trip to Russia, Pamela has plans for her father: she will rid him of his mistress and reunite him with his wife. Having tired of Hilda Lancicourt, Lord Kettlewell tacitly approves Pamela's first stratagem, but Lady Kettlewell's sudden appearance is even more a surprise than his daughter's arrival. Despite the fact that Richard and Rose have not spoken to one another in years, they are reconciled in minutes, but Priestley does not supply the scene toward which the play has been building. Instead, Lady Kettlewell rather casually informs her daughter of their decision: ". . . he and I have discovered that we're still very fond of one another, and I've forgiven him and admitted there were faults on both sides."[3]

With its ill-defined conflict arbitrarily resolved early in the third act, *The Roundabout* abruptly changes direction as Pamela's political commitment is exposed as superficial. The product of a broken home, she had embraced communism after a misunderstanding with a young man. With her parents reconciled and her beau back on the scene, Pamela too can return to the fold.

Moving in two directions at once, *The Roundabout*'s awkward political framework distracts rather than enhances, for high comedy finally depends on its wit, and here too the play is unsuccessful, as the following exchanges attest:

LORD KETTLEWELL: . . . He talks like a fool sometimes—and I'm not sure he doesn't look like one—but he's got his head screwed on.

SAUNDERS: That must be wretched for him. I've always been glad my head hasn't been screwed on. I like to keep moving it about. (274-75)

LORD KETTLEWELL: . . . If I'd a family, I'd be the head of it. None of this modern nonsense.

SAUNDERS: Modern nonsense is always something that's going on in other people's families. (279)

II   Laburnum Grove

Assigning the labels "High, Light and Broad" to the various styles of comedy, Priestley curiously suggests that the first "has never been popular with English writers and audiences," although he cites *The Circle* as a successful example of the form. Dismissing Light Comedy as "flimsy pieces" which serve as vehicles for popular performers, he asserts that his "own choice is Broad Comedy, which is stronger in situation and richer in its characterisation than Light Comedy, and more frankly farcical and less austerely intellectual in its approach than High Comedy. It is . . . peculiarly suitable to the English temperament, and as I consider I possess a fairly thick slab of this temperament, this is the field of comedy in which I have chosen to work."[4] *Laburnum Grove,* his first foray into the form, demonstrates that he had chosen wisely following the false start of *The Roundabout.*

The production of *Laburnum Grove* in the West End in 1933 marked the beginning of a long and rewarding association with J. P. Mitchelhill, owner of the Duchess Theatre, which would provide a home for many of his plays. The comedy also made clear to London's critics and audiences that they were dealing with an unpredictable dramatist. *Dangerous Corner* had suggested that a daring innovator had arrived to shake up the West End; *Laburnum Grove,* on the other hand, was a disappointment for some, albeit a charming one, in that Priestley the experimenter was there marking time. Subtitled *An Immoral Comedy in Three Acts,* the play is an amusing satire on suburban life, unconventional only in Priestley's inspired choice of protagonist, the criminal as family man.

George Radfern seems to be a typical hardworking breadwinner, running a small business in the City, growing tomatoes in his greenhouse in his spare time. His wife finds life with him conveniently comfortable, his daughter finds him perfectly dull. Nothing ever seems to happen in Laburnum Grove in Shooters Green, a North London suburb, where all the houses have quaint names and quaint occupants, until the evening that Radfern tells two men who want to borrow substantial sums of money from him, his brother-in-law, and the young man who wants to marry his daughter Elsie, that he has been counterfeiting bonds and notes for four or five years, ever since his wholesale paper firm was done in by a larger company. Elsie's intended beats a hasty retreat, but Baxley and Elsie herself see the provider whom they have been taking for granted in a new light. Elsie gets up early to cook his breakfast and Baxley polishes his boots, much to Radfern's surprise and pleasure: "You mustn't spoil me," he says, "just because I don't make an honest living."[5]

The fun of the play lies in an uncertainty which spreads from the characters to the audience: Is George Radfern really a criminal mastermind, or has the book he has been reading, *The Great Bank Mystery*, supplied him with all the details he needs to convince some hangers-on to pack up and clear out? Once the audience knows for certain in Act III that in his droll, off-hand manner Radfern has been telling the truth, is in fact "a crook," the play's comic effect diminishes, and the intentionally "immoral" conclusion becomes disquieting. When Inspector Stack informs him that Scotland Yard is on to him, that it is just a matter of time before the Yard will have enough evidence to arrest him, Radfern maintains an innocent stance: "I've been swindled myself in my time, but if ever I've injured any man, woman or child in this country, then it's news to me" (65). Evans comments that "one's acceptance of this . . . depends entirely on how far one accepts the premise that Radfern's illicit activity is no more illegitimate than the legal machinations of banks and speculators."[6] Radfern, Priestley's first complete dramatic character, is so thoroughly engaging, however, that all criticism, ethical or dramatic, is disarmed.

The weakness of the play lies in its supporting characters. Later, in *When We Are Married*, Priestley would effectively portray an entire comic group in credible human terms, but in *Laburnum Grove* Radfern is surrounded by conveniently drawn caricatures. Indeed, to add zest to Baxley, Cedric Hardwicke, the director, invented for him an insatiable appetite for bananas, his only characteristic (unmentioned in the text) which audiences could later recall. And the play defies logic in the naiveté of the loving Mrs. Radfern, who seems to know even less about her husband than Emilia knew about Iago. Nonetheless, the play demonstrates that Priestley can be engaging and penetrating at the same time. While it pokes sly, gentle fun at the humdrum existence which most men willingly endure, it indirectly points a cautionary finger at banks, big business, and government. *Laburnum Grove* is the first of many Priestley plays to focus directly on the family circle; and its implication that criminal action is necessary to provide for the group, to hold it together, is at once provocative and richly comic.

III   Duet in Floodlight *and* Bees on the Boat Deck

Once again imitative rather than innovative, Priestley in *Duet in Floodlight* in 1935 catches the cadences of the comedy of manners as practiced by Noel Coward. Where Priestley's play is again found wanting is in the quality of its wit. The opening exchange between a playwright and the actress with whom he is living is a fair sampling of the comedy's lack of sparkle as Keith comments on Julia's remarkable delivery:

KEITH: . . . But you could do the trick with me if you recited Bradshaw—even if it was only the local services of the Southern Railway.
JULIA: Oh—but especially the Southern Railway.
KEITH: Why?
JULIA: You're forgetting that the first time we really talked was on the Southern Railway.
KEITH: On a train to Bournemouth.
JULIA: A slow train, too.
KEITH: Yes, we were both furious because we had each caught the wrong train.
JULIA: There was the finger of Destiny. We could never have got to know one another so well on a fast train.
KEITH: No, there's something about a stopping train that unlocks the heart.[7]

For Priestley, the broader the comedy, the more comfortable the playwright. He is out of his element in *Duet in Floodlight*, forgettable nonsense about a couple who marry as a publicity gimmick, despise their overpublicized wedded bliss, then pretend to be divorced in order to meet again happily on the sly. If the play once more underscores his versatility, it also represents Priestley at his most trivial level in the theater, nor did the play's brief London run benefit from its author's new theatrical role as director alongside his friend Cedric Hardwicke.

Subtitled *A Farcical Tragedy in Two Acts, Bees on the Boat Deck* is described by its author as "an attempt to write political satire in terms of farcical comedy." Despite strong performances by Ralph Richardson and Laurence Olivier, who also served as codirectors as well as partners with Priestley in its 1936 production, the play was not well received. Priestley, who still has affection for it, suggests that the Lyric Theatre may have been too large, that the realistic ship setting may have worked against "the symbolism of the piece."[8] A sounder reason for its relative failure lies in an unworkable concept: political allegory and farce, an unmanageable mix. Even a comic genius like Chaplin nearly ruined the inspired lunacy of *The Great Dictator* (1940) with his too-earnest message. In *Bees on the Boat Deck* Priestley is never inspired, merely clumsy.

The S.S. *Gloriana*, owned by the White Albion Line, is out of service in a backwater of Trim Estuary. Gridley and Patch, her chief engineer and second officer, serve as watchmen until she can be taken out to sea again. Their job is not an easy one. Oblivious to the consequences, Fletherington, a confused and irresponsible research chemist, has developed a powerful new explosive and plans to test it by blowing up the ship. With a by-election about to take place in the district, Gaster encourages the explosion as a political protest, which perfectly suits Captain Mellock, giving him reason enough to denounce Gaster publicly. For Lord Cottingley, the ship's destruction is an opportunity to turn a quick profit. He will buy the *Gloriana* and insure her before the blast. But communism, fascism, and corrupt capitalism, despite the aid of pure science, are no match for the solid English virtues of brains and brawn. Gridley and Patch rout the villains and save the ship. Even brains and brawn, however, can be done in by bumbling bureaucracy. Like a perverse deus ex machina, a clerk from Head Office brings word of the *Gloriana*'s ironic fate: having outlived her usefulness, she is to be blown up!

Priestley's characters are a set of cartoon figures who rush wildly from stateroom to storeroom, up and down ladders, in and out of hatches, quoting Marx and Schopenhauer all the while. Politics are blurred by frantic action, which is overloaded by the antics of a drunken shopkeeper, an inept policeman, a missing witness, and a spoiled debutante. And the piece's inherent farce is denied a logic of its own, giving way instead to pleas for democratic action on the part of right-minded men. Gridley, Priestley's spokesman, was once aboard a sinking ship and watched the survivors "screaming, fighting, knocking hell out of each other to get into the boats."[9] He knows human nature, "and you can have it," he tells the younger Patch, yet his own solution to the problems which England shares with the world is finally overly simplistic: "I don't want a party, yours or anybody else's. I don't care about capitalists and proletarians, masses and bosses, red shirts, black shirts, brown shirts, green shirts. I want to see some men about, real men who know what sense is, and duty is, and order is. *(Shouting)* I'm getting on, my time's running out, and I'm tired of living among millions of howling monkeys. For God's sake, show me some men" (137). Even Gridley's passion is too strong for the play.

IV   Spring Tide *and* The Bad Samaritan

Spring Tide, a slight sentimental comedy written in 1936 in collaboration with George Billam with Priestley employing the pseudonym of Peter Goldsmith, also suffers under the weight of a burden it cannot support. Two themes are introduced at once, each detracting from the other's development. When Mrs. Porrett's West London boarding-house runs into financial straits, her lodgers pool their resources and move with her to a houseboat on the Thames owned by Mr. O'Hara, her oldest and wisest guest. Once the careers of all the young people take a successful turn, they pair off two by two, and Mrs. Porrett and O'Hara move back to the boarding-house to help a new group of youngsters try their wings.

Priestley's hope for a world in which people band together to bring out the best in one another is stated in the scene in which the members of the newly formed commune discuss a name for their organization:

MRS. PORRETT: . . . Here, what's this about combinations?
CHRISTOPHER: The name of our houseboat-pool-everything-company.
JILL: Let's have "Consols, Limited."
LUDLOW: Yes, because we consolidate and console one another.
CHRISTOPHER: . . . Objects of the company—?
WROTHERINGTON: To promote and pursue health, wealth, and happiness.
MRS. PORRETT *(happily)*: Sink, swim or float together, boys and girls.
ANDREW: Let's drink to it.[10]

What makes the commune work, however, is neglected in favor of the play's primary theme, which is summed up by O'Hara as he reads to Mrs. Porrett: "Listen to this. 'At the season of the spring tides, the young move in great swarms to their new feeding grounds, but enormous numbers of them perish on the way. . . .' He's talking about a certain sort of fish in the Indian Ocean, but he might be talking about these boys and girls you have here, Mrs. Porrett, mightn't he?" (8). Why some perish while others thrive, however, is never explored. Instead, all of the characters conquer the world as artists and entrepreneurs, or at the very least, as happy housewives.

The most intriguing element of *Spring Tide* is its Shakespearean structure. Act I presents a semblance of order, but when Mrs. Porrett tells the others that she can no longer pay her bills since they no longer pay theirs, Act II transports them all to the disordered world of the houseboat, where, in adversity, each one comes to terms with himself and the others. Act III returns them to the reordered world of the play's opening. A glaring weakness of the play is that the imposed structure arbitrarily forces the move. On the houseboat O'Hara becomes a convenient god-figure as he guides each of the young people through a moment of self-realization, enabling the play's fledgling dramatist to understand that he must write about what he knows, not what he imagines (a lesson Priestley learned in *The Roundabout*), and convincing a budding composer to tackle dance music before tone poems. The audience, however, is left to wonder why O'Hara has not had the good sense to offer his good advice within the confines of the boarding-house in Act I.

The Bad Samaritan, "a sardonic comedy, with a good basic idea, but . . . a messy third act,"[11] was performed in Liverpool in 1937. Priestley claims that the unpublished play is the only one he ever wrote "in the manner of the text-books, first building up a detailed synopsis, then clothing each scene with dialogue," but both play and method were abandoned during the out-of-town tune-up.

CHAPTER 12

Chekhovian Drama

DURING the period from 1933 to 1937 in which Priestley frankly sought commercial success in the theater with his early comedies, the artist in him found expression in two plays, more serious than the others, *Eden End* and *Cornelius*. The first was produced in London in 1934, a year after *Laburnum Grove,* and the second in 1935, three months before *Duet in Floodlight.* If *Cornelius,* despite glowing notices,[1] did not attract the following which *Eden End* won him, the latter proved to Priestley that there was as large an audience for a thoughtful drama artfully wrought as for a popular melodrama like *Dangerous Corner* or an infectious comedy like *Laburnum Grove;* and for the dramatist such a work offered the richer rewards of personal gratification. He had taken a lighthearted look at the family in *Laburnum Grove,* but in *Eden End* his probing is deeper as he considers seriously for the first time the group's hopes and dreams, its loyalties and betrayals. The play suggests that with the family's inevitable break-up, as its members grow apart and shed their responsibilities toward one another, there comes an end to Eden, a loss of innocence. That sense of loss infuses *Cornelius* as well, as the focus shifts from the family to a larger group of office-workers experiencing the break-up of a firm in the City.

The widening of the Priestley circle, eventually to encompass a nation and a world, is evident in *Cornelius,* a play underrated by its author, a dramatic comedy rather than a drama in that it sounds a stronger note of optimism than *Eden End.* Both plays, however, share an element which would return again and again in Priestley's plays, in *Time and the Conways, The Linden Tree, Summer Day's Dream*—a pervasive mood which links J. B. Priestley with Anton Chekhov.

I   Eden End

Eden End in northern England is the home of the widower Dr. Kirby, his daughter Lilian, who keeps house for him, and Sarah, the old nurse who raised his three children and has stayed on past her years of usefulness. Lilian has been keeping company with Geoffrey Farrant, who runs a nearby estate. Years before, Geoffrey had been in love with Stella, Lilian's older sister, but Stella, restricted by the limited horizons of Eden End, had gone off to make her way in the world as an actress. As the play begins, the youngest of the children, Wilfred, has come home on leave from the British West Africa Company. He feels a vague dissatisfaction with his holiday in Eden End. In Africa he had eagerly looked forward to it, yet now he finds himself missing Nigeria and his work just as Baxley in *Laburnum Grove* fondly recalls the responsibilities he never shouldered in Singapore. To pass the time, Wilfred fancies himself in love with a local barmaid.

A stable family situation is disrupted by the unexpected arrival of Stella, the prodigal daughter, sick to death of tiring railway journeys, uncomfortable digs, the disappointing life of the second rate actress who has little to look forward to. She has returned to Eden End as to a haven, aware that the girlhood which her home represents was the one happy period of her life. Stella, however, learns before the play ends with her going out again into the world, that youth cannot be recaptured: "We have our lives to get on with, to live them as best we can. There's no running away. No escape. No miracles."[2]

Before her departure, which signals a return to normalcy in the Kirby household, she upsets her sister by reawakening Geoffrey's love, and, inadvertently, causes Lilian to strike back by bringing to Eden End another actor, Charlie Appleby, Stella's estranged husband. When Geoffrey learns that Stella is married, he plans a life for himself in New Zealand, dashing Lilian's hope for a home of her own. Stella and Charlie will try to renew their life together with probably as little success as they have had in the past. Discovering that his barmaid flirts with all her customers, Wilfred will return to Nigeria, where he will impatiently look forward to his next leave.

Soon to die of a heart condition, Dr. Kirby, considering himself a failure, a mere general practitioner when he longed for something more, mistakenly anticipates a bright future which he knows he will never experience, but which he expects life to hold in store for his children, for the baby in the village whom he has just helped into the world. Yet despite the fact that no dreams come true in Eden End, that what life really promises is hardship and heartbreak, as Charlie, the one character who has fully come to terms with his own mediocrity, quite simply states, "It doesn't matter what women do, or who tells you lies, or whether you go to Africa or not, life's a very wonderful thing. . . . A wonderful thing. You can't get away from that" (108). That he is in his cups at the time does not diminish the truth of his observation. He has merely found a means to ease the pain which is part of life's wonder.

Priestley makes certain that his audience will be far wiser concerning the future of his characters than they themselves can be by making extraordinary use of dramatic irony by the simple yet effective means of setting the play in 1912. Not only the Kirbys but a world, too, is about to lose its innocence. As the doctor talks about the possibilities of a better world to come, the audience knows of the horror into which it will be plunged, from which it cannot fully recover. Time itself lends to Eden End its richest dimension.

On rereading *Eden End*, the author's own favorite among his plays, more than a decade after its first production, Priestley registered wonder at having written it "because everything in it is imagined—I have never known any people like the Kirby family—and I know nothing in my own life that would suggest to me this particular theme of the pathetic prodigal daughter."[3] Yet any reader of the first page of Priestley's appreciative book *Anton Chekhov* is given a clue to the play's source, which its author has conveniently forgotten: "When . . . I was asked to contribute to [the International Profiles series] . . . I agreed to do so on one condition—that my subject should be Chekhov. . . . A dramatist myself, I had long enjoyed both admiration and affection for Chekhov's plays."[4] *Eden End* is clearly Priestley's Chekhov play, and Priestley is the Russian mentor's most able English student. More than an imitation, Priestley in *Eden End* has made Chekhov's method his own as he masters a mood which depends primarily on a depth of characterization and a wealth of detail.

The characters of *Eden End* are combinations of Chekhov's own. Stella, the failed actress returning home from abroad, suggests both Madame Ranevskaya of *The Cherry Orchard* and Nina of *The Seagull* (1896), with a touch of Elena of *Uncle Vanya* (1898) as she attracts the man her practical, hard-working sister Lilian, like *Vanya's* Sonia and Varya of *The Cherry Orchard*, herself loves. Lilian even has a brief exchange with her Lopahin, Geoffrey, in which they discuss the weather when each has in mind that they should be discussing their personal relationship. Wilfrid is a younger but equally impractical Gaev, while Dr. Kirby is a combination of all of Chekhov's sad and wise doctors. His knowledge of his own imminent death suggests a strong parallel with Dr. Chekhov himself. Even the furniture, the pictures on the walls, seem to have a life of their own in the prodigal's eyes, as they do for the Ranevskys. That her china castle is still in the room pleases Stella as much as the noble cupboard's endurance astounds Gaev.

To emphasize an era of change, a stable innocent world hurtling into the uncertainties of the twentieth century, Priestley includes old Sarah. While he claims that she is "the only character in it I took directly from life,"[5] the nurse is reminiscent at first of Marina in *Vanya*, but as the play progresses she grows more like old Firs of *The Cherry Orchard*. She cannot accept her charges as adults and still worries about their dressing properly on going out in the rain and their having their tea on coming in again. She prefers the world as it was, even brings out the costume Stella wore in a local theatrical years before, which Stella symbolically tears as she tries it on. Sarah does not understand such new-fangled gadgets as motorcars and phonographs. Alone on stage as the others go off to the train station for Stella's departure at the end of the play, she stares in bewilderment, then retires to her room as a ringing telephone replaces Chekhov's breaking string.

Margaret Marshall once wrote about a performance of Chekhov's play, "Again I overheard the old remark that nothing happens in *The Cherry Orchard*. Nothing happens—except that a world comes to an end."[6] Commenting on the reaction to his own play, Priestley writes that "one frequent criticism . . . was that 'nothing happens in it.' "[7] The difference is one of scope. The Kirbys are believable characters due to a number of delicate touches which humanize them, but their home is not microcosmic. Eden End remains merely a provincial English town. It never takes on the overtones that make *The Cherry Orchard* a viable symbol for all the world. Significantly, after a highly successful West End run at the Duchess Theatre, the play quickly disappeared on Broadway.

Evans's accurate observation on the language of the two plays suggests a limiting factor of the Priestley work: "Both plays . . . show a similar deployment of effects, but in the final analysis they part company because the poetry achieved by the one is richer and more inevitably achieved than that of the other. In *The Cherry Orchard* the language is naturalistic in form—it impersonates the inconsequentiality, the fragmented character, of human conversation. . . . In *Eden End* the language is not an impersonation of naturalistic language. As in *Dangerous Corner* the characters speak dialogue which does not penetrate deep into the recesses of their minds and feelings, but reports."[8] Aside from the well-observed drunk scene, "the rhythm that is created in *Eden End* is too explicit and does not come inevitably from the inner source of character." Where *Eden End* requires a strong poetic idiom of its own, Priestley has his characters quote Stevenson and Wordsworth.

That which ultimately makes *Eden End* a play of consequence, if not a masterpiece of world drama, Priestley has described as "Chekhov's peculiar method":

What he does in effect is to turn the conventional "well-made" play upside down and inside out. It is almost as if he had read some textbooks on the art of playwriting and had then done the opposite of everything they recommended. It is common form in conventional drama to endow the leading characters, if only for the sake of the inevitable "conflict," with more power of will and sense of purpose than most of us can pretend to have. Chekhov reverses this. Instead of heightening and hardening the will in his characters, he depresses and softens it: most of them are even more uncertain and weaker than we are.[9]

Just as E. R. Wood suggests that one can answer the question, "What is . . . [*Eden End*] about?" with a Priestley quotation on *The Cherry Orchard*: "It is about time and change and folly and regret and vanished happiness and hope for the future,"[10] Priestley's own estimate of the value of Chekhovian influence on later writers can well stand as a final judgment of *Eden End*:

"Since his time we have had many Chekhovian plays. None of them rivals *The Cherry Orchard* or *The Three Sisters,* but they are not worse plays because of his influence, they are all better than they might have been."[11] *Eden End* may well be the best of those Chekhovian plays.

II   Cornelius

Priestley has commented that of all the actors he has worked with, he has a special regard for Ralph Richardson, and the actor has written that Charlie Appleby in *Eden End,* the first of his five Priestley roles, is "the best shorter part" he has ever had: "There I was given wonderful jokes all set to music—what more could one ask?"[12] Two of those characters, the title roles in *Cornelius* and *Johnson Over Jordan,* Priestley created expressly for him, and both are strongly influenced by the unique qualities, even suggest the speech patterns, of the actor whom the author thus describes: "He . . . has been at times, a superb comedian. But while he is essentially not a tragic actor . . . he is more complicated and deeper in his appeal than any comedian. Perhaps he could be described . . . as a moon-faced *wondering* tragi-comedian, earthy possibly but never really at home in the sad bad world we have inflicted upon this earth."[13]

Cornelius "took the shape it did," Priestley writes, "partly because I wanted to write a play for my friend Ralph Richardson, and partly because I wanted to write a play about an office and about business during the depression."[14] That Richardson may have acted the role to perfection is paradoxically reinforced by Priestley's comment that the actor was "never quite at ease with this City man," for *Cornelius* is a gentle comedy about a gentle man with a romantic imagination, out of his element in a changing business world, full of wonder about the world outside the office. Like the Chekhovian *Eden End,* it depends on characterization, atmosphere, and tone.

Briggs & Murrison, a small aluminium import firm in the City, reminiscent of Twigg and Dersingham of *Angel Pavement,* is on the verge of bankruptcy. A new world of high finance—of big-business conglomerates, complicated foreign currency deals, impersonal bankers, and impatient creditors—has passed it by. While Murrison, the senior partner, has gone off on a month-long sales trip to the north in a last effort to save the company,

Cornelius, the middle-aged junior partner, attempts to keep the office running smoothly, to jolly his staff into believing the firm can survive: "When the head of a decent firm like this goes himself—and when he's Bob Murrison, who knows the business inside out, who's got drive, who's got—well—charm, if you like, who they all know to be an absolutely first-class fellow—I tell you—something happens. You'll see."[15] Yet Cornelius knows in his heart that an era of personalized relationships, of trust and integrity in the commercial world, is at an end. Business has become "a game of snakes and ladders—but without the ladders. . . . And what's it all about?" he asks, "If we've to live by private trade, then let it be private trade. Why have they made it like a lunatics' obstacle race? Why are we condemned to scheme and scratch, in these cubby-holes? I tell you, a blind monkey could find a better life to live than we've lately had here" (44).

When Murrison, like Willy Loman, learns that personalized sales methods no longer work, that even his long-standing customers refuse to see him, he returns a broken man and kills himself. With the collapse of the business, Cornelius too considers suicide. Buoyed by the courage and indomitable spirit of the small group of men and women who work for him, have stood by him with love and loyalty, he, however, finds the capacity to carry on, to challenge the new world beyond the office door.

Not since Frank Wedekind's *The Marquis of Keith* (1900) has the protagonist of a comedy contemplated suicide after an actual suicide by another character. Yet from this unlikely material Priestley fashions one of his warmest and subtlest works, which defies arbitrary classification, for it is unlike any of his other comedies. Priestley himself seems not to categorize it as such, as he includes it in Volume III of his collected plays, which contains some of his most serious dramas. If one allows that Chekhov's plays are comedies, however, and the Russian author certainly thought so despite the disagreement of his director, Stanislavski, then *Cornelius* must be considered one as well. Its tone, affectionately humorous throughout, is more positive than that of *Eden End,* whose inhabitants face a bleaker world than they expect. Cornelius has within him the inextinguishable spark of life; he will survive.

The wealth of detail concerning the dull workaday world

suggests *Cornelius* as a forerunner of Arnold Wesker's *The Kitchen* (1956) and David Storey's *The Contractor* (1969), while the scene of the office-boy's leave-taking foreshadows a similar scene in Arthur Miller's factory-set *A Memory of Two Mondays* (1955), as a young man, impatient to find his own way, turns his back on an outmoded world. The relationships among the staff, their antagonisms and petty jealousies as well as their sympathetic understanding of one another are richly drawn with Chekhovian warmth and humor. Cornelius' rejection of Miss Porrin, gentler than Lopahin's treatment of Varya in *The Cherry Orchard*, and Miss Porrin's uneasy alliance with Judy Evison, reminiscent of a scene between Sonya and Elena in *Uncle Vanya*, are as accurate and unsentimental as their Chekhovian models and evoke a similar response.

Cornelius's employees are simple human beings, not articulate speechmakers. They rescue him from despair with heartfelt convictions, not neatly turned phrases, and in this respect the language of *Cornelius* works to better effect than that of *Eden End*. When Cornelius suggests that Murrison's suicide was a brave act, his faithful old clerk contradicts him:

BIDDLE: If you'll excuse me saying so, you're talking like a man who's tired and a bit sick. After all, who are we to say what life is and what it's worth?
CORNELIUS: We know what it's offered us.
BIDDLE: We know the bit we've taken, that's all. (58)

Discovering that Judy is about to marry an unscrupulous businessman, Cornelius, who fancies he loves her himself, is skeptical about her chance for happiness. Judy, however, is ready to face what she recognizes as a difficult future: "You need courage, a special sort of courage, if you're going to live properly" (65). Her simple statement of the play's theme, that despite adversity one can begin anew, is finally reiterated by the even more plain-speaking charlady, Mrs. Roberts: "Well, my motto is, it's never too late. You look after yourself, Mr. Cornelius" (67).

Effective supporting characters, however, cannot on their own make a play. At the very center of *Cornelius* stands a complex, contradictory human being, one of Priestley's finest creations, a man, like the author himself, who has looked on despair, has suffered rejection and loneliness, yet dares to live. His saving grace is that he has the ability to laugh at himself. Not as strong as he might be nor as wise as he should be, Cornelius brings life to his play, for the affection and loyalty he inspires in his staff are credibly communicated to his audience. As a portrait of fallible man, Cornelius is totally convincing.

CHAPTER 13

Time Plays

THE split in time in *Dangerous Corner* had been no more than a stage trick, but the dramatic irony which provided *Eden End* its strongest effect was more than mere device. By setting the play on the eve of World War I, Priestley relied on his audience's awareness of the inexorable movement of the clock to heighten the drama's stature. The audience rather than the dramatist transformed the Kirbys into a representation of England at the end of an era, for time provided them a knowledge of the future which was denied the family within the play. That Priestley would turn again to time as controlling factor and precognition as supporting theme was inevitable, for Priestley is admittedly "a Time-haunted man."[1]

I Time and the Conways

In 1937 Priestley was at work on another play that dealt with time, *I Have Been Here Before,* when the inspiration for *Time and the Conways* struck him: "I was lunching with my sister. . . . We were idly discussing old acquaintances and especially a family I had known before the War. Suddenly I saw that there was a play in the relation between a fairly typical middle-class provincial family and the theory of Time, the theory chiefly associated with J. W. Dunne, over which I had been brooding for the past two years."[2] So insistent was the idea that the dramatist plunged into what he knew to be the second act of the play, completing it in two days. This difficult act, with all of its technical problems, seemed to write itself, as though he were not so much its creator but "an instrument of creation" in temporary union with a mind outside his own (RG, 45), as though his Observer 1, in Dunne's terms, were in tune with his Observer 2. Once he had completed the necessary research for the period details of Acts I and III, the entire play quickly took shape.

As *Time and the Conways* begins, the year is 1919 and the scene is a sitting-room in the Conway home in a prosperous suburb of a manufacturing town. A party is taking place in an adjoining room. Kay, an aspiring novelist, is celebrating her twenty-first birthday with her widowed mother, five brothers and sisters, her friends and neighbors. Idealistic Madge is eager to be part of a brave new Socialist world. Dashing Robin, just released from the RAF, is ready to make his fortune in car sales. Beautiful Hazel is awaiting a prince charming, while excitable Carol, the youngest, is bursting to get on with the business of living. Only unambitious Alan seems content with a humdrum existence as clerk in the Rate Office. As the young Conways prepare to entertain their guests with charades, vivacious Mrs. Conway reveals herself as much a child at heart as the rest: "Now I'm ready—if you are. What a mess you're making. I knew you would. Let me see. *(Dives into the clothes, and scatters them far more wildly than the others have done. She finally fishes out a Spanish shawl and mantilla.)* Ah—here they are. Now I shall be a Spanish beauty. I know a song for it, too."[3] Although she dotes on her son Robin, the one who is happiest to see him home again is Hazel's pretty, foolish friend Joan.

The Conways, prefiguring the Alingtons of the novel *Bright Day,* are a happy family but have known suffering. They have recovered from the sudden loss by drowning several years earlier of Mr. Conway, who left them well provided. Having survived the war, they have every reason to expect a bright future. For Ernest Beevers, a young businessman who has settled in town after buying into a local paper mill, entry into the Conway home has obviously been his goal. Taken to the party by the Conways' young solicitor, Gerald Thornton, Beevers awkwardly follows Hazel around the house.

Once the charades are finished and costumes cleared away, everyone goes into the next room to hear Mrs. Conway sing, but Kay returns to the sitting-room, finds pencil and paper and begins to write. When Carol looks in on her, Kay tells her younger sister about her novel:

KAY *(that eager young author):* . . . a girl goes to a party—you see—and there are some things I've been feeling—very subtle things—that I

know she'd feel—and I want my novel to be very real this time—so I
had to scribble them down—

CAROL: Will you tell me them afterwards?

KAY: Yes.

CAROL: Bedroom?

KAY: Yes, if you're not too sleepy.

CAROL: I couldn't be. *(She pauses happily, one earnest young creature
staring at the other. And now we can just hear* MRS. CONWAY *in the
drawing-room beginning to sing Schumann's "Der Nussbaum". CAROL
is now very solemn, a little awed.)* Kay, I think you're *wonderful.*

KAY *(awed herself):* I think *life's* wonderful.   (151-52)

This is the happiest moment that any of the young Conways will
ever experience, but only Kay, with the special sensitivity of the
artist, is to be granted a vision of what the future holds in store.
When Carol goes out, Kay continues to write. Moved by the
music and a sense of creation, she switches off the lights, but *"the
room is not in darkness because light is coming in from the hall.
KAY goes to the window and opens the curtains, so that when she
sits on the window-seat, her head is silvered in moonlight. Very
still, she listens to the music, and seems to stare not at but into
something, and as the song goes soaring away, the curtain creeps
down"* (152).

When the curtain rises on Act II, it seems that the action is
continuous, *"for there is the light coming in from the hall, and
there is KAY sitting on the window-seat"* (153). When Alan
enters and switches on the lights, however, it is obvious that
several years have passed. Act II is in fact, as Priestley explains it,
"Kay's glimpse of the future, or, to put it in terms of Serialism, it
is Kay's Observer Two who sees what will happen, years ahead,
to her Observer One."[4]

The room has changed; Alan and Kay are older. It is again
Kay's birthday, but this time her fortieth. It is 1937, the year in
which the play was written, and there is a family crisis. Mrs.
Conway is in financial difficulties and has called her children
together. Like Madame Ranevskaya, whom she closely resembles, she would turn the homecoming into a party as she waits to
learn some harsh economic truths, but her children are not in a
party mood. Alan retains the serenity he displayed in Act I, but
Kay is suffering the pangs of an unhappy affair with a married
man. No novelist, she is a hack journalist. "What about you,
Madge?" she asks her hypochondriac sister, now a dried-up

schoolmistress, who has deliberately wounded her by inquiring about her work. "Are you building Jerusalem—in England's green and pleasant land?" (157). Hazel has not lost her looks, but there is a change in her. Now the wealthy Mrs. Ernest Beevers, she is subdued and fearful, terrified of the husband who has claimed his prize but never forgiven the Conways for snubbing him years before. Robin is now more seedy than dashing. Unable to hold a job, he has frittered away more than his share of the family's funds and has deserted Joan and their children. Conspicuously, the once lively Carol is not among the others, for she has been dead for sixteen years.

Mrs. Conway still has moments of impulsive generosity, can still win her children's love, but can hurt them with uncanny cruelty. Presenting Kay with a brooch which had been given her years before by her husband, she tells her daughter, "When you were younger, I never liked you as much as I did Hazel, but now I think I was wrong."

HAZEL: Oh—Mother!

MRS. C: I know, Hazel dear, but you're such a *fool* with that little husband of yours. Why, if he were mine—

HAZEL *(sharply for her)*: Well he isn't—and you really know very little about him.

MRS. C. *(as she looks about her)*: It's time the men were here. I've always hated seeing a lot of women sitting about, with no men. *They* always look silly, and then I feel silly myself. I don't know why. *(Notices* ALAN. *With some malice.)* Of course you're here, Alan. I was forgetting you. Or forgetting you were a man.   (161–62)

Once a good friend to the Conways, Gerald Thornton is now impatient with them as he informs them of the seriousness of the situation. When Hazel suggests that her husband lend Mrs. Conway the money she needs, Beevers coldly refuses. Furious, Mrs. Conway makes a grand but foolish gesture, for which her daughter will have to pay. Ordering Beevers out of the house, she slaps him across the face.

After further recriminations, a chastened Kay is left alone with her brother Alan, who proves to be the strongest, the most stable member of the family. He lights his pipe and attempts to cheer her up:

ALAN: You mustn't mind too much. It's all right, y'know. Like being forty?

KAY: Oh no, Alan, it's hideous and unbearable. Remember what we once were and what we thought we'd be. And now this. And it's all we have, Alan, it's *us*. Every step we've taken—every tick of the clock—making everything worse. If this is all life is, what's the use? Better to die, like Carol, before you find it out, before Time gets to work on you. I've felt it before, Alan, but never as I've done to-night. There's a great devil in the universe, and we call it Time. (176)

But Alan manages to comfort her before leaving the room. Alone, Kay looks out the window, her *"head raised. No sooner is she settled there than the curtain comes down"* (177).

As Act III begins, Mrs. Conway can be heard singing "Der Nussbaum," and Kay is discovered at the window just as she was left at the end of the first act. It is once again 1919 and her twenty-first birthday. The action continues as though Act II had never occurred, and it has not, as yet. As the scene progresses, however, it is obvious that Kay has an awareness the others cannot share. For Kay, as well as the audience, Act III has an unbearable poignancy; for the Conways, carefree again, are busily planting the seeds of their future unhappiness as they destroy one another in ignorance and innocence. Beevers is made to feel unwelcome by all but Carol; Alan, quietly in love with Joan, steps aside for Robin; and Mrs. Conway kills a budding relationship between Madge and Gerald.

When Mrs. Conway wants to tell their fortunes, Kay stops her, but it is Carol who unaccountably seems to have foreknowledge about her brothers and sisters:

CAROL *(sharply, pointing)*: Hazel will always have plenty of money.
MRS. C. *(amused)*: How do you know, Carol?
CAROL: I just do. It came over me suddenly then. . . . And I'll tell you another thing *(Points suddenly at* ALAN*)*. Alan's the happy one. (194).

After all the Conways confess to hopes and dreams that will never come about, Carol, unaware of her own fate, breathlessly plans her future. She will act, she will paint, she will design her clothes, she will cook, she will travel. When her amused mother asks her how she can begin doing all that, Carol replies, "I'd get it all in somehow. The point is—to live. Never mind about money and positions and husbands with titles and rubbish—I'm *going to live*" (195).

Deeply moved, Kay begins to cry and asks a bewildered Alan to speak the words that can comfort her. Mrs. Conway decides that Kay has had enough excitement on her birthday, and it is time for bed. She goes into the other room and softly begins to sing Brahms's "Wiegenlied." Carol switches out the lights and forms a group with Hazel and Joan as Alan joins Kay at the window:

ALAN *(quietly through the music)*: Kay.
KAY *(quietly)*: Yes, Alan?
ALAN: There will be—something—I can tell you—one day. I'll try—I promise.

The moonlight at the window shows us ALAN *looking at her earnestly, and we just catch her answering smile, as the song swells out a little. And then the lights begin to fade, and very soon the three girls are no more than ghosts and all the room is dark, but the moonlight—and the faces of* KAY *and* ALAN—*still lingers; until at last there is only the faintest glimmer, and the Conways have gone, the curtain is down, and the play over.* (197)

What Kay wants to hear at the end of Act III is what Alan will tell her in eighteen years, has already told her at the end of Kay's precognitive vision which is Act II: "There's a book I'll lend you—read it in the train. But the point is, now, at this moment, or any moment, we're only a cross-section of our real selves. What we *really* are is the whole stretch of ourselves, all our time, and when we come to the end of this life, all those selves, all our time, will be *us*—the real you, the real me. And then perhaps we'll find ourselves in another time, which is only another kind of dream" (177). Surely the book Alan has been reading, or will have read in eighteen years, is *An Experiment with Time* by J. W. Dunne.

Audiences with no interest in time theories have been profoundly moved by the dramatic irony of the third act of *Time and the Conways*.[5] If Priestley began the play in part as an explication of a theory, his insight into man's plight in a bewildering age together with his sense of drama transform the play into an effective rendering of the human condition. What Dunne contributes to the fabric of the work is a note of hope, an intimation of immortality. In the final analysis the audience, like the author, is grateful for something to cling to in the midst of life's pain. Pseudoscientific explanations are beside the point, and Priestley himself has made this clear with an amusing anecdote about Dunne's backstage talk to the cast of the play: "With that innocence which seems to belong to mathematicians and engineers . . . [Dunne] covered a blackboard with mathematical formulae and threw over his shoulder various references to Minkowski and the Michelson-Morley experiment with the speed of light. Pretending to know what he was talking about, the players gave a magnificent performance."[6]

Recalling the time split of *Dangerous Corner*, some critics believed that in *Time and the Conways* Priestley was still delving into an old bag of tricks. The dramatist himself sums up their attitude: "This play is a lot of fuss about nothing and merely has the third act played where the second act ought to be and then the real second act put last."[7] Performed chronologically, however, the three acts do not add up to a play with meaningful impact; yet as Priestley has designed it, "its whole point and quality are contained in the third act, when we know so much more about the characters than they know themselves."[8]

In *Time and the Conways*, Priestley reveals himself as a true innovator in the drama, liberating the stage from a limiting convention of realism, as he paves the way for such later works as Pinter's *Old Times* (1971) and *No Man's Land* (1975) in which past and present coexist on the stage. His audience's enthusiastic acceptance and understanding of the work convinced him that the time had come for even more daring experimentation. Soon Priestley would set himself more difficult tasks in play after play, challenging himself and his audience with the form and content of untried materials. But first there was a play to finish which had been inspired by the very theory which seemed to resolve a significant question which Dunne, had left unanswered: Can precognitive dreams reveal *alternatives* to the future?

Under the immediate spell of his first reading of P. D. Ouspensky's *A New Model of the Universe*, Priestley had undertaken to turn theory into drama in *I Have Been Here Before*, but the play proved troublesome. It would undergo several complete revisions before it would be ready for the stage. He had abandoned it temporarily for the writing of *Time and the Conways*. Now he returned to the problems of the more stubborn work. In 1937 the two plays had simultaneous London runs, *Time and the Conways* opening in August, *I Have Been Here Before* in September.

II   I Have Been Here Before

The action of *I Have Been Here Before* (the title is the first line of Dante Gabriel Rossetti's poem "Sudden Light," written in 1854) spans the three days of a Whitsun weekend. On Friday an exiled German professor comes to an isolated inn on a Yorkshire moor in search of a married couple and a single man. Informed that the only guest is Oliver Farrant, a young headmaster, Dr. Görtler amuses the landlord by saying, "This must be the wrong year."[9] Soon, however, a couple do arrive, Walter Ormund, a tired industrialist overwhelmed with despair, and his younger wife Janet, no longer able to cope with her husband's moods. The four guests at the inn experience a feeling of *déjà vu*. It seems as though they have met one another there before, but, supposedly, they have not, even though Ormund is one of the governors of Farrant's school, where the landlord's grandson is enrolled, and was responsible for the young man's acquiring the headmastership there. Curiously, Dr. Görtler seems to know all about the others, and Janet and Farrant are unaccountably embarrassed in each other's presence. The industrialist takes an immediate dislike to the teacher, but nevertheless suggests that Farrant accompany his wife on her outing the next day while he catches up with his work.

Janet goes off alone on Saturday morning for a walk on the moor with Farrant following. After discussing with Görtler a foreboding of oblivion, Ormund, contemplating suicide, goes to his car and removes his gun. Something prevents him from killing himself, but he fires the weapon, startling the landlord and his daughter. Janet and Farrant return separately, having avoided one another all day. Finding themselves alone, they experience an irresistible compulsion and embrace. Before they can separate, Ormund interrupts them: "There may be a storm. And it's nearly Whitsunday—the Feast of Pentecost—the Day of the Spirit" (247). He suggests that they ask Görtler how it will all end, as Janet comes to a realization: "He knew it had happened before" (248).

On Sunday Görtler tells the others about his experiments and his belief in recurrence and intervention. In a dream he has seen himself in exile in London in another life cycle. Living in the same shabby building are an unhappy young couple. The woman had left her husband, who had committed suicide. A business had collapsed, forcing many people into bankruptcy. The young man, unable to get work, is embittered; his love for his wife dies. By coming to the inn to warn them of their fate, Görtler is attempting to save them all, and Janet understands at last that she must not leave her husband.

In a long discussion based directly on Ouspensky, Görtler tells Ormund, "You can return to the old dark circle of existence, dying endless deaths, or you can break the spell and swing out into new life" (264). Ormund finally sees the cause of his bleak despair: "I think what I've resented most is that the only wisdom we have is wisdom after the event. We learn, but always too late. When I was no longer a boy, I knew at last what sort of boy I ought to have been. By the time we are forty, we know how to behave at twenty. Always too late. So that the little wisdom we get is useless to us," to which the professor quietly adds, "In your world. Not in mine" (264-65). With the realization that his suicide would cause Janet despair, lose Farrant the means of earning a living, even bring ruin to the landlord of the inn and his daughter who have invested their savings in his firm, Ormund decides to live. He allows Janet to go, wishing her happiness with Farrant. She kisses him goodbye as Görtler, too, his mission completed, prepares to depart:

DR. GÖRTLER *(after closing door)*: I too must be going now.
ORMUND *(with a slight smile)*: Having concluded the experiment. *(Pause.)* I am still wondering whether I believe a word of it.
DR. GÖRTLER: It is very difficult at first, like all new knowledge. *He is staring curiously at* ORMUND.
ORMUND: You look at me as a doctor looks at his patient.
DR. GÖRTLER *(calmly)*: Yes, because if my theory is correct, you are now in the unusual and interesting position of a man who is moving out on a new time track, like a man who is suddenly born into a strange new world— (267)

Ormund invites the landlord to join him in a quiet smoke. They light their pipes and smoke companionably as the curtain falls.

I Have Been Here Before is a well-made play which does not move well enough. Despite Priestley's intention "to present dramatically a kind of Everyman of my own generation . . .

[who] would represent the deep distrust of life felt by so many moderns" (RG, 50), it remains unconvincing melodrama. The Gothic overtones of its opening suggest that within the framework of a conventional thriller, the author intends, as in *Benighted*, to probe the depths of some more meaningful material. An audience in the theater, however, has certain expectations of a genre. A work that begins as a tale of suspense with the introduction of a mysterious foreigner, possibly a spy, ought to follow through with a reasonably contrived climax rather than an explication of an incredible theory. The electric atmosphere of the opening is replaced by a leaden didacticism. Priestley has not dramatized Ouspensky; he mouths him as Görtler and Ormund lecture one another. With the exception of the landlord, a minor role, the characters have no recognizable touches of humanity, and their only motivation is Priestley's contention that they have been there before.

Perhaps the play suffers from the manner in which it was written. Usually able to complete a play in a week to ten days, Priestley found himself struggling with *I Have Been Here Before*. He wrote several drafts, changed his conception of Görtler from "a transient from some other sphere" to a foreign professor (RG, 51), and even incorporated some suggestions offered by Jed Harris, an American director. That the author, usually secretive about unproduced plays, showed a version to James Barrie suggests an uncharacteristic insecurity (RG, 51). All the delays took him further away from the initial impact that Ouspensky had upon him, and distance enabled the dramatist to grasp the flaw in the mystic's reasoning: "In the way he presents it, his eternal recurrence simply will not work. . . . As soon as changes are introduced, with some men rising and others falling, the exact recurrence of a time is not taking place. The complete repetition, with which he begins, is destroyed by the elaboration of his theory. What he offers us finally is not recurrence and it is not eternal" (MT, 269). Losing confidence in the theory, Priestley lacks conviction in the play.

He has since written: "A novel or a play cannot really be *about* Time. . . . Time is a concept, a certain condition of experience, a mode of perception, and so forth; and a novel or a play, to be worth calling one, cannot really be about Time but only about the people and things that appear to be *in* Time. Some novelists and dramatists may be unusually aware of Time, but they have to

write about something else" (MT, 122).[10] In *Time and the
Conways* that "something else" is humanity, but *I Have Been
Here Before* is primarily about circles and cycles. Its
undeveloped secondary theme, Ormund's responsibility to a
community of interdependent men, would find fuller expression
in Priestley's later plays.

III   People at Sea *and* The Long Mirror

People at Sea finds Priestley adrift in a sea of shoddy
melodrama. Produced in 1937, the lifeless play about eleven
survivors on a fire-swept ship in the Caribbean demonstrates
once again Priestley's annoying habit of occasionally sinking a
work by overloading it. *People at Sea* might have worked as
suspenseful and exciting entertainment with a credibly developed plot, but the dramatist, in his most pretentious vein here,
pauses repeatedly for disastrous forays into the nature of reality
and heavy-handed social commentary, none of which arises
naturally from the contrived situation. The comments on life as
dream or movement in a fourth dimension seem mere leftovers
from the two time plays which immediately precede it, while
real people at sea are probably more concerned with the
problem of getting rescued than the problems of the lower
classes.

Priestley tips his hand early with the entrance of Professor
Pawlet, who, like Cornelius, smokes the pipe which designates
him his author's other self. "If we survive . . . we can experiment
in social organization,"[11] he tells the rest and even points out that
they form a "microcosm of society" (97). The sensible professor
and Mrs. Westmoreland are nearing the end of their lives; the
middle-aged Valentine Avon and Diana Lismore, author and
actress, have wasted theirs in a welter of illusion; Frank Jefferson
and Nona Stockton represent the brave new world eager to
confront reality; and Ashford Myricks, an American millionaire,
the principal representative of those "who've had it all their own
way," finds himself pitted against those "who've never had a
chance" (113), the wily crewman Boyne and Diana's desperate
maid, Miriam Pick.

When Boyne and Miriam devote their energies to robbery and
murder rather than saving themselves on a ship still prey to fire
and heavy seas, the play's logic goes overboard. Before *People at*

Sea completes its erratic course, the professor demonstrates how to deal effectively if crudely with the criminal classes by shooting Boyne; Miriam commits suicide with Carlo Velburg, a man in the Pirandellian quandary of having no passport, therefore no official existence; and Diana and Valentine abandon drugs and drink for one another. Like Christine and Krogstad in Ibsen's *Doll's House,* they are fully aware of their weaknesses, and, together, will overcome them. Myricks, who actually prefers cooking to high finance, cheerfully receives a radio message informing him that his entire fortune has been wiped out in the market, and Mrs. Westmoreland learns that life begins anew with the information that her daughter has presented her with a grandson. Having gained new insights about the real world from the excruciating ordeal, the professor realizes that his philosophical treatise may be worthless and passes the time awaiting a rescuing ship by tearing up the manuscript.

Three years later provincial theatergoers might have themselves experienced feelings of *déjà vu.* For in 1940 Priestley wrote *The Long Mirror* for Jean Forbes-Robertson, whose luminous performance as Kay Conway remains one of his "Particular Pleasures."[12] The play was not performed in London until 1952, but the actress who inspired *The Long Mirror* frequently toured in it throughout the 1940s. The appeal of the leading role to a performer is understandable, for the character of Branwen Elder combines the wisdom of Candida, the impulsive romanticism of Marchbanks, and the eerie other-worldliness of the title character of Barrie's *Mary Rose.*

The Long Mirror is in fact an inversion of the basic situation of *I Have Been Here Before.* Branwen, a painter, arrives at a hotel in North Wales, expecting Michael Camber, a composer whom she has never actually met. Camber arrives and momentarily mistakes Branwen for Valerie, his wife. Camber and Valerie have been separated but now meet to attempt a reconciliation. Branwen reveals that she not only knows the details of Camber's peripatetic present, but his past too, and his intimate thoughts as well. After attending a concert, she had suddenly been aware of being with him in spirit. She has since been living two lives, her own and his. When Camber recognizes that he too has had a vague awareness of Branwen's spirit from time to time, had in fact married Valerie, mistakenly thinking it was she who embodied that spirit, painter and composer decide to go off together. Valerie, however, confides in Branwen, telling her that her love for her husband is her only reason for living. To prevent Valerie's death, Branwen reveals to Camber the depth of his wife's love. Camber leaves with Valerie, whose need for him is greater than Branwen's. The painter has made the ultimate sacrifice, but she will continue to live through her art.

Love transcends space as well as time in *The Long Mirror*, but too many themes struggle for prominence, none of them realized in this "rather thin 'fey' piece"—Priestley's own accurate description.[13] While Ouspensky's theories provide *I Have Been Here Before* with at least a mechanical movement, *The Long Mirror* is a time piece out of all working order. As Rex Pogson suggests, that Priestley may have based it on an actual extrasensory relationship neither justifies the play nor makes it credible.[14]

Over the years Dunne and Ouspensky would again be relied upon, their ideas combined, as Priestley continually returned to the theme of time in his drama. Thirty-one years after *Time and the Conways* and *I Have Been Here Before*, in *Anyone for Tennis?* (1968), a television play, he wrote about a man who commits suicide, thus moving himself out of Time One into Time Two. There he learns that he must relive his Time One experience until he achieves the purgation of Time Three, where events may be remade. And in 1974, at age eighty, Priestley announced the completion of a new play for the stage, *Time Was, Time Is.* But prohibitive production costs for a play set in 1914 and the present and requiring a cast of fourteen forced its shelving.[15] Yet, for Priestley, Time will always be.

CHAPTER 14

Mature Comedies

W HILE preparing *Time and the Conways, I Have Been Here Before*, and *People at Sea* for the London stage late in 1937, Priestley was asked by the *News Chronicle* to provide a test piece for amateur dramatic societies competing in its drama contest. That he did so, effortlessly, with *Mystery at Greenfingers* is further proof of the craft at his command and the ease with which he employed it. *Mystery at Greenfingers*, a comic trifle, may have encouraged the dramatist, in the midst of writing his most serious plays and contemplating his most ambitious experiments, to consider a return to comedy—for Priestley a generally difficult form. "I have usually spent far more time and trouble," he writes, "done far more re-constructing and re-writing, demanded far more additional rehearsals, in the comedies than in the serious plays."[1]

Only one of his mature comedies, *When We Are Married*, proved a commercial success, rewarding him in 1938 for the effort he spent reworking it. Two other comedies, *The Golden Fleece*, "originally written just before the war," and *Ever Since Paradise*, "originally written in 1939" (II, xi), were put aside for later revision. Under an earlier title, *Bull Market, The Golden Fleece* was performed at the Bradford Civic Playhouse and the Glasgow Citizens Theatre, but never in London. Its hotel setting, however, may have inspired the film which Priestley wrote and produced in 1950, *Last Holiday. Ever Since Paradise*, an underrated Priestley play, one of his most intriguing theatrical experiments, eventually opened in London in 1947 to a hostile press but enjoyed a deserved success on the continent later on (II, xii).

I   Mystery at Greenfingers

A refreshing change of pace from the complexities of *Time*

and the Conways and *I Have Been Here Before* and the pretensions of *People at Sea, Mystery at Greenfingers* (produced in London in 1938 by the Bournemouth Little Theatre Club, the contest winners) is an engaging burlesque of the mystery play which provides easily actable roles and requires a minimum of elaborate effects.[2] Set in the staff room of a snowbound hotel, the play concerns the disappearance of a female guest which leads to the uncovering of a drug ring. A tweedy elderly woman, much like Agatha Christie's Miss Marple, and a young lady, whose acid tongue hides a heart of gold, solve the mystery while the detective dithers, the cook grows hysterical, the assistant manager falls in love, and two bug-eyed maids view the frantic proceedings with alarm. Innocent fun, the play is remarkable only in the deftness and economy with which Priestley sketches his characters, all of them at least as convincing as the "shop-soiled lot" with which he admits having peopled *People at Sea* (III, xi).

II   When We Are Married

When We Are Married exhibits Priestley's farcical side at its broadest and best. During a long London run which began in October 1938, the *Yorkshire Farcical Comedy,* as he calls it, even exhibited the author as actor for twelve performances as he took over the part of Ormonroyd, the drunken photographer, on twenty-four hours' notice. Not a professional actor, Priestley was quickly at home in the role because the milieu of *When We Are Married* is a careful recreation of the Yorkshire of his boyhood.

For a long time Priestley had wanted to write a comedy about the area as he knew it thirty years earlier. When his wife read a French short story "describing how a couple who were celebrating the anniversary of their wedding suddenly discovered they had never been married at all," the seed was planted, but it sprouted in very English soil, the town of Cleckleywycke, with two more couples to triple the fun. "Trying to remember every droll thing about that old Yorkshire, I let it rip," he recalls, and then admits that he laughed as he wrote it at great speed, "not because I thought I was being very witty, but because memories of favourite words of that period, such as 'flabbergasted,' came back to me, and it was such fun introducing them all into the text."[3] And audiences have appreciated the infectious fun of the play's many revivals ever since, for in *When*

We Are Married Priestley himself happily takes the advice he had offered to the young dramatist of *Spring Tide* a few years before—write what you know.

On their twenty-fifth anniversary three couples learn that the young parson who had performed the ceremony had not yet received authorization to conduct marriages. Alderman Joe Helliwell, Councillor Albert Parker, and Herbert Soppitt, pillars of the community of Cleckleywycke and "big men at chapel too"[4] are in the process of warning Gerald Forbes, the organist at Lane End Chapel, that his behavior is unseemly—he had been seen in the company of a young lady—when Gerald stuns them with the graver news that they have all been living in sin for a quarter of a century. What was to be a gala celebration with a reporter and photographer from the *Yorkshire Argus* in attendance turns into a comic nightmare when they realize that Mrs. Northrop, the Helliwell's char, is already spreading the word at the local pub. Before Ormonroyd, the photographer, who acts as deus ex machina, can inform them that he was the groom in the one other ceremony in question and has discovered that the registrar's signature on the marriage certificates had actually legalized the proceedings—that they have in fact been married all the time, some predictable but delightfully managed events take place. Henpecked Herbert lets Clara know that he is to be in charge henceforth, docile Annie informs Albert how dull life with him has been, and Maria turns her housekeeping accounts over to the town's painted lady, Lottie Grady, with whom Joe has had his "bit o' fun" at Blackpool (210). If their relationships will never be quite the same again, all of them will be better for the experience, and Cleckleywycke may even become a better place to live, at least a more tolerant community.

Priestley provides stronger characterization than usual, with dialogue underscoring essential personality traits. The following exchange, for example, demonstrates the accuracy of Mrs. Parker's view of her smugly complacent husband, who can hardly believe that he is the one being described:

ANNIE: . . . I don't think I want to be married to you.
PARKER *(staggered)*: *What!*
ANNIE *(slowly)*: You see, Albert, after twenty-five years of it, perhaps I've had enough.
PARKER *(horrified)*: 'Ad enough!

ANNIE: Yes, had enough. You talk about your duty. Well, for twenty-five years I've done my duty. I've washed and cooked and cleaned and mended for you. I've pinched and scrimped and saved for you. I've listened for hours and hours to all your dreary talk. I've never had any thanks for it. I've hardly ever had any fun. But I thought I was your wife and I'd taken you for better or worse, and that I ought to put up with you—

PARKER (*staring, amazed*): *Put up with me!*

ANNIE (*coolly*): Yes, put up with you.

PARKER: But what's wrong with me?

ANNIE (*coolly*): Well, to begin with, you're very selfish. But then, I suppose most men are. You're idiotically conceited. But again, so are most men. But a lot of men at least are generous. And you're very stingy. And some men are amusing. But—except when you're being pompous and showing off—you're not at all amusing. You're just very dull and dreary—

PARKER: Never!

ANNIE (*firmly*): Yes, Albert. *Very* dull and *very, very* dreary and stingy.

PARKER (*staring at her as if seeing a strange woman*): 'As somebody put you up to this?

ANNIE: No, I've thought it for a long time.

PARKER: How long?

ANNIE: Nearly twenty-five years. (207–208)

An occasional exchange heightens the absurdity of casual conversation, comically demonstrating man's failure to communicate:

SOPPITT: Now stop tormenting him, Annie.

PARKER (*indignantly*): Tormenting me! Nobody'll torment me. And I like that coming from *you*, Herbert, when you've been a by-word for years.

CLARA (*angrily*): A by-word for what?

PARKER: For years.

CLARA: Yes, but a by-word for years for what?

PARKER: Oh! Hen-pecked! . . . (209)

The passage indicates that long before Harold Pinter and Samuel Beckett had thought to do so, Priestley was already mining the rich vein of music-hall crosstalk which so delighted him in his Yorkshire youth.

The character with the most indelible Yorkshire stamp upon her is not one of the unfortunate couples, but the irrepressible char who deflates the pompous town officials even before they appear: "And d'you know what I say? I say—to 'ell with 'em!" (155). Mrs. Northrop's clear gaze pierces the pretensions around her and guides the audience to a proper perspective as well. The wives may be in awe of their husbands, but Mrs. Northrop treats them all like the wayward children they are:

MARIA (*rather grandly*): There's a tray with glasses on—just bring it in—
MRS. NORTHROP (*indignantly*): What—me? How many pairs of 'ands—
HELLIWELL (*peremptorily*): Now then—just tell thingumptyite—Ruby—
to bring in the port wine.
MRS. NORTHROP: What—on top o' your tea? You'll be poorly. (161)

Some of the values of a hypocritical middle class are found wanting in *When We Are Married*, but all the right ones are finally upheld in a sociological probing that is always delightful if not very deep. And every middle-class member of the audience can accept without qualm the message which the play delivers so painlessly and artlessly that it becomes unexpectedly moving in the mouth of the slightly drunk, totally bewildered photographer: "Why don't you live and let live? We're all in the same boat. We all come 'ere and we don't know why. We all go in our turn and we don't know where. If you are a bit better off, be thankful. An' if you don't get into trouble an' make a fool of yourself, well be thankful for that, 'cos you easily might. What I say is this—we're all human, aren't we?" (218).

Gareth Lloyd Evans, correct in his assertion that *When We Are Married* "is perhaps the only play of Priestley's which totally convinces one of the complete identification of character and language and situation," may be overgenerous when he suggests that it is "in parts, as trenchant as Molière."[5] More modest is Priestley's own assessment of its worth: "Actually, behind its farcical bustle, the little piece is not a bad sly sketch of provincial manners and attitudes."[6] The truth lies somewhere between, but the promise of *Laburnum Grove* is fulfilled in *When We Are Married*, which ranks as the dramatist's major achievement in the realm of broad comedy.

III   The Golden Fleece

The Golden Fleece, a play about "sudden vast gains in speculation," was put aside for a time, the author believing that it "would seem old-fashioned or unreal to wartime audiences" (II, xi). Priestley is probably correct in his assumption that the "rough-and-ready" piece, as he calls it, would not succeed in London, for the play, a comic satire on a capitalist society, is forced and mechanical.

The central character, the bland, easygoing night porter of the Golden Fleece Hotel in Cheltingate Spa, obviously a combination of Cheltenham and Harrogate, has given himself the name Will Lotless, since he had a lot less once he had served out a prison term for forging securities. That the pleasant middle-aged hotel employee was once a wizard of high finance, especially of its shadier aspects, makes Lotless a direct descendant of George Radfern, the counterfeiting family man of *Laburnum Grove*. In *The Golden Fleece*, however, Priestley has an untenable thesis to prove, and he must manipulate his protagonist to the point where, unlike Radfern, he loses credibility: money buys power but the powerful are all unhappy tyrants. An engaging but passive character must be transformed into a monstrous, bullying financier.

Lotless has reformed since his conviction. To keep his hand in and his mind sharp, however, he reads the financial news and keeps track of his imaginary dealings. When Molly Cudden, a hotel chambermaid, asks him to look over some papers an uncle has left her, he discovers that she has a fortune in negotiable shares. With her consent, he takes over the handling of her affairs and turns a lowly worker into a powerful millionaire. Molly, deploring the change in Will's personality, soon discovers that she was happier making beds. She turns her fortune into a public trust to be managed by the government, keeping for herself only enough to start a clinic for a young doctor and the hotel, which she already owns thanks to Lotless, which, at her insistence, he will run: "But it'll be a new kind of hotel for Cheltingate, for people who've been working too hard and not just eating too much, for men who are some use in the world, for women who deserve to be waited on for a change—for real people."[7]

The play's social satire is blatantly obvious, with hotel workers, who are wholly good, exploited by the nasty rich, who hate them for having what they themselves have lost—a capacity to enjoy life. Alec, the idealistic young doctor, describes the typical guest of the Golden Fleece: "It wouldn't matter if there was just one of her, but there are thousands and thousands of her—like—like stuffed old frogs—crocodiles—dinosaurs. This country's full of 'em. And there they are, doing no good to anybody, not even to themselves—and because they have the money, demanding services all day long from other people. That's what you see everywhere in this country—the living waiting upon the half-dead" (313). And he sees his employer, a wealthy old doctor, as another parasite in a stagnant society: "Instead of being a man of science, which he pretends to be, he's something between an old charlatan and a rich old woman's butler. He doesn't speak or even think the truth. He doesn't care about anything but fat fees and fat dinners. He's an example of what's wrong with this pussy-footed, rich old man's country" (342–43).

The most notable aspect of *The Golden Fleece* is Priestley's attempt to make his political and social theories the basis of light comic dialogue just as they were the basis of the plot of *Let the People Sing*. The following key exchange during Molly's birthday celebration is an adaptation of the same material which Priestley had originally written as a radio talk for the BBC on an ideal society founded on what he calls "Liberal Socialism," which also underlay the novel of the same period:

WILL (*as if beginning lecture*): Money! Money! It's a servant that's become a master. . . . Money—was intended to be simply a sign, a token, a convenience—something like a—well, a railway ticket. That's all. But what's happened to it? Got all out of hand. Become a source of power. The way we allow people to handle money as power, it's just as if we let 'em handle battleships and bombing squadrons for their own private benefit. . . . Now the first thing you have to do is to take most of the power away from money. In fact, private money should be just pocket money. That's the only kind of money I believe in—pocket money. Everybody should have pocket money and nobody should have any other kind.
MOLLY: What's the difference?
WILL: Pocket money is just short-range, personal money, to be spent on—whatever you fancy. You can't use it to make me do something for you in a year's time, as if you had a pistol at my head. You can't send it out to increase itself, while you sit back and watch it grow—
MOLLY: But you said the other night that's just what we were doing. . . .
WILL: But I'm telling you now how things ought to be, not how they are. We're only doing what everybody tries to do. We're not doing anything wrong. . . .
MOLLY: Now say it's all very well, all this clever talk about how things

ought to be, but if we think something's wrong, then we oughtn't to do it ourselves. Somebody's got to make a start, haven't they?

WILL: No. It's a question of a system, not just of people themselves.

MOLLY: Everything depends really just on how people treat each other. If people aren't willing, and kind, and hopeful, then it's all up. But if they are, then it's all right. . . . I think that where the trouble starts is that some people are dead against happiness. They can't have it themselves, so they're going to spoil it for other people. They don't like life at all, these folks—they'd like to be safe an' dead, only they don't know it, or perhaps they never wanted to be born—an' so whenever they see a bit of life springing up, they want to tread on it. . . . (343–45)

To prove the point the celebration is interrupted by the hotel's indignant guests who are mortified to find the staff enjoying themselves.

The passage in *Midnight on the Desert* where these ideas are expanded makes it possible to compare Priestley the essayist with Priestley the dramatist. In the autobiography the ideas are brilliantly worked out in a smooth-flowing style. The reader is convinced that Priestley's state is no utopian dream, but a real possibility in a more reasonable world:

And we make an important distinction, completely lost in your world, between necessaries and luxuries, what is urgently needed to maintain life and what makes it more fun. . . . But the point is, that all necessaries are produced by the state itself, which decided that it could not have individuals claiming possession of such vital things; whereas most luxuries are produced by private enterprise. It is the difference between water and wine. The state naturally owns and distributes the water supply, but private persons, who take more interest in such matters, sell you a bottle of wine. Or bread and cake. There is a standard government bread—pleasant, wholesome, unexciting stuff of which everyone has a share; but we do not want government cake, for cake is a matter of personal taste and personal service, so you can still buy cake, real home-made cake, in little shops. We still have money, because it is more convenient than a system of rations and credits, but of course it plays a much smaller part in the life of the community. It is more like boys' pocket-money, to be jingled and spent. You cannot hoard it very long, or treat it as a commodity and deal in it. There are no financiers, no money jugglers, in my country, and they seem as remote to us now as medieval barons or brigands. To the people in my country it would seem just as silly for a man to be able to command great power by artful dealing in money, as it would seem to you to find a man who had made himself powerful by collecting vast piles of those coloured counters and chips you use in card games. In fact, in my country money is rather like those coloured counters . . . except that it enables you to buy flowers, wine, silk shirts, books, pictures, or whatever you fancy. But it cannot touch the necessaries of life, and is not a source of power.[8]

Somewhere in the transition from essay to dialogue, Priestley loses conviction. Words which ring true as the author's own are strained in the mouths of unrealized characters. The essay bears its truth with grace and wit, whereas the play is neither comic nor profound. In *The Golden Fleece* Priestley offers an entertaining Cinderella story but delivers instead an earnest tract.

IV   Last Holiday *and* The Rose and Crown

The Golden Fleece is one of the few Priestley plays never to reach London. Abandoning it, he considered the ingredients more suited to another medium (II, xi): the life of a hotel could better be explored by a camera that could follow guests and staff from room to room and over the grounds. *Last Holiday,* for which he also served as coproducer, is Priestley's film which borrows the resort setting and a few minor characters from the play. Written expressly for actor Alec Guinness in 1950, Priestley considers the script his most significant work for the medium. He had adapted some of his own plays to the screen, and had even appeared in the prologue and epilogue added to *They Came to a City* in its 1944 film version.[9] In addition he had concocted some light film comedies, uncredited, for a favorite music-hall performer, Gracie Fields, written additional dialogue for an adaptation of Daphne DuMaurier's novel *Jamaica Inn* in 1939, and supplied the morale-building story for a wartime film, *The Foreman Went to France,* in 1942. But *Last Holiday,* an ironic comedy which ends with the death of its protagonist, is his one original film which intelligently explores some major Priestley themes.

A lonely, middle-aged farm-implements salesman learns that he is soon to die of a rare, incurable disease. Taking his savings, he goes to an exclusive small hotel to give himself a taste of the posh life during his last days. The new locale seems to change his personality as well as his luck. He makes friends easily and offers them sound advice. In turn he is offered good jobs along with love and affection. He even wins £400 on a horse. But George Bird is not dying. The diagnosis was made in error. When he learns the truth, he is overjoyed. Returning from a visit to his doctor, he swerves his auto to avoid hitting an old dog on the road to Fallow End and is killed in a crash with a lorry.

Last Holiday strongly underscores Priestley's Chekhovian view that man wastes his life by taking it for granted. As the salesman dies, he says, "Not bad at all . . . good thing . . . not bad . . . good." At least for a few days he had sharply experienced an awareness of life, a wonder denied most people. Even as he is returning to the hotel, the other guests are abandoning their favorable view of him. "He's just like the rest of us," one of them says. Had he lived, he might have been. George Bird was only touched with grace by a too rare understanding that life is fleeting.

A secondary theme related to the first, that people from varying backgrounds can pull together to create an harmonious community, provides the film its most successful scenes. When the hotel workers go out on strike, Bird rallies the guests. They cook, tend bar, wait on tables, and man the reception desk. An excitement builds as the diverse characters share a common bond and discover the joys of a job well done. As Bird tells them, "We haven't just passed the time. We've filled it." The guests— among them a cabinet minister, an inventor, and an ex-RAF officer involved in currency smuggling—are, however, an uninteresting collection of stock characters, and their situation is too stagey to accommodate a fluid camera.

The film's most distinguished feature is the remarkably modulated performance by Guiness in the difficult role of a man who can accept his death once he accepts his life, a development of the character of Harry Tully in Priestley's short 1947 morality play set in a North-East London pub which supplies the one-act's title, *The Rose and Crown*. When a man identifies himself as Death's representative and reveals that he has not filled his day's quota, Harry, understanding the stranger's words, "And if Life is a rose, then Death is a crown,"[10] volunteers, for he is the only one among the locals who has actively sought and achieved life's joy.

V Ever Since Paradise

Although Priestley considers his broad comedies to be his best work in a lighter vein, *Ever Since Paradise* demonstrates his eventual mastery of what was at first an elusive form for the dramatist—high comedy. The play, described as *A Discursive Entertainment, chiefly referring to Love and Marriage, in Three Acts,* is a "gay charade" (II, xii) which stylishly examines the roles of the sexes in achieving, or, more often than not, failing to achieve, wedded bliss. A male-female relationship is explored in comic scenes buoyed by some of Priestley's sprightliest dialogue and abetted by music which underscores the kaleidoscopic moods of the participants, three men and three women, all of them alert to the faults of the opposite sex but blind to their own. Paul and Rosemary reenact the highlights, some of them indeed low points, of their life together, while William and Helen, a witty older couple, comment on their inexplicable yet highly conventional behavior. Philip and Joyce echo the attitudes of William and Helen as they provide a musical accompaniment on two pianos. The young people meet, fall in love, win parents' consent, marry, quarrel, console themselves at first with obnoxious friends then incompatible lovers, plan for divorce, then rediscover the love which first brought them together. Making no profound observations nor offering sound solutions, *Ever Since Paradise* delightfully reaffirms what every one knows: starting with Adam and Eve, man and woman have been the bane of one another's existence, yet life apart is no life at all.

What makes the play unique among comedies of manners is that Priestley has chosen to explore a universal theme in an experimental form, marking it as one of his most innovative pieces. The two actor-musicians sit at pianos on either side of a bare stage. The commentators occupy chairs near the pianos. Behind them are dark curtains which, when opened, reveal an inner stage where the young couple perform their scenes. William and Helen leave their positions as commentators to move in and out of the curtained area as they assume whatever roles are required of them, either Paul and Rosemary's parents or their various friends. In additon to commenting on the action, they introduce the scenes, suggest the mood of the music to be played, and give directions to the light man. William, amusingly undercutting the dramatist's more sober side, even gives the play a timelessness by beginning to explain Priestley's theories in response to Rosemary's comment that "behind the little *Now* there's this big *Now*, in which all at once you've met a man and loved him for years and lost him. . .":

WILLIAM: . . . It's a question of movement along the fourth dimension—
HELEN: What is?
WILLIAM: These two Nows—two different kinds of time. Now imagine yourself travelling with the speed of light—a hundred and eighty-six thousand miles a second—along the fourth dimension—
JOYCE: No.
PHILIP: No.
HELEN: No thank you, William.
WILLIAM: I thought you wanted to know.
HELEN: Not just now, thank you. Some other time. . . .[11]

Whereas Evans suggests an affinity in method between *Ever Since Paradise* and an older play, Wilder's *Our Town* (1938),[12] the Priestley comedy is actually prophetic in suggesting another theatrical form which would soon be in vogue. Almost point for point the play seems to follow the guidelines set forth by Bertolt Brecht for an "epic theater" as opposed to a "dramatic theater."[13] The narrators, the episodic action, the shift from prose to verse, the endings of scenes revealed as they begin, the emphasis on *how* a relationship breaks down rather than *what* happens to the couple, the accent on the theater as theater all suggest devices of epic theater. Even the intent seems to mirror Brecht's. Like Brecht, Priestley would engage thought rather than feeling and accomplishes his aim in a similar way, achieving Brechtian alienation by detachment: "Can't observe properly unless you're detached," William insists (450).

In effect, however, Priestley and Brecht part company. Brecht remains the didactic dramatist moving an audience to action. Priestley calls for no action, merely recognition. Instead of mobilizing the masses, *Ever Since Paradise* sets out to entertain them. The similarities between the two dramatists are in fact coincidental. Priestley, resenting the epic label, denies any Brechtian influence on his work and claims to have seen his first Brecht play on a visit to East Berlin sometime after the German's death in 1956, at least seventeen years after the first version of *Ever Since Paradise* was written and ten years after its first performance.[14] He considers the German a dramatist of limited ability with a "bogus reputation" who had to promote a particular style because he could write in no other way. "Here's a man," he says, "who makes a virtue of his limitations."

According to Priestley, dramatists of the nineteenth century like Ibsen and Dumas *fils* who broke away from the romantic tradition had to learn to achieve their effects more economically, and writers of his own generation followed suit in developing a concentrated modern drama until Brecht announced a counter-movement: "Then suddenly Bertolt Brecht appears with his 'epic theater.' It's like putting up a sign saying 'Joe's Bar'!" What especially annoys Priestley is a dramatist's daring to set down rules to be followed in play after play. If *Ever Since Paradise* employs epic devices, it is because a particular subject struck Priestley as requiring a particular handling. For Priestley *Ever Since Paradise* is an exercise in form, not a manifesto for a new drama. Except for some refining of the form in *Dragon's Mouth* in 1952, Priestley has abandoned it in his later plays. Yet its introduction in the late 1930s in the work of a British writer possibly influenced by an American dramatist suggests an inevitable flow in the development of modern drama which carried Brecht and his colleague Erwin Piscator along with it. The Germans did not by themselves release the tide.

Breaking fresh ground with the marital debate of *Ever Since Paradise* in 1939, Priestley had considered the subject matter too frivolous for wartime; yet when the play was finally performed in London eight years later, the critics were still not ready for the inevitable. They had probably expected a comedy of manners in the tradition popular since the Restoration, the kind of work, witty but conventional, then associated with Maugham or Coward. They were not prepared for "something new" (II, xii), a daring and innovative framework for an entertaining comedy. Whether one labels it epic or not, *Ever Since Paradise* was ahead of its time.

CHAPTER 15

Experiments and Innovations

I NVITED to write a play for the Malvern Festival in August 1938, Priestley remembered an idea that had come to him a few months earlier on a magical trip to Rainbow Bridge, Utah, near the Grand Canyon. Stopping in New York on his westward journey, he had been favorably impressed by Thornton Wilder's *Our Town*, which poignantly suggests the interrelatedness of all the inhabitants of an imaginary locale which stands for all of small-town America. One day in the life of Grovers Corners, New Hampshire, when even the dead return to comment on the living, evokes the past as well as the present, all time existing at once. Priestley considered the play "beautifully written and produced with a touch of genius . . . the American Theatre being truly and grandly creative."[1] *Our Town* would strongly influence him as he too sought a theatrically effective but simple means of delving into the subconscious to explore the oneness of all mankind, the Jungian theme which underlies three extraordinary theatrical experiments: *Music at Night* (1938), *Johnson Over Jordan* (1939), and the later *Dragon's Mouth* (1952).

I   Music at Night

Temporarily putting aside the play which would become *Johnson Over Jordan*, Priestley raced to complete *Music at Night* against a deadline set by the Malvern Festival committee, contrary to his usual working method. As his own manager, he generally spent as much time on the writing of a play as it required. Some plays, like *Time and the Conways*, seemed to write themselves, and he set them down quickly. But the speed with which he was forced to write *Music at Night* hampered his creative imagination. He would not, in fact, have undertaken the work at that time had he not believed in the principles of the festival, in the spirit of collaborative daring it evoked in author and audience. As he wrote in an essay entitled "A Note From the Workshop," printed in the festival brochure, "A dramatic festival should be . . . a laboratory for the dramatist who wishes to make experiments. The people who attend such a festival should be the very last persons to take into the Theatre with them some conventional cut-and-dried notions of what a play should be. They should be on the side of the dramatist who is trying something new."[2]

In *Music at Night* Priestley "would attempt to dramatise the mental adventures of a group of people listening to the first performance of a piece of music" (RG, 180–81). The play would move in a progression "from the surface of the mind to deeper and deeper levels of consciousness." "Towards the end," he writes, "I would try to present dramatically my feeling . . . that we are not really the separate beings we imagine ourselves to be." Since the form of *Music at Night* would present an audience with an unusually demanding challenge, he decided to make the characters recognizable stock figures, "because you cannot have everything new all at once in the Theatre or the audience will be completely baffled." With "one eye on the calendar," he began the play easily enough, but the further he progressed, the more difficult became the problem of finding language suitable for the expression of unusual ideas at a subconscious level: "In the final scene . . . I used verse that the characters had to chant, sometimes singly, sometimes in chorus, and I soon discovered that after years of prose my verse, which did not pretend to be poetry but only heightened dramatic speech, was wretched stuff" (182).

Both at Malvern and in London, where it was presented a year later in revised form, *Music at Night* "appeared to be better understood and appreciated by audiences," Priestley claims, "than it was by most dramatic critics, who set their faces against this fancy stuff."[3] Yet the disappointing critical reception seems to have colored the author's own view of the work. More impressive than even Priestley suggests, *Music at Night* weaves a magical theatrical effect as its language develops brilliantly from the idle gossip of its opening to the evocative incantation of its climax. As David Hughes suggests, the words may "lack the massive horsepower to soar into celestial poetry," but "the play, tightly constructed and controlled with a fine sense of dramatic timing, is quite strong enough to survive this stumbling rocky patch of writing."[4] The reaction of the usually perceptive Gareth Lloyd Evans typifies earlier comments on the play. He complains that "the characters are metaphors which are intended to create a total image, but their metaphorical nature is at the mercy of Priestley's insistent refusal to allow them to leave the earth. They become theatrically schizophrenic because part of them seems utterly bound to the 'actualities' of the present-tense while another part becomes intermittently conscious of a deeper 'reality.' "[5] Yet this seems a willful misunderstanding of the intent of a play which in fact charts a movement from present-tense actuality to a consciousness of a deeper reality. Even Hughes does not fully credit Priestley with what is a significant achievement through language in *Music at Night* and a major breakthrough in theatrical form. Employing words instead of music, Priestley composes a complex three-movement concerto which produces the same profound effect as a musical composition that transports the listener outside of himself.

On an evening just before the war, Mrs. Amesbury invites some influential friends to her home to hear the first performance of a concerto for violin and orchestra. David Shiel, the young composer, is to play a rough transcription of the orchestral parts on the piano as accompaniment to the violin solo of his sympathetic but cynical friend, Nicholas Lengel. In addition to Shiel's wife Katherine, the guests are Charles Bendrex, an ailing cabinet minister; Philip Chilham, a gossip columnist; Peter Horlett, a communist poet; Ann Winter, the young girl who loves him; Sir James Dirnie, a wealthy industrialist; and Lady Sybil Linchester, his present mistress who has also had a brief affair with Shiel. After some strained introductions, Bendrex is impatient to hear the concerto: "Now for some music . . . the only art that's really detached. It doesn't lead you back to the newspapers. It doesn't drag in the rest of the world. You can lose yourself in it." To which his hostess responds, "That makes it all the more dangerous sometimes. . . . It can break down those careful barriers we build up inside our minds."[6] And those barriers are indeed broken. The diverse group engaged in coldly polite chit-chat at the opening of Act I converge by the end of Act III, or the third movement of the concerto, into one heart and mind, the very soul of mankind, sharing what Jung has termed the collective unconscious.

What seems at first the idle thoughts of some listeners sharing the experience of a piece of music becomes the reality of all humanity as *Music at Night* explores the truth of Katherine's enigmatic observation, "But perhaps what we think is happening inside is really happening outside. We may think about life all the wrong way round" (346). But hostess and guests remain very much locked in themselves, at least during the first act, or first movement, which the composer marks *"Allegro Capriccioso"* (347). In soliloquy Mrs. Amesbury tries to understand that she involves herself in such soirees to give her empty life some purpose, while Katherine implores the rest to like her husband's work. Chilham, with the columnist's practiced eye, notices that Katherine dislikes Lady Sybil and imagines himself the detective solving the mystery of the faded beauty's murder. Looking about him, aware of his humble beginning, Chilham insists that his life is more glamorous than that of the rest, his own success more remarkable. While the music transports Ann to a tropical isle, Peter is busily concocting poetic propaganda. Dirnie, tiring of Sybil, imagines a life with Katherine, and Sybil remembers her rejection of Shiel. In an imagined after-dinner political speech, Bendrex for once has the courage to tell the dreary truth: "You do not know, you cannot understand, what is happening in the world. The Government does not know and cannot understand what is happening in the world. Speaking for myself . . . I have not the least comprehension of what anything means anywhere any more. The last time I made any sense at all out of the world was in July nineteen-fourteen. Since then I have not been able to make head or tail of anything that has happened three miles from Westminster" (360).

The mood deepens in Act II as Shiel prepares his listeners for the *Adagio*: "Of course it's all rather sad" (363). The music conjures up memories of time past. Whereas Kay in *Time and the Conways* had a prevision of what was to be, the guests now recall what has been. Lengel remembers his love for Katherine, who in turn relives a happier moment in her life with Shiel and cries out in alarm, "David, David, come back. Everything—come back" (367). For Bendrex the music becomes an elegy for his straw boater, symbol of a time of innocence, as his long-dead valet brings him the hat. As Ann professes her love for Peter, the poet loses his assurance and begins to doubt the validity of his mechanical verses. Chilham suffers as he recalls the mother he deserted, and Dirnie remembers a friend he betrayed. Sybil relives a moment of childhood happiness, while her dead sister and Mrs. Amesbury's dead son look on, like the characters in *Our Town,* unable to reach out to ease the pain of the living. Shiel returns to his carefree student days in Vienna, but the reality of Vienna on the eve of war intrudes. As Mrs. Amesbury prods herself to make an effort, to "keep going—keep going," her words take her back to that past moment which is the source of her present despair. The sound of an airplane engine is heard as her son Rupert takes up her words with increasing agitation: "Keep going. . . . Keep her going, you bloody fool! That strut's gone! Bank her, bank her! . . . Look out!" (370). For a brief instant present and past are inextricably one. Music has wrought its magic on time.

As Act III begins, Shiel announces the final movement: "*Allegro—agitato—maestoso nobile,* which means that it starts in a nice brisk cheerful style, to wake you up, then it becomes very agitated—y'know, worrying about life, and then it turns all grand and noble, just to end up with" (386). Again the musical program dictates the scene. A surge of joyous music unites the listeners who find their common ground as men and women. In a paean to life, language heightens to poetic prose as Ann, Sybil, Katherine, and Mrs. Amesbury extol the wonders of womanhood, while Dirnie, Peter, and Chilham praise man for his wondrous accomplishments. An intimacy grows among the group in a crescendo of happy laughter. Suddenly a terrible cry of pain interrupts the mood. Shaken by a heart spasm, Bendrex is overcome by a fear which slowly but inexorably invades the thoughts and hearts of the rest. They too know pain, the anguish of guilt, of sinking into hellish misery.

Again the mood changes as a triumphant chord is sounded, and Shiel appears among the rest, *"looking impersonal, strange, majestic."* He speaks in a calm, impersonal tone: "James Dirnie may be in Hell, but what is James Dirnie? Nothing. And what is David Shiel? Nothing. In this world of appearances, yes, something—but only one faulty nervous system among billions, a name, a date or two . . . a rotting bag of tricks. In the real and greater world, David Shiel is a mere appearance, a part, a mask, a shadow. So I tell you—sink deeper, deeper. Forget and then remember. Go down and down and discover what you are" (394).

The music *"announces a final majestic theme,"* the lights

change, the room disappears, and a wide sky becomes visible behind the characters. The effect, Priestley writes, *"should suggest humanity itself outside time"* (394). The language further modulates into an expressionistic ritual chant as the characters find within themselves traces of man's time in caves, on bare hills, through ice and flood. At last a oneness is forged: one time is all time, one man is all men. They hail the one great heart and mind:

> Forgetting much, remembering more, we find
> The one great heart, the ever-enduring mind,
> All love, all wisdom. So let nothing sever
> This link, this binding vision. Keep us for ever. (396)

The concerto ends, and the characters are again in Mrs. Amesbury's music-room; but the music has worked a subtle change in them. There is now sympathy and understanding as they speak to one another. Sybil and Dirnie no longer wish to hurt one another. Peter seems ready to embrace another human being rather than one more cause. Since Bendrex appears to be asleep, the others retire to another room so that he will not be disturbed. But Bendrex has died during the concerto. Alone on stage, he is joined by his valet, who gives him the boater once again. Putting it on, Bendrex *"suddenly becomes a smiling middle-aged man and strolls off"* (399). The curtain falls.

Despite its limited character development and absence of plot, *Music at Night* engages the intellect and sways the emotion. The audience shares the characters' epiphany. Not since Strindberg has a dramatist successfully restricted himself to a work for the stage structured on a musical composition. Whereas Strindberg deliberately chose a reduced scale for his chamber pieces, Priestley, more ambitiously, has worked out an affirmation of life within the pattern of a full-scale concerto. *Music at Night* triumphs over its self-imposed obstacles and expands the language of theater, and such language would not be heard again until the final scene, an incantatory acceptance of death as part of life, of Michael Cristofer's Pulitzer Prize play, *The Shadow Box* (1977).

Although there was interest in presenting *Music at Night* in London, Priestley had already determined that another experimental work, *Johnson Over Jordan*, actually begun before, should appear there first. In August 1939, a year after its appearance as part of the Malvern Festival, *Music at Night* went into rehearsal in London, but the war broke out before its opening and all theaters were closed. Priestley is proud that once permission to reopen was granted, *Music at Night* had "the honour of being the first play to be done in London" during World War II.[7]

II Johnson Over Jordan

February 22, 1939, the first night of *Johnson Over Jordan,* was a landmark occasion in the London theater, a dramatic presentation in expressionistic form in a commercial theater which had long resisted dynamic change. While some energetic noncommercial theatrical groups such as the Stage Society and Gate Theatre had experimented with new forms developed on the continent, the West End theater continued to cater to a public for whom "a visit to a Theatre is a larky night out."[8]

For a long time Priestley had wanted to make maximum use of the resources which the theater offered. So many of his previous plays had called for a simple single setting, not merely for matters of economy but because his work was firmly based in the naturalistic tradition London audiences expected and comprehended. But he had begun to look beyond that tradition in searching for a suitable framework for a drama stressing that timelessness which is one of his favorite themes, and he was eager "to break away from the flavourless patter of modern realistic English dialogue" (JOJ, 130). Already in *I Have Been Here Before,* he claims he had begun to cheat naturalism by gradually heightening the dialogue to the point where the characters were no longer speaking as people actually do in real life. Films had proved to be the perfect medium for "very small-scale realism" and would soon be intelligent and sensitive enough to drive naturalism out of a theater which could not compete with them (JOJ, 131). In *Johnson Over Jordan* Priestley prodded the English commercial theater into a new era of self-discovery, even demanding of it intricate musical effects requiring a full orchestra and some complicated but essential ballet sequences as he took his characters outside time and presented them four-dimensionally.

Johnson Over Jordan is "a biographical morality play" which explores the life of a common man, an English Everyman. "What I wanted to do," Priestley claims, "was to give an account, in dramatic form, of a man's life in a new way, taking an ordinary middle-class citizen of our time and then throwing a new light on him and his affairs, and giving to my record of his rather commonplace life an unusual depth and poignancy" (JOJ, 120). Many critics, James Agate among them, incorrectly described it as a play about death,[9] but *Johnson Over Jordan* is in fact a play about life with a character's death directing its dramatic framework. Reading Evans-Wentz's study of the Tibetan *Book of the Dead,* Priestley had become fascinated with an account of the *Bardo,* a prolonged dreamlike state after death filled with hallucinatory visions in which "the dead man does not know that he no longer possesses a body of flesh and blood, and he mistakes characteristic thought-forms for genuinely objective entities, much as we do . . . in our dreams" (JOJ, 121). Priestley, however, rejected the overly complex *Bardo* with its forty-nine symbolic days for a simpler westernized version in which Robert Johnson moves back and forth in time as he examines the quality of the life he has just departed.

In some respects Robert Johnson of *Johnson Over Jordan* is close kin to the protagonist of *Cornelius,* and Priestley also intended it from the first for his favorite actor, Ralph Richardson. At the end of *Cornelius* the disenchanted business man contemplates suicide but opts instead for a new life in a new world. *Johnson Over Jordan*—one might even regard it as a sequel—leads its protagonist—like Cornelius, a manager of a small business firm—to the threshold of another world, to an acceptance of death as the natural end, not to be feared, of a life richly and worthily lived. Alive, Cornelius had been out of his element in a changing business world. Deceased, Robert Johnson, wanders through an exaggerated, distorted landscape of documents, ledgers, tax forms, the endless red tape of the business world thrust at him by clerks and secretaries *"lit from below"* and casting huge confusing shadows *"making very quick movements in a stylised fashion"* with the irritating effect of projecting *"a whole modern business man's day within one minute."*[10] It is a nightmare world he cannot cope with, yet his concern with the material, a desire for money even after death, forces him to confront it. At first his concern is for his wife. Will she receive his insurance benefits? However, after reliving various unpleasant moments, becoming like the officer in Strindberg's *A Dream Play* a badgered schoolboy again, confused by life's contradictions, reminded of his petty deeds and thoughtless actions, questioned about his neglect of his own health, his family's well-being, the world's welfare, money becomes no more than a means of entry into the world of bright lights, hot jazz, and beautiful girls. He flees the central offices of the Universal Assurance and Globe Loan and Finance Corporation in which his dead self has been mired for the refuge of the *Jungle Hot Spot*.

In a second act, reminiscent of Ibsen's Peer Gynt in the land of the trolls, Johnson confronts his animal nature as he mingles with men and women in grotesque, piglike masks. He molests a young girl and stabs a young man, only to learn that they are his own son and daughter, a valuable but costly lesson. A mysterious figure, who, like Peer's Button Moulder, reappears throughout Johnson's spiritual journey, informs him that "there are no human instruments created solely for our satisfaction. . . . There are only persons. They are all sons and daughters" (313). A repentant Johnson calls himself a swine, but the forgiving figure of death tells him he has been merely a fool and sends him on to the Inn at the End of the World.

Through a window at the inn in Act III all who have illuminated Johnson's mind and touched his heart reappear to him—a favorite cricketer, a beloved pantomime artist, an understanding schoolmaster, characters from books, and members of his immediate family. Johnson recognizes Jill, whom he had first met at a dance as Peer had Solveig, as his wife and the mother of his children. Like Solveig, she is eternal woman: "You are the essential Jill, whom I was for ever finding, losing, then finding again" (330). His love for her is lasting, despite a scene of petty marital bickering concerning the state of their garden which is similar in tone to the couple's squabbling over cabbage for dinner in *A Dream Play*. At last Johnson is deeply aware of the wonder of life, its lost opportunities and prosaic joys:

> I have been a foolish, greedy and ignorant man;
> Yet I have had my time beneath the sun and stars. . . . (335)

With the recognition that he has been a less than perfect being, Johnson is granted entry into an unknown universe encompassing a myriad of stars.

Generally effective, Priestley's adventurous play bogs down, however, in the overly sentimental scenes in the inn. Its optimistic ending, with its hope of salvation through life's affirmation, seems mere contrivance; for Johnson's spiritual ramble lacks direction. Ibsen's Peer Gynt travels in a circle to find at last what he failed to recognize at the start of his journey; and the circle determines the structure of the play, even dominates its imagery. The spiritual growth of Strindberg's daughter of Indra reflects that of the men she meets—the naive officer, the worldly-wise lawyer, the cosmically knowing poet; and her maturation takes place within the shadow of the unifying symbol of the growing castle. Johnson, however, moves arbitrarily from scene to scene. That the countenance of his guide, the mysterious figure, grows brighter as the play progresses marks little actual development in Johnson's character, and his final reward is unearned. Of the two experimental plays, *Music at Night* is firmer in its structure, subtler in its handling, more imaginative in its invention.

Despite a moving performance by Ralph Richardson, stirring music by Benjamin Britten, and inventive choreography by Antony Tudor, *Johnson Over Jordan* was a commercial failure. Even more bewildering to Priestley was the play's hostile critical reception. James Agate, considering it "a mish-mash of *Outward Bound* and *Liliom* done in the demoded Elmer Rice manner," dismissed it as a return to expressionism.[11] Yet only a year before its production Priestley himself told an interviewer that he had "never seen an expressionistic play that said anything that couldn't be said better—to him—by apparently real people."[12] For Priestley, the realistic portrayal of his protagonist, despite the distorted trappings of his environment, rescued the work from the dreaded label, which ought to be applied, he felt, only to plays with flattened characters and "purely symbolic figures."[13] As Morton Eustis reports, "Priestley dislikes pure symbolism, whether in poetry or prose."[14] Yet his explanation of what he was attempting suggests that Agate was justified in calling the play expressionistic: In *Johnson Over Jordan* and *Music at Night* "I took such dramatic technique as I possessed as far as it would go, using the most objective form there is for material that was entirely and deeply subjective."[15]

Like all expressionistic works, *Johnson Over Jordan* distorts surface reality to find a form to release a subjective view.

Priestley projects his innermost feelings into Johnson's subconscious, and Johnson sees as Priestley feels. Aside from Johnson
himself, the characters are types. All of them, including Johnson,
speak a heightened language, sometimes lyrical, sometimes
halting, and Johnson joins them in an exploration of a dream
world devoid of time, devoid of space, to discover the ultimate
worth of man. *Johnson Over Jordan* is finally overwhelmed by its
failings, but its highly theatrical expressionistic style struck an
important blow in the fight to free the London stage from a
stultifying conservatism, and the theater was richer for its
protagonist's brief passage.

III   Dragon's Mouth

With the exception of *Desert Highway,* Priestley's drama of
the war years and the postwar period was marked by a return to
more conventional forms. But he was to play the bold
experimenter one last time in the fifties. In New York in 1951, he
was lured to Brooklyn one night by his old friend Cedric
Hardwicke, who was appearing there as the Statue in a staged
reading of the *Don Juan in Hell* section of Shaw's *Man and
Superman.* Hardwicke, Charles Boyer, Agnes Moorehead, and
Charles Laughton, who had also directed the performance, had
been touring the United States under the auspices of producer
Paul Gregory. The group had performed in England earlier that
summer; but Priestley, who, following the unenthusiastic advice
of the English critics, had not attended the performance, was
unprepared for what awaited him. Familiar with Shaw's interlude, Priestley was overwhelmed by the manner in which it was
performed with no scenery and a minimum of movement by
actors in evening dress pretending to read at lecterns. More
amazing still was the response of the young Brooklyn audience,
who seemed to hang on every word of the difficult, almost
unplayable piece with its intricate debates and complex set
speeches. When critics were later to accuse Priestley of merely
copying Shaw in his own attempt at a "platform piece," as
Priestley was to call *Dragon's Mouth,* the author would respond,
"No, it was not the Shavian content but the Laughton method"
that first fascinated him and then inspired his own experiment
with the form.[16]
Priestley considered the staged reading to be "something new

and exciting, a production almost reduced to a bare platform, that brought both the dramatist and the actors much closer to the audience . . . than they were in the ordinary theater." He saw in it the possibility "of a new and powerful form of writing, producing, acting" (DM, viii). And when his enthusiasm was matched by that of English poet and archeologist Jaquetta Hawkes, later Mrs. Priestley, with whom he discussed Laughton's method after a performance in a Manhattan theater, the two agreed to collaborate on an original platform piece for Gregory and Laughton. What they both found intriguing was the possibility of a spartanly staged performance that could convert "a town hall into a new kind of theater" (DM, xii). A platform piece could be effectively performed anywhere with such flexibility that it could "be enjoyed by four thousand people in a great concert hall or by fifty people in a village institute" (DM, xviii). Citing the popularity of Dickens readings and the sudden enthusiasm for the plays of Christopher Fry, Hawkes was aware of "a trend back toward an enjoyment of words, whether they are listened to for the sake of their sound and imagery, or for the totally different pleasure of debate—the tossing to and fro of ideas" (DM, 95). According to Priestley, "Radio has given people a taste for debate . . . but radio has also robbed people of oratory, if only because in politics the broadcast talk in the fireside manner has driven out impassioned platform speeches in the grand manner" (DM, xvii). The new form would combine "debate and oratory . . . setting them both . . . in a dramatic framework." They saw *Dragon's Mouth* as "something like a return . . . to Classical and Elizabethan Drama" cunningly heightened by amplified sound (DM, xvii–xviii).

The collaborators set to work on a piece with four characters representative of the four "functions" of Jung: thinking, feeling, sensation, and intuition. According to Hawkes, "Jung's belief is that all human beings have elements of all these functions . . . but always with one or two dominant. . . . If one function is so absolutely dominant in the personality that the others are held together in abeyance then an incomplete human being will result." *Dragon's Mouth* illustrates Jung's belief that it is "the moral duty of all . . . to strengthen their undeveloped functions and so achieve the 'fully integrated personality'" (DM, 100).

Matthew, a successful businessman, and his glamourous wife Nina have invited two friends, Stuart, a man of letters, and

Harriet, the personnel manager of one of Matthew's companies, to join them on a yacht bound from Venezuela to Trinidad. When one of the crew dies and two others are taken ill, the yacht takes shelter in a safe but sinister cove called Dragon's Mouth, where a port doctor has taken blood samples. As the piece begins the four await the results of the tests, which they will receive by shortwave radio. In the first half they have vague fears of death, but once a message is received that one of them is afflicted with an incurable disease, the four spend the second half pondering the certain death of one member of their intimate group. To add suspense, Priestley relies on a device he had used before in *People at Sea* and *Desert Highway*: the radio breaks down before they learn which one is to die. As the piece ends, the victim has not yet been revealed; but the Jungian concept of the four functions provides a basis for the closing scene. Mutually promising to rediscover the one who dies within those who are spared, the four affirm through thinking, feeling, sensation, and intuition the need for the fully integrated personality at the same time that they make "a simple declaration of close friendship" (DM, 101).

Priestley and Hawkes each took two characters and wrote their long speeches while the experienced dramatist worked out the linking passages and provided the dramatic frame. Their early fears that their distinct styles would be incompatible were proven groundless as some critics incorrectly assumed that Priestley had written the two male characters and Hawkes the females. Matthew is unmistakably the Priestley male, bluff and assured, but Stuart, the desiccated don, is Hawkes's creation. Neither writer has laid claim publicly to the women characters, and while they are seemingly very different, Nina, completely feminine, and Harriet, a success in a man's world of high finance, the two lose their distinct voices as the piece progresses. The eventual blurring of the male voices as well suggests the weakness of the work. The collaboration works too well. The authors' disparate styles merge into a bland and finally characterless prose.

Impatient to learn the effect of the piece, Priestley himself undertook the production of *Dragon's Mouth*. The tour of one-night stands was badly publicized and mismanaged. Many of the halls in provincial towns were unsuited to the nature of the piece, and London's Winter Garden Theatre was too large. Yet, as Ivor Brown suggests, *Dragon's Mouth* showed "what can be done to find new premises for a new style of play-craft."[17] Priestley, however, "is not a follower-up," as Brown points out. He was not to attempt another platform piece, nor would it attract imitations. For the collaborators, the experiment in form was its own justification. Oddly enough, when the two again collaborated on a play two years later, the result was a decidedly conventional comedy of manners set in Austria in 1809, in which a countess, trapped in a loveless marriage, becomes aware of life beyond her castle's walls. A lifeless effort, the unpublished *The White Countess* expired in London within a week.

CHAPTER 16

Wartime

O F the five plays which Priestley wrote during the Second World War, only two, *Desert Highway* and *How Are They at Home?*, both produced in London in 1944, deal with situations arising from the global conflict. The former is a serious drama set in a war zone abroad, the latter a frothy entertainment set at home; but the two share a common bond as well as a common theme. They are both functional plays whose impetus is a sense of duty rather than a spark of creative genius, and both express, albeit mechanically, Priestley's commitment to community. Priestley's workmanlike contributions to the war afforded soldiers and civilians alike some comfort and release from tension, but neither play has lasting merit. Two earlier plays, *Good Night Children*, a slight comedy written in 1941, and *They Came to a City*, a utopian drama written in 1943, are not directly related to the war, a fact which probably hindered the former's chance of success. *They Came to a City*, on the other hand, found a wartime audience receptive to its undeveloped but comforting ideas. Of the plays of the period, only *An Inspector Calls* reveals the dramatist as master of his craft. Written during the last winter of the war, it eventually benefited in production from the mood of uncertainty and disillusion which marked the postwar years.

I   Good Night Children

The surprisingly short London run of *Good Night Children* following a successful provincial tour taught Priestley that sacred institutions are not to be mocked in time of war. A comic satire on bureaucracy and befuddlement in the BBC, the play was mistimed, for Britons were well served by radio during the war. Radio united and comforted them as it kept them informed.

Some of its vital work was done by Priestley himself in his popular "Postscripts." That the same patriotic Englishman could suggest that Britain's broadcasting system was "cock-eyed . . . half-witted . . . wasteful, pedantic and stupid"[1] did not sit well with some of his countrymen. Eventually Priestley would admit that the piece is something "of a private joke" with too special an "appeal to an inner circle."[2]

While a typically Priestleyan cross-section of English society ranking from Sir Reginald Runton, deputy-assistant director-general, to Percy King, the Cockney effects man, rehearse, broadcast, court, and squabble, a typical day in a regional broadcasting studio unfolds in *Good Night Children*: a children's program is nearly wrecked by a quarrelsome pair of performers; and the cast of locals for "Down Here in Barset . . . Another fascinating medley of folk-lore and song from a fragrant corner of old England" (226) fails to show up. All the while two young producers, Paula and Martin, progress, like Beatrice and Benedick, from raillery to love, occasionally pausing for some trenchant commentary: "It's not broadcasting itself. I suppose at best it's a rather limited medium, but it can be turned into something vital, moving, quite beautiful sometimes. . . . What's wrong is the organisation itself, the machine. It doesn't care— and the people who run it don't care—for that precious vital impulse which makes the artist an artist. And so that impulse just fades away and dies" (290).

Priestley dexterously maneuvers a large cast of characters through the brisk proceedings, some of them arch, one of them hilarious. The latter involves a doddering old codger who plays an ancient musical instrument, an episode which, two years later, would be transformed and expanded to involve stranger men and stranger instruments in another media satire, the more successful novel *Low Notes on a High Level*.

II They Came to a City

They Came to a City, one of Priestley's most popular plays if not one of his favorites, demonstrates that on occasion the dramatist accurately gauged the mood of a nation at war. Written in 1942, the play enjoyed a long London run after a successful tour, and that success was repeated in numerous productions by repertory companies and amateur groups at home and abroad. The play offers a promise of a better world, and a wartime audience demanded nothing more, not even the details of the imagined Utopia.

They Came to a City is an idealistic fantasy involving nine people, again a representative cross-section of all classes of English society, who unaccountably find themselves outside the wall of an unidentified city. For the most part, the older, well-heeled members of the group are satisfied with the world from which they have been mysteriously transported and are eager to return to their dull but patterned conservative routines. Those who have not fared so well, have never found what they have been searching for, are ready for the adventure of exploring the new. When the door of the city opens at the end of Act I, all of them decide to have a look around, although the financier among the group simply wants to get to the nearest post office to complete a business deal.

By the end of Act II, which takes place at sunset of the same day, all nine members of the group have come out of the city. The hardworking charlady, however, tarries outside the wall only long enough to pick up her market basket. She returns to the city to take up a new life in which she will continue to work hard but will be better cared for. Several affecting scenes follow.

A henpecked bank clerk from Leamington has had a wonderful day in the city, but his joyless wife has not. He is eager to go back inside, but she refuses to join him. He starts to go, but falters. The ties between husband and wife are stronger than whatever promise the city holds in store. He will return to an unfulfilling life in Leamington, but will live to regret it.

Philippa, daughter of the widowed Lady Loxfield, explains to her snobbish mother that she must leave her and go back into the city, where, for the first time, she has truly felt alive. She cannot resume the empty life her mother leads in dreary resort hotels. Lady Loxfield stoically accepts the loss of her daughter and is soon chit-chatting with the play's representative of the landed gentry, Sir George Gedney, about their mutual acquaintances.

Joe, a disillusioned merchant seaman, and Alice, a practical-minded waitress, find in the city not only the life which they have long been seeking but love as well. Nevertheless, they too decide that they cannot stay. They return to their former world unwillingly but dutifully in order to tell the truth about the wondrous place which they have been privileged to visit, to

counter the lies which those who have willingly abandoned the
city are sure to tell of it. The world to which they return is
undeniably full of wrongs, but their day in the city has convinced
them that with effort those wrongs can be righted.

Anyone expecting enlightenment about a utopian world is
bound to be disappointed in *They Came to a City,* for Priestley
has solved the difficult task of describing the workings of the city
by merely sidestepping the issue. The hours which his characters
spend within the walls of the city take place in the interval
between the play's two acts. A drink in a bar in a theater lobby
may offer some comfort, but is hardly a satisfying solution to the
world's problems. During the play, however, the audience must
make do with the few clues the characters give them: on learning
that he spends his days hunting and fishing, the inhabitants of the
city had asked the aristocrat if he were a savage; they consider
the financier's method of making money a crime and had notified
the police; and their belief in social justice had caused them to
laugh at Lady Loxfield's offer of charity.

The fullest account of the city is Joe's. He describes it as a
place "where men and women don't work for machines and
money, but machines and money work for men and women—
where greed and envy and hate have no place—where want and
disease and fear have vanished for ever—where nobody carries a
whip and nobody rattles a chain. Where men have at last stopped
mumbling and gnawing and scratching in dark caves and have
come out into the sunlight."[3] Joe's words may seem as empty as
they are idealistic to anyone seeking political, economic, or social
solutions in *They Came to a City,* but Priestley would point out
that such a person has missed the point of the play, which he
claims to be a work of "symbolic action" concerning differing
attitudes of mind toward postwar change: "What is important in
the play is not the city but the respective attitudes of the
characters toward it."[4] The chief difficulty is that the various
attitudes of the stereotyped characters are thoroughly predictable throughout. The only unpredictable element about *They
Came to a City* is its popular appeal. Perhaps an audience during
the war merely needed assurance that a better world existed—if
only in the clouded imagination of a playwright who seems in this
instance more calculating than committed.

III   Desert Highway

Desert Highway, Priestley insists, "was never intended to be a contribution to the Theatre." Presented in London for a limited period, "it was specially written, as a gift to the Army." With a cast of soldier-actors it toured army camps and a few "ordinary" theaters, "where all profits and royalties were given to a book fund for the Services."[5] To Priestley's astonishment, the play enjoyed a vogue immediately after the war, when, against his advice, an inexperienced young manager successfully toured it.

The play deals with a tank crew lost in the Syrian desert. The men have enough rations for a day or two, but are unable to establish radio contact. Sighted by an enemy plane, they are strafed with machine-gun fire, and the youngest member of the crew, a Gloucestershire farmer, is mortally wounded.

In Act II, the next morning, the youth dies. The plane returns and drops a message. If the crew shows a sign of surrender, the plane will drop supplies to keep the men alive until they can be picked up by the advancing German army. The survivors, a Jewish sergeant from London, a cynical corporal educated at Oxford, a Yorkshireman, a Welshman, and a Cockney, argue about the worth of man and the reasons for the war. The Jew convinces the others that the Nazi persecution of his people is "something quite different from ordinary prejudice":

JOSEPH: . . . They want to destroy, once and for all, that idea which the two tribes of Judaea have never quite lost—the idea of the great invisible Lord of Hosts, the one God of righteousness, to whom every man belongs, and to whom every man is precious, and who should reign on earth, through man's free choice, as He reigns in Heaven.

DONNINGTON: And why should they want to do that?

JOSEPH (*passionately*): Because while that idea is still working in men's minds, the iron empires of fraud and force, of police and machines, of torture and murder, can never feel secure.[6]

Joseph turns from an explanation of what they are fighting against to consider what they are fighting for ". . . the real democracy, which is something more than having an occasional vote. It's the belief that all human beings are precious to God, and that therefore all human beings must be precious to each other, and that the will of God shall be done on earth as it is in heaven" (259–60). The men agree that they must not surrender. As the play ends, they hear an approaching plane but are uncertain whether it is the enemy's or one of their own.

Between the two contemporary acts Priestley has inserted an interlude to be enacted by the same performers in the same locale in the desert, but the year is 703 B.C. A caravan of traders *"of indeterminate Near Eastern nationality"* (227) and their learned Egyptian scribe meet the Israelite guide who will lead them through the mountain passes on their way to Jerusalem. As a ravaging Assyrian army is reported approaching the vicinity, some Aramaean soldiers demand the youngest trader as a sacrifice to Baal. Only the Israelite opposes them, but the others hand the youth over. Before he is bound, the Egyptian (Donnington, the Oxford man) and the Israelite (Joseph) argue the reasons for a nation's defeat:

DONNINGTON: . . . The Northern kingdom fell simply because it couldn't stand up against the powerful Assyrian army. Purely a military problem. Nothing to do with the worship of images at all.

JOSEPH: You did not listen to the words of the prophet Amos. . . . He said to the greedy nobles and the false priests: "Ye who turn judgment to wormwood, and leave off righteousness in the earth—" . . .

DONNINGTON *(smiling)*: . . . Turning judgment to wormwood, leaving off righteousness, worshipping images—what have they to do with the facts of the military problem?

JOSEPH *(with emphasis)*: Because a kingdom in which judgment has turned to wormwood and there is no righteousness is like a fruit that has gone rotten, and will crumble at a touch. (238)

The interlude ends with the word that the young trader has been killed. The Israelite stands apart from the rest: "I was wrong to say that we must leave this place. Why should we make haste? We go from one place of evil only to another, and our iniquity goes with us . . ." (243).

Even in this specially constructed wartime product, Priestley refuses to be bound by chronology. By moving backward in time in the middle of *Desert Highway*, the dramatist suggests that mankind has made little progress over the ages, but a few men will always see the right and fight for it. The interlude and the rest of the play are made one through language. The near-biblical speech of the former becomes the impassioned fervor of the latter as Joseph, prophetlike, exhorts the others to endure for God and man.

But *Desert Highway* forces a parallel which is basically unsound; thus a bold technical experiment is undercut. A scant two years after the war, Rex Pogson recognized the difficulty: "In Act II Priestley tried the impossible task of finding common ground between soldiers of 1943 and 703 B.C. The result was some woolly idealism which was scarcely distinguishable from jingoism. Surely Priestley cannot have believed that the late war had any pretensions as a religious crusade."[7] Priestley's own fervor is social rather than religious, aroused by the exploration of the relationship of man to man. Even in his time plays he had consistently avoided relying on an omnipresent deity for ready-made solutions. When man invokes God, an unusual occurrence in his work but the very center of *Desert Highway*, Priestley is less comfortable and less convincing.

IV   How Are They at Home?

Designed as light escapist entertainment for servicemen abroad, *How Are They at Home?* proved to be serviceable fare for undemanding audiences at home as well. The play is a made-to-order concoction padded with musical numbers and punctuated with uplifting speeches about the better world to come. While the troops at the front fight for that world, the women they have left behind are working toward it too in factories and on farms. With good united against evil, geographical boundaries are meaningless: an Austrian refugee does her share as cook and an American officer proves a none-too-bright but capable ally. But what is more important, class distinctions disappear as well. When the earnest but bewildered major from Indiana comments, "I thought Lady Farfield was a member of your old privileged classes," Hilda, the Yorkshire lass who works alongside her on the assembly line, leaps to her defense: "If yer'd seen 'er coming through 'ere 'alf an hour since, after she'd been cleanin' her auto-bike, in 'er mucky old overall, yer'd 'ave thought she was Black Jack from the boiler 'ouse."[8] Lady Farfield herself stresses the invigorating spirit that is a direct result of the war: "I've met people—and made friends—that I couldn't have known before. I understand a lot of things—important things—that I didn't begin to understand before. I can face the future properly and in the right spirit. I feel that—in my own very humble way—now I can help—and not hinder—the new England most of us want" (404).

That Oliver Goldsmith and Anton Chekhov lend Priestley a hand in the proceedings merely demonstrates that in time of war everyone must be made to do his share. Two RAF officers arrive at Farfield Hall to be billeted and are greeted by an ancient butler, like Firs, living in the past. In an inversion of *She Stoops to Conquer,* Group-Captain Camyon and Squadron-Leader Acton are led to believe that the large country house is still manned by numerous servants as the frivolous lady of the manor parties her way through the war. Thus begin the mistakes of a night, but the horrified officers are eventually disabused. At last they come to see Farfield Hall as exemplar of "Democracy with its sleeves rolled up" (430). Too slight to have found favor in a normal world, *How Are They at Home?* is unobjectionable as a topical farce frankly fulfilling its mission, like the wartime novels, *Black-Out in Gretley* and *Daylight on Saturday,* as morale-builder for a nation at war.

V   An Inspector Calls

During the winter of 1944-45 Priestley wrote *An Inspector Calls* "at top speed."[9] Its air of inevitability and a uniformity in manner and tone enabled him to finish it within a week. As no London theater was available at the time of its completion, Priestley sent a copy of the script to Moscow to underscore his approval of the Russians' serious regard for the theater, an attitude approaching his own. The play was simultaneously presented there by two companies to great acclaim. Soon it was produced throughout the Soviet Union and in various state theaters in other countries. Eventually it was presented in London in October 1946 as part of the Old Vic season, but in its native land the play was greeted with surly indifference and dismissed as a mechanical contrivance overly reliant on coincidence.

In Moscow the Russian director Tairov had provided the seemingly naturalistic work with a symbolic production making full use of a large raked stage. The set consisted of a carved ceiling sloping down toward a heavy door. There were no walls, "only a dimly-lit space beyond the brilliantly illuminated acting area." According to Priestley, the setting enabled the audience to grasp the true nature of the play, that it concerned more than its immediate and continuous action. The London production, however, "was less brilliant and experimental" and "far more solidly rooted in English life," with a heavy set full of realistic detail. "Against this weighty naturalism," Priestley believes, "the play's symbolism tends to be underemphasised; so that perhaps there is an excuse for those London daily grumblers who really thought the play is merely concerned with a bit of excitement in one night in 1912 and is not an attempt to dramatise the history of the last thirty years or so, making everything cast a long shadow."[10] Some critics regarded *An Inspector Calls* as they had Priestley's first play, *Dangerous Corner*—a mere recapitulation of the events leading up to the death of a character who never appears.[11] Priestley, however, offers something more, a further development of the theme of man's interdependence on other men, the responsibility of one man for all men. Sharing with *Dangerous Corner* the seemingly conventional form of a melodramatic thriller, *An Inspector Calls* is in fact a deeply committed social drama with a focus on one man's family, which insists inevitably on the family of man.

At a quiet family dinner party in an industrial city in the North Midlands on a spring evening in 1912, the Birlings are celebrating the engagement of their daughter Sheila to Gerald Croft. The coming marriage is especially fortuitous as it signals the merging of the firms of Birling & Company and Crofts Limited. Instead of competing, the rival companies may soon be "working together—for lower costs and higher prices."[12] With Sheila, her mother, and her brother Eric out of the room, Mr. Birling confides to Croft that he expects to be named on the next Honours List "so long as we behave ourselves, don't get into the police court or start a scandal—eh?" (272). A few minutes later the maid ushers into the room an Inspector Goole who is new to the district. A young woman, Eva Smith, had swallowed a strong disinfectant and has died in agony in the Infirmary. After examining her diary and some letters, the Inspector has come to question the Birlings regarding the circumstances prior to the suicide. One by one the Birlings are shown a photograph of the girl, and each in turn obviously recognizes her.

By the time Inspector Goole takes his leave of the shaken family, every member of the party has become implicated in the tragedy: Mr. Birling had sacked the girl for her part in a strike at the factory. Sheila, annoyed by her supposed impertinence, had had her discharged from her job in a dress shop. Changing her name to Daisy Renton, Eva Smith had become Croft's mistress until the arrangement proved an inconvenience. She had then taken up with Eric and become pregnant by him, but Eric could only support her by taking money from his father's firm. Rather than accept stolen money, the girl had asked for assistance from the Brumley Women's Charity Organization but had been denied by the interviewing committee, chaired by Mrs. Birling, who felt strongly that the man who got her into trouble should shoulder responsibility for her fate. Having "been turned out and turned down too many times" (302), she had ended her life.

Before his departure, Goole forcefully states the theme which has emerged from the family's steadily mounting denials, charges, countercharges, and confessions: "One Eva Smith has gone—but there are millions and millions and millions of Eva Smiths and John Smiths still left with us, with their lives, their hopes and fears, their suffering, and chance of happiness, all intertwined with our lives, with what we think and say and do. We don't live alone. We are members of one body. We are responsible for each other. And I tell you that the time will soon come when, if men will not learn that lesson, then they will be taught it in fire and blood and anguish" (311).

Mr. and Mrs. Birling and Croft, however, are more concerned with their reputations than their share of guilt and responsibility. It occurs to them that Goole may have shown each one a different photo. Eva Smith may not have been Daisy Renton. On learning that there is no Inspector Goole on the police force and no girl has died in the infirmary that day, they are overjoyed. An elaborate hoax has been played on them, but as there is no threat of a public scandal, the Birlings can carry on as if nothing had happened, an attitude which appals both Sheila and Eric. Fate, however, has one more joke in store. The telephone rings and Birling answers it: "That was the police. A girl has just died—on her way to the Infirmary—after swallowing some disinfectant. And a police inspector is on his way here—to ask some—questions—" (323). The five characters are dumbfounded as the curtain falls.

An Inspector Calls is one of Priestley's tautest, best con-

structed dramas. An electric tension builds from Goole's
entrance to the extraordinary final moment which takes the
characters full circle as the action, as in *Dangerous Corner*,
seems to begin anew. This time, however, the characters are
aware of the unending coil in which they are hopelessly caught.
What seems throughout a naturalistic play suddenly moves
outside time as once again the present simultaneously becomes
past and future. The play illustrates no particular time theory;
rather, time effectively reinforces theme: man must take full
responsibility for his actions as well as their consequences. He
builds his future as he lives his present. Even the *raisonneur*, the
enigmatic Inspector Goole, is taken outside time as his very
existence is called into question: is Goole a policeman or merely
an imposter? Still another possibility exists: Goole is the
embodiment of the Birling's collective guilt called forth by man's
need to account for his actions, to inspect himself—a need which,
if he could, he would deny. Goole is one of Priestley's most
enigmatic organizers, and *An Inspector Calls* is a brilliant if ironic
twist on the common cause, the plot device which he makes use
of in so many of his works.

Returning to an earlier style of apparent naturalism in the
well-constructed play of continuous action, in *An Inspector Calls*
Priestley displays a firm and vigorous hand. In one respect only
does the play suffer in comparison with his earlier work. Like
Eden End, *An Inspector Calls* is set in 1912, which enables the
playwright once again to mine a vein of dramatic irony. Having
placed the Kirby family of *Eden End* in a world on the brink,
Priestley had trusted his audience to bring an added dimension
to the play. He felt no need to nudge them with speeches
obviously foreshadowing the coming war. The dramatic irony in
the opening scene of *An Inspector Calls*, on the other hand,
intrudes clumsily on the play's exposition with such lines as
these: "Nobody wants war. . . . There's too much at stake these
days. Everything to lose and nothing to gain by war," and an
obvious reference to the "absolutely unsinkable" *Titanic* as
Priestley awkwardly injects the play with contemporary rele-
vance: "In twenty or thirty years' time—let's say, in 1940—you
may be giving a little party like this . . ." (271-72). Once
Inspector Goole makes his entrance to initiate the play's rising
action, however, the dramatist paces his surprising revelations

with astonishing control, and his characters never lose credibility. Yet the lapse of the opening seems a sign that Priestley no
longer trusts completely his audience's intellect or intuition.

CHAPTER 17

Cautious Optimism

B Y 1939 Priestley had finished an act and a half of a play to be called *The Linden Tree* about an old man who returns from a trip to the East accompanied by an Oriental philosopher and a mysterious girl.[1] Abandoned at his wife's suggestion that he was barking up the wrong tree, the play was to have ended with a quiet scene in which old Linden, like Stephen Dawlish in the later *Summer Day's Dream*, dispenses wisdom to his grandchildren. *The Linden Tree*, 1947, retains only the title of the abandoned play, but the final scene in which Professor Linden, one day after his sixty-fifth birthday, quietly reads a passage of his history manuscript to his daughter Dinah, the only member of the family to stand by him, is among the most memorable and moving in all of Priestley's works. "What he reads," according to E. R. Wood, "is an important assertion of the dual nature of Man, a view of our present economic troubles in a philosophical perspective that gives strength to the thinking of Professor Linden, and which adds a special resonance to the major works of J. B. Priestley himself."[2]

His only major work for the theater in the difficult years of postwar recovery, *The Linden Tree* shows signs of disillusion. Priestley recognizes that the spirit of community is flagging in a war-weary world, but that spirit must be revitalized if the family, the nation, the world are to survive. In two seriously intended plays, *Home Is Tomorrow* in 1948 and *Summer Day's Dream* in 1949, as well as three less consequential works, the libretto for Arthur Bliss's opera *The Olympians* that same year and the comedies *Bright Shadow* the following year and *Treasure on Pelican*, written in 1951, the dramatist reveals his uncertainties concerning the future, yet he remains a cautious optimist.

205

I The Linden Tree

Unlike the false start about the Lindens which was written amidst the scenic splendors of Arizona, the final version of *The Linden Tree* was written during the rigors of a bitterly cruel February in 1947, when, short of fuel and snowbound, Priestley "had to work, eat and sleep in one small room in my house in the Isle of Wight."[3] Although the play opened in London that summer, *The Linden Tree* reflects in theme the harsh conditions under which it was written. By August the snow had melted, but the British still faced shortages and disillusionment—the high cost of the victory of war. "No play could have been made out of less promising material," Priestley admits. "It opened no magic casements for anybody. It confronted our audiences with their own drab scene." Yet none of his plays "was ever given a more solid welcome by both Press and public than this one was,"[4] the last success that a serious Priestley drama would enjoy.

The Linden Tree represents Priestley's return to the Chekhovian style and subject matter of *Eden End*, but is subtler and ultimately more complex. Whereas the earlier work reflects the passing of a former world, the latter confronts a world in flux. No dirge for a lost age, *The Linden Tree* marks the passing of the old, but suggests that its legacy must not be rejected by the new, to which the play tentatively extends a welcoming hand. Its leitmotif is the Elgar Cello Concerto, which is heard throughout much of the play's second half as Dinah, the youngest of the Lindens, plays one of its themes herself and listens to a recording of another movement as her father comments on the music's hopeful melancholy:

A kind of long farewell. An elderly man remembers his world before the war of 1914 . . . gone, lost for ever—and so he distils his tenderness and regret, drop by drop, and seals the sweet melancholy in a Concerto for 'cello. And he goes, too, where all the old green sunny days and the twinkling nights went—gone, gone. But then what happens? Why, a little miracle. You heard it. . . . Young Dinah Linden, all youth, all eagerness, saying hello and not farewell to anything, who knows and cares nothing about Bavaria in the 'Nineties or the secure and golden Edwardian afternoons, here in Burmanley, this very afternoon, the moment we stop shouting at each other, unseals for us the precious distillation, uncovers the tenderness and regret, which are ours now as well as his, and our lives and Elgar's. Burmanley to-day

and the Malvern Hills in a lost sunlight, are all magically intertwined. . . .[5]

The family has gathered ostensibly to celebrate Professor
Linden's birthday, actually to convince him to give up his post as
professor of modern history at the University of Burmanley.
Having reached the supposedly compulsory age, he has been
asked to retire, but chooses to remain, as have other members of
the staff older than he. But Linden, a true humanist, like Tuby
and Saltana of *The Image Men*, is a nuisance to "the new
educational machine" which would suck "the blood and mar-
row" out of what should be and once was a "great common
enterprise" (475). Yet Linden is not at odds with the world
around him. Together with Dinah, he loves the life of
Burmanley, a typical provincial city in Labour England, thrives
on it, recognizes there the seeds of a brighter future, while his
wife and other children can only see a drab and dismal place full
of surly shopgirls:

MRS. LINDEN: . . . Nobody cares how things are done—they just slop
  about and take the least possible trouble—and if you dare to
  complain, they don't hesitate to be rude at once . . . it's quite
  hopeless here now.
DINAH *(handing cups)*: I don't believe it *is* hopeless at all.
MRS. LINDEN: You don't know what we're talking about, child.
DINAH: I do. People in shops—and waitresses—and all that. And I think
  they're all right—nice and matey—considering.
MRS. LINDEN: You don't remember anything better.
MARION: Just what I was going to say. You're too young to be in this,
  Dinah.
PROFESSOR: I'm not, though. And I know what you mean. I remember
  when most of these people you're talking about were terrified that
  one or two complaints would throw 'em out into the street and back
  to the Labour Exchange. You could see that fear in their eyes, hear it
  in their apologetic voices, and I hated it so much that I never dared to
  make any complaints.
MRS. LINDEN: You were always much too easy-going.
PROFESSOR: No, no. But now I can grumble like mad, and they can
  grumble back at me, and I feel much better about it. (434-35)

Mrs. Linden leaves her husband to go to London with their son
Rex, an Epicurean who has made a killing on the stock exchange
but is haunted by a sense that time is running out. Their daughter

Marion returns to her French husband and his cozy, aristocratic, Old World and comforting Catholic faith. Another daughter, Jean, a doctor, uncertain of her loyalties, goes back to her hospital to work toward "a world as efficient, sterilised and scientific as an operating theatre," but she may eventually heed her father's warning, "Don't confuse science with life" (453). Recognizing that "somebody's got to stay," Linden refuses "to walk away from real life, give it up as a bad job" (459-60). Dinah, whom Susan Cooper sees as "a more fully developed portrait of the bubbling, doomed young Carol of *Time and the Conways*,"⁶ and Mrs. Cotton, the Linden's *"woman-of-all-work,"* a direct descendant of Chekhov's Firs and Sarah of *Eden End*, remain with him.

Priestley's drawing of Mrs. Cotton suggests how much he has learned about characterization since *Eden End*. In the earlier work, Sarah provided comic relief as a relic of the past unable to enter the modern world. Mrs. Cotton, on the other hand, finds herself in a bewildering world—like Sarah she has trouble with such gadgets as telephones—but she will cope; they are of Dinah's world, not hers. Her love for her young charge, however, makes that world worth bothering about. As the play opens she tells a visitor, "Nothing's right now, nor ever will be, if you ask me. Half the sitting-room ceiling come down yesterday" (405). A house may literally and symbolically be falling down around her, but when Mrs. Linden walks out late in the play, Mrs. Cotton knows what must be done. When Dinah begins to fret about Monday's meal, she takes charge: "It's only Saturday now . . . Leave it to me. An' don't look so solemn about it—'cos it's no use—it's all 'it or miss, these days, an' mostly miss—an' if you start takin' it all serious, you'll soon be off your rocker" (464). Mrs. Cotton may herself be slightly "off her rocker," but her particular view of the postwar world seems shrewd enough, and, like her employer, she remains undaunted in a difficult situation.

While the family members each represent a particular approach to life, Priestley does not make the mistake in *The Linden Tree* that mars the later *Dragon's Mouth*, in which four static characters mechanically mouth four opposing points of view. The Linden children are skillfully fleshed out with redeeming characteristics which humanize them. As Wood observes, "Rex has charm despite his unattractive views and way of life. . . . Jean appreciates her father and Dinah, and Marion

has misgivings about deserting them."[7] Mrs. Linden's exasperation with her husband is tempered by her genuine love for him.
That both her exasperation and love are understandable
reactions in the circumstances is a tribute to Priestley's
characterization of his protagonist. For Linden is more vulnera-
ble than he pretends to be, and some of his optimism is sheer
bluff. Yet he can overlook the pain which the others cause him to
take up his role as husband and father as he presides over a
family game of Black Sam which Priestley tellingly handles with
maximum effect. Unlike the fussy, time-consuming charades
which the Conways play, the Linden game is emblematic,
underscoring the pivotal position of the professor who tilts at
windmills: "Give us our counters, Rex—that's your job . . . while
the old man, with his patience, shuffles the cards. Patience . . .
patience . . . and shuffle the cards . . ." (444).

Professor Linden's patience, however, is not reserved for his
family. In his relationships with his students, even the unpromis-
ing ones, Linden reveals the gentle goading of the born teacher
whose understanding and enthusiasm eventually penetrate the
fog of undisciplined minds, making clear to his students, just as
Priestley clarifies his theme for his audience, the professor's
view of history—that the past has shaped a present in which are
planted the seeds of a future. In *The Linden Tree,* his last major
achievement in the theater, a patient dramatist once again
explores what has been for him an obsessive theme and
revitalizes it in a disturbing but compelling manner which will
surely speak as forcefully to future generations as it did to its
immediate audience.

II Home is Tomorrow

The unfavorable reception of *Home Is Tomorrow* bitterly
disappointed Priestley, for the play's theme is an expansion of
the dominant issue of several of his later works. Whereas *An
Inspector Calls* explores the relationship of community and
family and *They Came to a City* that of community and nation,
Home Is Tomorrow, as does the novel *Salt is Leaving,* projects
Priestley's vision of community onto the international scene.
Despite Priestley's claim that "its production was mistimed,"
that it would have been better understood ten years later,[8] the
play remains an ambitious but confusing melodrama.

While the minor characters—a French economist, a Chinese educator, and a Czech doctor—are colorfully infused with honest human ambiguity, the central characters—an earnest English diplomat heading a United Nations agency in charge of a Caribbean island, his bored wife, and the assistant from New England who doggedly loves him—are drawn with bold but unconvincing strokes. Their triangular involvement, meant to mirror the play's larger issues, actually reduces the work to a matinee drama about a philandering wife and her understanding, faithful husband. When Ann tells Sir Edward that a relationship between the two of them would be fulfilling because they are so alike, he explains that he loves his wife Jill for the very reason that she complements him, is in fact his opposite. Jill can lead him "to the other side of things, the enchanted place."[9] Yet Sir Edward, Jill, and Ann—all of them cut from the same Anglo-Saxon cloth—inadequately counterpoint the relations between progressive industrial nations and undeveloped exotic territories.

Home Is Tomorrow avoids the vague idealism of *They Came to a City* by insisting that developed nations can actually aid less affluent countries by curbing disease, building and staffing schools, and lending technical assistance. What hampers the development of the backward island is a twofold opposition—the natives' traditional values and suspicion of foreigners, as well as a power struggle among industrialists once a rare mineral useful for encasing uranium in atomic piles is discovered there. That opposition becomes overwhelming once its forces combine. When a ruthless manufacturer enables a native dictator to reassert his control over the islanders, the UN agency, having lost the support of Great Britain and the United States, finds itself impotent. Sir Edward tells his adversary, Lerma, "You see this island as so many deposits of beryllium silicate. I see it as a community of people, who sooner or later cannot help but live by faith, hope and love" (398), but the time is not yet ripe for that better world toward which he has been struggling. In an abrupt and inconclusive resolution, the native leader shoots and kills Sir Edward, and the play ends with an ambiguous symbolic action. As he slumps over his desk, he knocks a globe to the floor. His secretary, a native girl educated in England, emotionally torn by two cultures, carefully replaces the globe on his desk and sits *"as if awaiting further orders"* (402).

Priestley rightly refuses to patronize the natives in his play, but he has failed to provide sufficient characterization of a single one of them. Instead, the audience must accept on trust what the foreigners say—that their vibrancy, their joy of living are traits which the sophisticated inhabitants of developed nations would do well to emulate. Education and sanitation need not signal an end to vitality, Priestley maintains, and the play successfully conveys the sensual excitement of a tropical milieu, with an offstage fiesta an effective background to its climactic confrontation. But the Europeans resolutely command center stage in *Home Is Tomorrow*, while the islanders who might clarify the play's major issues recede into the shadows.

III   Summer Day's Dream

Gareth Lloyd Evans suggests that in a sense *Summer Day's Dream* is "a play about those people who have seen the City in circumstances of harshness and deprivation, but who are trying to live by the example it has set."[10] Yet even closer in theme to *Summer Day's Dream* than *They Came to a City* is *Home Is Tomorrow*, in which a Caribbean island is exploited by world powers who care more for profits than people; for in *Summer Day's Dream*, it is England itself, survivor of a nuclear war, which is the backward nation, prey to the might of Russia, the money of the United States, and the technology of India. Written in 1949, the play is a pastoral fantasy set in 1975, by which time, Priestley—temporarily abandoning the caution which now tempers his optimism—suggests natural man will again embrace the land and learn to live simply off the fruits of the earth.

With their country devastated by a Third War, the English survivors have come to terms with their lot. They raise animals, farm the land, and barter for their needs. They have not, however, reverted to a wholly primitive state of barbarity. In fact, art thrives among them. The young people are poets and musicians as well as farmers. In their spare time—and they have more now than in the past—they entertain themselves with performances of the plays of Shakespeare. They have no use for the gadgets which seem necessities to the other peoples of the world, the "TV-comms" and "atomicars." Instead, they make do with green fields, a sky of stars, the scent of roses, and love and compassion. If the simple life was once forced upon them, they have come to understand that they are victors in defeat.

In a decaying country house on the South Downs live Stephen Dawlish, a wise, pipe-smoking, old codger born in 1895 (Priestley was born in 1894); his daughter-in-law Margaret, a mystic who moves through life as in a dream foretelling what is to come; and his grandchildren—Rosalie, a poet, and Christopher, who farms when he can spare time from his music. Their bucolic paradise is threatened when Dr. Bahru, an Indian representative of the Chemical Research Department of the South Asia Federation; Franklyn Heimer, Vice-President of the American Synthetic Products Corporation; and Irina Shestova of the USSR Foreign Trade Commission descend upon them when the controls on their helicopter jam. They have been on the Downs to investigate the feasibility of using the chalk there in the processing of a new synthetic substance and are about to recommend the erection of a manufacturing plant and the establishment of an entire industrial complex.

With their equipment out of order, the foreigners must remain the guests of the Dawlishes for three days before filing their reports and arranging for transportation. In the interim the enchanted green world works its magical spell, which the dramatist underscores with quotations from *A Midsummer Night's Dream* and *The Tempest*. Like the characters in *The Tempest*, the visitors have arrived as the result of an accident, and Chris, who recites Caliban's lines, ". . . when I waked, / I cried to dream again. . ." (III.ii.145-46),[11] calls Irina "a castaway on a mad island" (419). Irina, Bahru, and Heimer all dream of childhood or remember their youthful days. Tensions disappear as their humanity is rekindled. Irina, likened to the Snow Queen on her entrance, even melts in the warmth of Chris's love. Like Garbo's Ninotchka, the commissar becomes a woman. Through it all, old Dawlish, a rustic philosopher, serves as master of the revels. Like Prospero, who retires to Milan, ". . . where / Every third thought shall be my grave" (V.i.310-11), he prepares himself for his death in a ritualized incantation at the end of the play: "I see the hawthorn that the Roman stared at . . . and soon I shall have gone with the Roman . . . leaving the green old tavern of the world" (475). By then the visitors have gone back to a harsher world where duty rules, but they have been touched by their contact with the green world. No report will be filed.

Summer Day's Dream disarms criticism. Its languorous, dreamlike setting, a unique landscape in Priestley's world, casts its own magical spell, and the dramatist has found a perfect language to enhance it in the heightened dialogue of Chris's protestations of love and Dawlish's canny philosophy. Yet his characters engage in straightforward argument as well, as in an exchange in which the theme of *An Inspector Calls* is further developed:

MARGARET: Ask him what he can make out of our chalk that will be better than the life you will murder here.

BAHRU *(sharply)*: I do not like this way of talking. It has nothing to do with him—or with us. We are scientists—

MARGARET *(cutting in)*: And so it has nothing to do with you. You are not responsible—you are scientists. Dr. Bahru, we have stopped believing that dangerous lie.

BAHRU *(stung)*: Mrs. Dawlish, in these days I doubt if you have any scientists here.

MARGARET *(sharply)*: Then all the better. Now we can all be responsible for what we do, and nobody can any longer say "It has nothing to do with me." (454)

In *Summer Day's Dream* Priestley has evoked an almost irresistible world, but in the final analysis the play suffers from a case of wooly-mindedness. In *Home is Tomorrow* Priestley insisted that the technology of the modern world could help an underdeveloped island to become a *better* place, but in *Summer Day's Dream* the outside world has absolutely nothing to offer to natural man living in a state of grace. Nuclear holocaust, the play implies, is a blessing in disguise. It is to Priestley's credit that one must be distanced from the play's seductive mood before the mind is reengaged.

IV   The Olympians

In 1949 Covent Garden presented a comic opera with music by Arthur Bliss and a libretto by Priestley. *The Olympians* takes place in the South of France in 1836. Hector, a young poet, summarizes the legend on which the plot is based:

When men ceased to trust the ancient gods, they lost their power but not their immortality. They then became a troupe of traveling players, wandering the roads for ever. . . . And every now and then, when the moon is full and the night is filled with magic, then their ancient power returns, their godhead shines . . . for a little while . . . who knows how long? . . . or whether it is all a dream? . . .[12]

In the dreamlike action of the opera, the band of strolling players in fact become gods again as they aid two young lovers in overcoming a wealthy father's objections to their marriage. The libretto, in some ways a forerunner of Anthony Burgess' *The Eve of St. Venus* (1964), consists of prose and an easy-flowing if undistinguished verse divided into solo arias and ensembles for the principals as well as choral passages. There is opportunity for dance—Mercury mimes his entire role—as well as spectacle as the gods' former powers are restored. After some comic misunderstandings are smoothed over with the help of an earthy priest, a glorious wedding celebration takes place.

Amidst the frolicking charm of the piece Priestley injects meaningful themes which, wisely, he does not attempt to develop. Lengthy discussions of life as dream, of earth as man's only paradise, of power through art, the very concerns of *Summer Day's Dream,* could only unbalance the fragile work. Instead, Priestley hints at mysteries beyond the text but allows his collaborator to explore those mysteries through the music.

V Bright Shadow

The character who plays detective in *Bright Shadow,* described as *A Play of Detection in Three Acts,* amusingly offers a defense of the genre:

PETER: . . . Do you read detective stories?

IVOR: No. I prefer my fiction to be rather more intelligent and sensitive—to be literature.

PETER: Highbrow type, eh? Well, I've tried some of this new literature of yours, but most of it seems to be filled with people who don't accept any responsibility and run screaming when they remember any awkward questions. So when I've time to read, I make do with detective stories.

IVOR: Rather crude, aren't they'?

PETER: Yes, no doubt. But they do try to make sense out of the problem they offer you—and don't run away from it. Something's settled in the end.[13]

But neither the genre nor the play needs Peter's defense, or

Priestley's. The murder mystery is acceptable fare in the commercial theater if handled with a modicum of skill. *Bright Shadow*, first produced by the Oldham Repertory Theatre Club in 1950, provides something more. The situation is credible and the characters neatly defined. Before a not unexpected but reasonable denouement, some pertinent questions are posed to the same postwar audience which Priestley challenged in *The Linden Tree, Home is Tomorrow,* and *Summer Day's Dream:* Who are we? What have we been up to? How could we have let it happen? Wisely, the dramatist forces no analogies and supplies few answers. The murderer and his motive are revealed, but, like Martin Caplan in *Dangerous Corner*, the victim remains an enigma.

Diana Risborough, whose death three years earlier Peter Warton has come to investigate unofficially, seems to have been all things to all people. As Peter complains, "Every time anybody talks about her, I get an entirely different picture. Now she's this—now she's that" (40-41). Yet her very complexity suggests her humanity. Even in death, she holds the dynamic center of the play. Diana's young cousin, Lesley Dereham, falls in love with Peter, but once the mystery is solved, she rejects him. Diana's specter is too strong:

LESLEY: It wouldn't work. I've thought about it—oh, I won't pretend I haven't—but I know it wouldn't work.
PETER: Why not?
LESLEY: Don't you see there'd always be a shadow between us . . . and the worst kind—a bright shadow. What's the use? You were in love with her. (66)

Lesley, however, is mistaken. Peter never loved Diana, had never laid eyes on her. He has undertaken the investigation, not for himself, but for a friend. Embrace and quick curtain.

With tongue in cheek, a relaxed Priestley has been having fun with characters and audience alike. The key to his mood here is the use he makes of the jovial, knowledgeable pipe-smoker in the play. Generally such a figure can be relied on for a display of uncommon good sense, as Priestley parodies his public image and casts his own bright shadow across his work. This time, however, that character is the murderer!

Like *Dangerous Corner,* from which he has borrowed

extensively, *Bright Shadow* has a mistaken suicide and theft, even a secondary character who is homosexual. But Diana's pervasive spirit, not unlike Martin's, more closely resembles that of another willful and impulsive woman who others wrongly believe has taken her own life, Daphne DuMaurier's Rebecca, another example of the multiple personality. Lesley even startles the others by impersonating Diana just as the second Mrs. De Winter astonishes her husband by appearing at a costume ball in a gown identical to one which Rebecca had worn. And Mrs. Probus, who adored Diana, seems a benign Mrs. Danvers as she makes up her former mistress's room, keeping illusion alive for Diana's father, who cannot accept the reality of her death. *Rebecca's* influence on *Bright Shadow*, however, is finally unimportant. One might make as convincing a case for *Dangerous Corner* as the source of DuMaurier's 1938 novel. What does matter in *Bright Shadow* is Priestley's demonstration that even a detective play designed primarily for repertory companies can benefit from style, wit, and a few ideas at its core.

VI   Treasure on Pelican

According to the director of the first stage production of *Treasure on Pelican* in Cardiff in 1952, "There is no intended analogy in the behaviour of the characters and happenings in the world of to-day, although the parallel between the 'formal meetings' and all the 'meetings' taking place in all quarters of the globe, on practically every subject, is obvious."[14] That the play's meetings, like most international conferences, end in impasse, however, suggests that Priestley has in fact pointed the work to reflect a lack of progress in human understanding. The following exchange indicates that the play parallels a general world condition if no specific political situation:

LOGAN: . . . I want to read some newspapers. I miss the news.
SIR GILBERT: . . . But it wouldn't really *be* news.
LOGAN *(staring at him)*: Why not?
SIR GILBERT: Because it would mostly be about a lot of people all behaving like us.[15]

Treasure on Pelican, a comedy of greed and mistrust reminiscent of Chaucer's "The Pardoner's Tale," marks

Priestley's deepening disillusion in the postwar world. Eight men and women, Priestley's familiar cross-section of English society, have traveled to the Caribbean Sea in search of buried treasure and have found it on a small uninhabited island. The play begins as the group toasts their accomplishment. They have had a great adventure, worked together to overcome nature's obstacles, solved all technical problems, and achieved their goal. Human nature, however, wrecks the moment of triumph. How to divide the spoils now that imagined riches have become the material reality of gold and gems? The camaraderie of the group's first formal conference is replaced by fear and suspicion. Watches are set up to guard the treasure, which is nonetheless stolen but eventually recovered. When a medicine case containing poison disappears, some of the party begin to feel a queasiness which may be the result either of the contaminated food or the unhealthy disclosures about one another: Simpson has done time in prison, Trout was dismissed from the service, Logan has made his money in unscrupulous financial deals, and even Sir Gilbert has had a brush with the law for molesting a young girl amidst the antiquities of the British Museum. By the end of the play a formal meeting is conducted with guns drawn. Violence is imminent when the British Navy paradoxically rescues the group by arresting them, for according to law the treasure belongs to the Crown.

Priestley has covered this ground before: money is power and power corrupts; but the dramatist is not at ease with a cast of scoundrels. He has dealt with the subject in an earlier comedy, the unsuccessful but more inventive *The Golden Fleece*. There the audience observed a good man bedeviled by the forces of evil—the world of finance—but redeemed by the solid virtues of England's common man, in this instance in the guise of a forthright and thoroughly honest charlady. On the other hand, the characters of the more pessimistic *Treasure on Pelican*, representatives of all classes of society, have no redeeming qualities whatsoever, aside from Sir Gilbert's questionable charm, and therefore cannot save themselves. Only a deus ex machina can save the day. But *Treasure on Pelican* does not fully engage its author's craft nor his interest. At the time of its Cardiff performance Priestley was already engrossed in the complex managerial problems of the pre-London tour of the more ambitious, highly experimental *Dragon's Mouth*.

CHAPTER 18

Last Plays

I N 1946 Priestley had written:

I left other kinds of writing, which offered me a safe living and far more peace of mind, to work in the Theatre because I believed the Theatre to be important. And more than once, irritated, bored or depressed by the chaotic conditions and the horrible waste of time and effort, I have told myself that I would write no more for the Theatre, would compete no longer in its nightmare obstacle race, but always I have returned because I have never been able to rid myself of the conviction that the Theatre, representing the communal art of drama, was far more important, far more deeply significant, than most people ever imagined.[1]

Yet a decade later Priestley had virtually abandoned the "nightmare obstacle race." He has since explained why. To be successful in the theater, one must work closely and patiently with others, and he was fast losing the required patience.[2] If writing the experimental *Dragon's Mouth* had been a satisfying experience, the actual production had proved frustrating. He was to make an occasional foray into the commercial theater in the late fifties and early sixties, but first Priestley devoted himself to a form of playwriting which avoided the complications of production and management—the one-act play designed for the amateur theatrical group.

I *One-Act Plays*

Priestley had published two one-act plays in the late 1940's, *The Rose and Crown* (1947), previously mentioned, and *The High Toby* (1948), a sentimental comedy in the style of Sheridan in which Captain Anthony Waite thwarts his uncle and former guardian, Sir Jasper Gregg, from robbing him of his fortune by posing as the highwayman, Scarlet Ned. Written expressly for

218

Pollock's Toy Theatre, *The High Toby* was published with delightful cut-out scenery and characters by Doris Zinkeisen.[3] In 1953 and 1954 four more one-acts appeared in quick succession: *Private Rooms*, *Mother's Day*, *Try It Again*, and *A Glass of Bitter*.

Private Rooms, A One Act Comedy in the Viennese Style is a skillful pastiche of the continental comedies of manners of Arthur Schnitzler and Ferenc Molnar, *gemütlich* and ultimately poignant. A famous aging actor and a middle-aged actress woo, respectively, a ballet dancer and a young poet in adjoining rooms in a Central European capital. Inevitably the play ends with the youngsters going off together as the older couple understand, as do the protagonists of "The Pavilion of Masks," that their charms depend upon their public rather than their private personae. "We have to fight and conquer Time in our work. Yet the people who applaud us just for doing that would be the first to blame us for—well—this,"[4] the actress realizes as she indicates the rooms around them, the setting for their folly.

Including *Mother's Day* in his anthology of one-act plays, Donald FitzJohn recognizes the strong points of the piece: "The unfailing theme of the underdog getting the upper hand is given a new and amusing twist. The dialogue is pungent, and as they speak it the characters come warmly to life."[5] As in *The Rose and Crown* and *A Glass of Bitter* Priestley demonstrates an ear sensitive to the speech patterns of the urban lower class in *Mother's Day*, a domestic fantasy about tyranny and role-playing within the family circle, as Mrs. Pearson and Mrs. Fitzgerald briefly exchange bodies to enable the latter, the stronger personality, to subdue the family of the former, who has for years been treated as a household drudge. The overly sentimental *A Glass of Bitter*, on the other hand, is Priestley's least convincing one-act.[6] In the play a suburban husband pretends for his wife's sake to know nothing of her former involvement which led to the birth of an illegitimate son who has grown up to a life of crime. Not concerned with the young girl she was, he loves the woman she is.

In one respect *Try It Again*, set in an English country house, is Priestley's most significant short play. Despite the stilted dialogue reminiscent of his early comedies of manners, *Try It Again* contains Priestley's credo as dramatist. A heated argument between a man, his wife, his mistress, and his mother is interrupted by a foreign producer-director who forces them to try their scene again. Kramer, the intruder, has always believed that "in work or in life . . . nothing good can be founded on lies, that real creation and happiness depend on truth."[7] He avoids a possibly tragic denouement by transforming a melodramatic situation into a more psychologically convincing one by "tidying up the scene . . . making it a bit more civilized. . . . And truthful" (117). Eventually the mother confronts the destructive implications of her possessive tendencies, while the mistress goes off with Kramer, leaving the married couple, who still love one another, to reshape their lives. According to Hugh Miller, in *Try It Again* "Priestley's craft recalls his notable *Dangerous Corner*,"[8] but the play does not depend on a loop in time despite Kramer's superficial resemblance to Dr. Görtler of *I Have Been Here Before*. Instead, it is a small-scale inversion of Pirandello's metadrama, *Six Characters in Search of an Author* (1921), as the director imposes truth and order on the chaos of the characters' own making.

II   Mr. Kettle and Mrs. Moon

Of *Mr. Kettle and Mrs. Moon*, a full-length comedy of a bank manager who discovers that such simple pleasure as beating drums is preferable to life in a teller's cage, David Hughes comments: "This latest exponent of the importance of never falling victim to a routine of dry half-conscious hours and flabby relationships is saved only by the superficial boyishness of its humour; beneath the surface one detects a cynicism, a decision to resuscitate an old and well-tried way of making people roll in the aisles."[9] The critic suggests that Priestley is looking backward, repeating himself, yet in a sense the mildly amusing farce about a rebellion against stifling middle-class values demonstrates that the writer is still in tune with his time. If in the case of *Mr. Kettle and Mrs. Moon* the frame in which he attempts to dramatize sound ideas and firm convictions is too slight to support them, his attitude is not far removed from that of much younger dramatists like John Osborne and Arnold Wesker, who would soon sound their angry voices in decrying the sterility of twentieth-century life. It is that anger, however, which was to produce the theatrical climate in which Priestley would no longer feel comfortable. He could not excoriate an audience, but he could still attempt to awaken them, to arouse their thought as he entertained them, and he continued to aim his work at the mass audience of the commercial theater rather than the specialized audience of a coterie theater far removed from London's West End. Significantly, Tony Richardson, who would be instrumental a few months later in initiating a new theatrical wave with his production of John Osborne's *Look Back in Anger* at the Royal Court Theatre in 1956, directed the London production of *Mr. Kettle and Mrs. Moon* at the Duchess Theatre in 1955. It was not the play's easy laughter to which the young director was responding, but its serious commentary on a value system which was turning contemporary living into joyless existence.

George Kettle begins a wet Monday by donning his drab business suit. Instead of going to the bank, however, he buys a child's shooting game and a drumstick. Returning home and changing his clothes, he spends the morning playing with his toys, an action which bewilders the police superintendent and infuriates one of his clients, but delights another, Mrs. Delia Moon, who, like George, has begun to wonder if life holds nothing more than "the factories and the smoke and the fog and the dirt and the dingy streets and the dreary little shops" of the Midlands town of Brickmill.[10] Both Delia and George, however, eventually get to the root of the problem. It is not the town that is ultimately stultifying; it is the people there who live "by turning into haters of a full warm existence, into large grey rats just gnawing away at the good life" (295). Superintendent Street soon demonstrates the truth of the thesis when he reveals himself to be one of "the grey rats," close kin to the "Grey Ones" of Priestley's short story, when he explains why he has taken an interest in a case which hardly comes under his jurisdiction: "When I left him here this morning—all free and easy, having actually enjoyed playing a kid's game with him, and him not caring tuppence—the thought of him suddenly put my back up. I'd got to get back to my work. And he ought to get back to his. Why, where would we all be if . . . ?" (303). By the end of the play, George and Delia go off in search of the answer to Street's unfinished question.

Stock characters can frequently save an author and his audience from turgid, time-consuming exposition. Priestley knows that stereotypes offer instant recognition and enable the dramatist to get on with his play, and he has often exploited their possibilities in order to give his more fully developed characters greater credence. Uncharacteristically, in *Mr. Kettle and Mrs. Moon* Priestley neglects to individualize any of his pawns. The pleasant eponymous characters are actually as colorless as their adversaries, all of whom blur into a monotonous gray. The one character whom Priestley has not employed before is an ear, nose and throat man who has just qualified as a psychiatrist. While his inane professional jargon is the source of much of the humor of the third act, he is merely a pale copy of the meddling alienist incisively caricatured by Pirandello in *Enrico IV* (1922).

By being too good-natured a comedy—Priestley has called it a play of "cheerful anarchy"[11]—*Mr. Kettle and Mrs. Moon* defeats its author's intent. Osborne and Wesker demand self-recognition from their viewers, but Priestley jollies his to the point where the audience laughs at "the grey ones" without an awareness that they are themselves implicated in the satire. The play is too predictable, making no demands on the audience as invention lags. The opening exchange between George and his char tells it all:

MRS. TWIGG: . . . Mr. Kettle? What's the matter? Have you been taken bad?

KETTLE: No, I've been taken good.   (250)

Neither the audience nor the characters need exert themselves unduly from that point on.

III   The Glass Cage

The performance of *The Glass Cage* at the Picadilly Theatre on April 26, 1957, was to be the last London premiere of a Priestley play. Six years later he would enjoy the success of a collaborative effort with Iris Murdoch, *A Severed Head*, but the play based on her novel was more Murdoch than Priestley. *The Glass Cage*, too, seems to be the work of another hand. It is a play about people who have more hate in their hearts than love, and Priestley is at a loss to delineate characters whose feelings are so foreign to his own.

Three young Canadians have been brought up by their part-Indian mother to hate the relatives who may have swindled their father. Revenge has been the driving force of their wasted lives.

Only after recognizing that their resentment and envy have locked them within a glass cage are they able to free themselves to explore the world beyond the walls. Their movement from hatred to love, however, is clouded in a confused melodrama in which the author's own sympathies shift from scene to scene. Uncharacteristically, the play consists of one shrill confrontation after another, all in the stilted language of the following scene in which one character shouts and bullies another to make the point that life must be more than shouting and bullying:

DAVID *(angrily)*: Don't talk to me like that. . .

JEAN: . . . And don't talk to her like that. . . . Why don't you stop worrying about that bad-tempered old Israelite you call God—and try to understand your own daughter?

DAVID *(angrily)*: Any more of that blasphemous talk—and you leave this house tonight. . . . Even if *you* don't know what's sacred. . .

JEAN *(cutting in fiercely)*: I *do* know what's sacred. . . . And what's sacred isn't somebody's idea about who made the universe—what do *we* know about the universe? . . . None of that guesswork stuff is sacred—only people—life. And the least we can do is try and understand it—and love it—and not just shout at it and bully it.[12]

Written for a Canadian theatrical family, the play is set in Toronto (where it was first presented) in 1906, but the time of the action seems arbitrary. *Eden End* and *An Inspector Calls* gain an ironic dimension by being set in 1912, before the start of World War I. *The Glass Cage,* on the other hand, has only some tired platitudes to offer a contemporary audience. Perhaps Priestley removes it a half-century in time in order to introduce some outdated attitudes on which the play's unconvincing action depends. *The Glass Cage* is transparent enough to reveal that Priestley's heart is no longer in his work for the theater.

IV *Unpublished Plays for Stage and Television*

Since World War II only two Priestley plays, *The Linden Tree* and *Mr. Kettle and Mrs. Moon,* had enjoyed substantial runs. He had had high hopes for several others, especially *An Inspector Calls, Ever Since Paradise,* and *Home is Tomorrow,* only to have them dashed the morning after they opened when he read the reviews of critics who seemed to wilfully misunderstand his intent, even the mood of his plays. Yet *An Inspector Calls* had been hailed abroad, and provincial audiences had responded well to *Ever Since Paradise* and *Home is Tomorrow* before the plays were brought to London. The alarming fact was that it was no longer economically sound to nurse a play along, to let it find its audience despite poor notices. In the 1930's he had transformed *Dangerous Corner* from an instant failure into a highly profitable success by ignoring the critics and keeping the play running; but by the 1950's the theater was more a luxury than ever. People needed the assurance of the critics before investing their funds on an untried evening's entertainment. This was especially true in the case of serious plays, and as far as Priestley was concerned, the gentlemen of the press were shirking their responsibility: "They have shown themselves to be increasingly suspicious of and hostile to any change and experiment in either the form or content of the drama. Time after time, when attempting something new, I have found that the opposition came not from managers, producers, actors or audiences but from the critics, the very persons who ought to be delighted to welcome a little originality and experiment in a Theatre cluttered up with clichés."[13]

Aside from the critics, a further stumbling block for Priestley was the ever-changing shape and sound of the language, to which, as a man of letters, he is obviously sensitive.[14] This led the dramatist to consider himself out of touch with the younger audience, a concern less limiting for him as novelist and essayist. Nonetheless, Priestley has attempted yet another medium. In 1951, five months before it was staged in Cardiff, *Treasure on Pelican* was in fact first presented on television. Just as he had formerly written scripts for films, he has also tried his hand at scripts originally intended for television, but has not permitted their publication.

The first of these was *Now Let Him Go* in 1957, "a frontal assault on petty authorities," according to *The Times*,[15] about an artist dying in a railway hotel, loosely based on an episode in the life of Tolstoy and transplanted to a dreary town in northern England. A more ambitious television play was *Doomsday for Dyson* in 1958, containing violent dream sequences in the style of *Johnson Over Jordan* in which Dyson, an Everyman figure, dies in a nuclear holocaust, wanders through a devastated London where he finds politicians carrying on business as usual, and is arraigned before a tribunal for his own responsibility for the disaster. In addition several of his earlier plays received television productions, among them *Laburnum Grove* and *Mr. Kettle and Mrs. Moon* in 1957, *Home is Tomorrow*—retitled *The Fortrose Incident*—in 1959, and *The Linden Tree* in 1974 in honor of his eightieth birthday.

Priestley has all the while continued to write the occasional play for the stage. Sixteen months before the production of *The Glass Cage*, he authorized a performance of *Take the Fool Away* in Vienna in 1956. Described by Ivor Brown as the "picture of a clown at large and bewildered in a highly mechanized and authoritarian society,"[16] the play, enthusiastically received at its premiere, has neither been published nor produced in London, but was presented in Nottingham in 1959. Another unpublished play written in 1955, *The Golden Entry*, has never reached the stage. Instead, the ironic comedy about an art dealer who goes bankrupt in an age in which "atom bombs at fifty million pounds a time" are preferred to works of art,[17] was broadcast in a radio adaptation. In 1963 *The Pavilion of Masks*, a high comedy, was staged in Bristol. Instead of attempting a London production, however, Priestley transformed the work into a Graustarkian novella. Together with another comic short novel first conceived in dramatic form, it was published in 1975 in *The Carfitt Crisis and Two Other Stories*. Deserted by the theater audience, Priestley finds he can still rely on the loyalty of older readers of his novels.

V   A Severed Head

Priestley might not have returned to the West End theater had not his friend Iris Murdoch encountered difficulty in adapting her acclaimed 1961 novel, *A Severed Head*, to the stage. When her first version proved unwieldy, she sought Priestley's advice. It seemed to the experienced dramatist that Murdoch's adaptation would require a running time of twenty-four hours and a theater the size of the Albert Hall![18] As neither of these struck him as portents of success, Priestley suggested that they collaborate on a practical, playable version. After a trial run in Bristol, their play opened in London in 1963 to the enthusiastic response of the public as well as the unpredictable critics.

Priestley believes that success was achieved by their coarsening of the novel, which meant that the play is simpler to follow, therefore easier to understand. His thoughts on the subject, on the differences between novels and plays, reveal a professional craftsman's approach to the problems of form.[19] A play, he insists, must be coarse in order to evoke a communal response from perhaps a thousand spectators who must sit together for two or three hours. The novelist, who gently leads one reader through his work, does not have the same problem. The dramatist must insure a continuing, in fact a growing interest, by providing theatrical effects which become stronger as the play unfolds. A third act must have even stronger effects than a second act for the obvious reason that the audience has been seated a long time.

Murdoch's intricately patterned novel of the musical-chairs love affairs of three men and three women is closely linked with Oriental mythology. Honor Klein, a Cambridge anthropologist, moves in and out of the lives of her psychoanalyst half-brother, Palmer Anderson; his mistress and occasional patient, Antonia Lynch-Gibbon; the mistress's wine-merchant husband, Martin; the husband's sculptor-brother, Alexander; and the young university lecturer Georgie, who becomes in turn the mistress of each of the men. The lightness of their loving, their uncommitted sexual encounters, are contrasted with the strong and passionate relationship which evolves between the merchant and the anthropologist. The theme of incestuous love, as old as the Japanese myths which Martin traces in his reading of *The Golden Bough*, is emphasized in each relationship as each character plays the role of surrogate father, mother, son, or daughter according to the coupling of the moment. Only Honor, like the severed head on whose tongue primitive tribes placed pieces of gold in exchange for the utterance of prophecies, enables Martin to come to terms with the knowledge of self so that the two can enter into an interpersonal relationship which stands apart from the frivolous game of *la ronde* which the others play. The novel's patterning and the myths on which it is based are deemphasized in the play so that *A Severed Head* on stage becomes more sharply a comedy of manners and less insistently a puzzler of the intellect.

In language, characterization, and construction, the adaptors, with the more experienced Priestley undoubtedly leading the way, had to simplify, to provide shortcuts, to consider the mechanics of stage setting, to provide not only highly charged moments of action but even witty lines to evoke greater laughter. Such Murdoch epigrams as "One doesn't have to get anywhere in a marriage—it's not a public conveyance," remain,[20] but the adaptors have added such exchanges as the following:

PALMER: . . . Hers [her life] has been standing still for too long—she is due to move on.
MARTIN: You talk as if you were a policeman and she was a lorry— (25)

The construction of the play is tighter than that of the novel as the adaptation makes use of fewer locales in building from moment to moment. The first appearance of Honor occurs earlier as she unexpectedly walks into Palmer's house to discover Antonia holding in her arms both her husband, Martin, and her lover, Palmer, kissing each in turn. The three spring apart, as Martin, leaving, joins together the hands of Palmer, Antonia, and Honor. Thus two of the play's many triangles are quickly rendered into visual patterns. The scene of the shifting triangles is theatrically effective, but the subtlety with which the smaller patterns merge to form a greater one in the novel is lost on stage.

Perhaps the clearest example of the heightening which the stage demands is the scene in which Honor dramatically severs the head of a bust with a Samurai sword. In the novel she merely uses the sword to cut in two some linen table napkins. The change provides the play with its most vivid moment and also apparently solves for most of the audience the vexing riddle of the title, but Honor remains an enigma. Her action is in itself too startling to underscore the notion of separation of head and body as the basis of self-knowledge. It does, however, take an audience's breath away.

As a play, *A Severed Head*, for all its changes, remains a map of Murdoch country, peopled by sophisticates involved in sexual intrigue. This is by no means the usual Priestley landscape, but he has left his mark on the work, for it is the dramatist's craft which holds the scenes together. It is craft which coarsens the work, yet without that craft *A Severed Head* would be unplayable. It is exemplified by the scarf of the opening scene which causes a momentary rift between Martin and Georgie in her rooms near Covent Garden and is later picked up and commented on by Honor in Martin's house in Hertford Square. That scarf, not to be found in the Murdoch novel, is unmistakably

Priestley's, but it is as essential to the dramatization of *A Severed Head,* and as coarse, as is the strawberry handkerchief in *Othello.*[21]

CHAPTER 19

Conclusion

IN a letter acknowledging a gift copy of *Adam in Moonshine,*
Priestley's first novel, Edmund Gosse seemed to be offering
the author some veiled advice as early as 1927: "I have enjoyed
your excursion into the world of moonshine, and must tell you
so. . . . Nevertheless I hope you will not abandon criticism, a
field in which your successes are preeminent."[1] Five years later,
writing to congratulate Priestley on the success of *Dangerous
Corner,* his first play, Michael Arlen adopted a curiously
ambiguous tone: "It's very nice to think of you barging into the
theatre" (WL, 21). While Priestley has not commented
specifically on these letters, he surely understands what they
were attempting to communicate. He has expressed it himself:
"In this age . . . versatility does not enlarge a writer's reputation
but reduces it";[2] and in *Instead of the Trees,* which he subtitles *A
Final Chapter of Autobiography,* he writes, "For years I have
been standing in my own better light, overshadowing my better
self."[3]

In a sense contradicting what he wrote earlier in *Margin
Released,* Priestley now makes it clear that he takes no pride in
being called, no matter how kindly, a man of letters—"a term
applied . . . to any number of book-sodden dreary old hacks. It
suggests at once somebody who is boring and out-of-date and can
be ignored by eager young readers. . . . I must . . . stand up
here and shout, *I am not that kind of man at all*" (IT, 25). He has
indeed produced distinguished work in a wide variety of literary
genres, and some of his efforts are of course more successful than
others. The truth of the matter is that all creative artists must
ultimately be evaluated on the basis of their best work. This is as
true of Shakespeare as it is of Priestley. And to have written
Angel Pavement, Bright Day, Eden End, Time and the Conways,

and *The Linden Tree* is an accomplishment of which any writer would be proud.

From his earliest appearance in the literary world, Priestley has demonstrated an intelligent and sensitive awareness of both the function of literature and the forces at work in an ever-confusing world. In his fiction he belongs squarely to the comic tradition exemplified by Fielding and Sterne, philosophically tempered by the inspirations of the nineteenth-century Romantics. In his drama, deriving first from Ibsen and Chekhov, he is at last the innovator, manipulating and manipulated by Time. For the reader who feels that his writing provides little more than entertainment, Priestley has contempt, believing that such a reader is a "fit subject for comedy himself" (IT, 27). His best works are indeed those that show man to himself while revealing the texture of the life that goes on about him. The favorite of all his novels is *The Image Men,* in which his modern Quixotes, Cosmo Saltana and Owen Tuby, are "parts of myself suitably enlarged" (IT, 37). If *The Image Men,* a work of his later years, does not exhibit quite the same artistic polish evidenced by *Bright Day,* an earlier work about a youthful time akin to his own, it is no less convincing a portrayal of the forces inhibiting the individual spirit.

And Priestley has not been ignored by other writers. Whereas T. S. Eliot and Iris Murdoch both sought his advice as an accomplished dramatist (WL, 25), John Osborne belligerently and erroneously reacted to him as a stuffy member of the Establishment in *Look Back in Anger,* failing to understand that in many ways Priestley anticipated the "anger" which Osborne's own drama exemplifies. Praising Priestley in *The Novel Now,* Anthony Burgess, on the other hand, cautioned readers against overlooking the very elements that make Priestley's work modern. A glance at the numerous editions of his novels and the frequent productions of his plays indicates the respect in which he is held by his public, an esteem to which the celebrations in honor of his eightieth birthday in 1974—the dinners, the exhibitions, the broadcasts, the reprints, and the revivals—further testify. Indeed, Priestley is one of England's national treasures, perhaps third in line behind the Queen and champion jockey Lester Piggott!

In both his novels and plays of the 1930's Priestley considered the State a vehicle which fell short of its potential. In the 1970's he found that he had not much changed his mind about the inhibiting aspects of a bureaucratic machinery that threatened the liberty of its subjects with sound ideas but questionable practices. He writes, "The State, in my book, was always a big clumsy bully. . . . And if . . . the very notion of a liberal freedom-loving democracy is shrinking and in peril, then I can hardly be blamed if I alternate . . . between a general grumpiness and downright anger" (IT, 35). All of his works, from whatever decade, reveal a thoroughgoing awareness that ultimately fallible man, not an impersonal State, has the power to remedy his situation. If man has not yet accepted his responsibility, it is not for want of Priestley's urging, for there glows through all his novels and plays a romantic yearning for a world as it might, could, and should be. In recent years Priestley's vision has darkened—but only slightly. Once the cautious optimist, he now styles himself "a life-enhancing pessimist" (IT, 69).

One word more: Priestley's style. It is direct, forceful—even heroic. Priestley uses language lovingly to convey information, feeling, thought. There is never any attempt to confuse a reader or theatergoer into believing that there is more to the statement than the statement says despite the occasionally poetic resonance. His intentions are clear, for to be understood is, for Priestley, to engage in the most rewarding skill of all—to live vitally in community. And if his reputation has suffered as a result of his versatility, Priestley is unconcerned. He has done what he has had to do, and his is the credo of the professional writer: "I have tried to do my best for over half a century, often keeping my impatience quiet by turning from one form to another, quite different. We have to do what we can with ourselves, rather like a man who has inherited a circus. And after all the circus might make some good friends."[4]

Notes and References

With the exception of *The Plays of J. B. Priestley* (London, 1948–50), three volumes, identified throughout these notes as *Plays*, full bibliographical information is supplied for each novel and play when it is first mentioned in an extensive discussion. Subsequent references to each novel and play are identified parenthetically in the text.

Chapter One

1. *Margin Released* (New York, 1962), p. 9; subsequently identified parenthetically as MR.
2. *The Times,* July 10, 1970, p. 10.
3. "On Education," *Essays of Five Decades,* ed., Susan Cooper (Boston, 1968), p. 213.
4. "Touch of Frost," *Outcries and Asides* (London, 1974), p. 113.
5. *Instead of the Trees* (London, 1977), p. 21.
6. Frank Swinnerton, *The Georgian Literary Scene* (London, 1950), p. 372.
7. *A Visit to New Zealand* (London, 1974), p. 139.
8. *Theatre Outlook* (London, 1974), p. 34.
9. Quoted in *New York Times,* April 6, 1974, p. 2.
10. Ibid.
11. "Faint Carpet Figure," *Outcries and Asides,* p. 101.
12. Susan Cooper, *J. B. Priestley: Portrait of an Author* (London, 1970), p. 10.
13. *Midnight on The Desert* (London, 1937), p. 245; subsequently identified parenthetically as MD.
14. *Man and Time* (London, 1964), p. 76; subsequently identified parenthetically as MT.
15. J. W. Dunne, *An Experiment with Time* (London, 1927), p. 44.
16. Ibid.
17. In *Over the Long High Wall* (London, 1972), p. 77, Priestley claims that he was finally successful in getting Dunne "to abandon the 'infinite regress' of Times and Observers that damaged his Serialism" just before World War II.
18. P. D. Ouspensky, *A New Model of the Universe* (London, 1938), pp. 425–26.
19. "A Braggy?" *Outcries and Asides,* p. 37.
20. *New York Times,* April 6, 1974, p. 2.

21. "A Wrong View of Literature," *Outcries and Asides*, pp. 88-89.
22. *Instead of the Trees*, pp. 25-26.

Chapter Two

1. Colin Wilson, "A Hell of a Talent," *Books and Bookmen*, XXI (January 1975), 26.
2. Anthony Burgess, *The Novel Now: A Guide to Contemporary Fiction* (New York, 1967), p. 102.
3. Ivor Brown, *J. B. Priestley, Writers and Their Work* series, No. 84 (London, 1964), p. 38.
4. Wilson, p. 26.
5. *Midnight on the Desert* (London, 1937), pp. 9-10; subsequent references are included parenthetically in the text.
6. *Margin Released* (New York, 1962), p. 194.
7. William Wordsworth, "Preface," *Lyrical Ballads*, in *The Prose Works of William Wordsworth*, ed. W. J. B. Owen and Jane Worthington Smyser, three volumes (Oxford, 1974), 1850 version, p. 140.
8. *Saturn Over the Water* (London, 1961), p. 37.

Chapter Three

1. *Margin Released* (New York, 1962), pp. 180-81; subsequently identified parenthetically as MR.
2. Reprint of original review, *Times Literary Supplement*, January 28, 1977, p. 2.
3. *Adam in Moonshine*, in *Four-in-Hand* (London, 1934), pp. 154-55.
4. *Times Literary Supplement*, January 28, 1977, p. 2.
5. *Benighted* (London, 1927), p. 218.
6. Susan Cooper, *J. B. Priestley: Portrait of an Author* (London, 1970), p. 49.
7. *Angel Pavement* (New York, 1930), p. 2.

Chapter Four

1. *Margin Released* (New York, 1962), p. 191; subsequent references are included parenthetically.
2. Ivor Brown, *J. B. Priestley, Writers and Their Work* series, No. 84 (London, 1964), p. 19.
3. *Faraway* (New York, 1932), p. 257.
4. David Hughes, *J. B. Priestley: An Informal Study of his Work* (London, 1958), p. 117.

5. *Midnight on The Desert* (London, 1937), pp. 49–50.
6. *They Walk in the City* (New York, 1936), p. 391.
7. *Rain Upon Godshill* (London, 1939), p. 136; subsequent references are included parenthetically.
8. *The Doomsday Men* (London, 1938), p. 251.

Chapter Five

1. David Hughes, *J. B. Priestley: An Informal Study of his Work* (London, 1958), pp. 167–68.
2. *Midnight on The Desert* (London, 1937), pp. 141–42; subsequently identified parenthetically as MD.
3. *Let the People Sing* (New York, 1939), p. 323.
4. Hughes, p. 170.
5. *Black-Out in Gretley* (New York, 1942), pp. 263–64.
6. *Margin Released* (New York, 1962), p. 193; subsequently identified parenthetically as MR.
7. *Daylight on Saturday* (New York, 1943), pp. 209–10.
8. *Three Men in New Suits* (New York, 1945), p. 216.
9. Hughes, p. 182.
10. Susan Cooper, *J. B. Priestley: Portrait of an Author* (London, 1970), p. 29.
11. Ivor Brown, *J. B. Priestley, Writers and Their Work* series, No. 84 (London, 1964), p. 20.
12. *Bright Day* (New York, 1946), p. 166.

Chapter Six

1. *Jenny Villiers* (New York, 1947), p. 157.
2. Ivor Brown's British Council pamphlet in effect lists the novel with Priestley's drama in the bibliography.
3. *New York Herald Tribune,* January 16, 1938.
4. *Margin Released* (New York, 1962), pp. 94–95.
5. David Hughes, *J. B. Priestley: An Informal Study of his Work* (London, 1958), p. 117.
6. *Festival* (New York, 1951), pp. 183–84. The novel was originally published as *Festival at Farbridge;* see bibliography.
7. *Low Notes on a High Level* (New York, 1954), p. 137.
8. *The Magicians* (New York, 1954), p. 121.

Chapter Seven

1. Anthony Burgess, *The Novel Now: A Guide to Contemporary Fiction* (New York, 1967), p. 102.
2. *Saturn Over the Water* (London, 1961), p. 173.

3. *The Shapes of Sleep* (New York, 1962), p. 181.

4. *Salt is Leaving* (London, 1966), p. 220.

5. *The Thirty-First of June* (New York, 1962), p. 53.

6. *Lost Empires* (Boston, 1965), p. 349.

7. *It's an Old Country* (London, 1967), p. 230.

8. "My Two Heroes," *Outcries and Asides* (London, 1974), pp. 64–65.

9. Susan Cooper, *J. B. Priestley: Portrait of an Author* (London, 1970), pp. 195–96.

10. Cooper, p. 194.

11. Anthony Burgess, "Having the Last Word," *The Observer Review*, March 20, 1977.

12. *Out of Town, The Image Men* (Harmondsworth, Middlesex, 1968), p. 21.

13. J. B. Priestley and Jacquetta Hawkes, *Journey Down a Rainbow* (Harmondsworth, Middlesex, 1969), p. 50.

Chapter Eight

1. *Snoggle* (London, 1971), p. 138.

2. *Found, Lost, Found,* or *The English Way of Life* (London, 1976), pp. 131–32.

3. *The Other Place and Other Stories of the Same Sort* (New York, 1971), p. 12.

4. "Dedicatory Letter," *The Carfitt Crisis and Two Other Stories* (London, 1975), p. vii.

Chapter Nine

1. *An Inspector Calls* (London, 1947), p. vi.

2. *Thoughts in the Wilderness* (New York, 1957), p. 182; subsequently identified parenthetically as TW.

3. Gareth Lloyd Evans, *J. B. Priestley—The Dramatist* (London, 1964), p. 189.

4. *Literature and Western Man* (New York, 1960), p. 284.

5. *The Art of the Dramatist* (London, 1957), pp. 8–9; subsequently identified parenthetically as AD.

6. *Summer Day's Dream,* in *Plays* (London, 1950), III, 422.

7. John Osborne, *Look Back in Anger* (New York, 1971), pp. 8–9, 82.

8. Evans, pp. 117–18.

9. *Letters of J. M. Barrie,* ed. Viola Meynell (New York, 1947), pp. 291–92.

Chapter Ten

1. Morton Eustis, "On Time and the Theatre: Priestley Talks about Playwriting," *Theatre Arts Monthly*, XXII, no. 1 (January, 1938), p. 45.

2. *Margin Released* (New York, 1962), p. 210; subsequently identified parenthetically as MR.

3. James Agate, *Ego 9* (London, 1948), p. 54.

4. Quoted in *New York Times*, November 20, 1932, Section 9, p. 2.

5. *The Art of the Dramatist* (London, 1957), pp. 84–85; J. B. Priestley and Edward Knoblock, *The Good Companions* (London, 1935), p. 85.

6. Agate, p. 54.

7. *Three Plays and a Preface* (New York, 1935), p. viii.

8. *Plays* (London, 1948), I, viii.

9. Ibid., p. vii.

10. *Dangerous Corner*, in *Plays*, I, 5.

11. *New York Times*, November 20, 1932.

12. Ruth Holland and J. B. Priestley, *Dangerous Corner* (New York, 1933), pp. vi–vii. According to Priestley, the novel uses "the version of the beginning and end of the play I wrote for the American production, in which the wireless play is eliminated." In the Broadway production, but not in the novelization, the surname Caplan, perhaps considered too Jewish, was changed to Chatfield.

13. Gareth Lloyd Evans, *J. B. Priestley—The Dramatist* (London, 1964), p. 82.

14. Tyrone Guthrie, *A Life in the Theatre* (London, 1960), p. 58.

15. Evans, p. 81.

16. *New York Times*, November 20, 1932.

Chapter Eleven

1. *Plays* (London, 1949), II, vii.

2. *English Humour* (London, 1976), p. 25.

3. *The Roundabout*, in *Four-in-Hand* (London, 1934), p. 335.

4. *Plays,* II, viii–ix.

5. *Laburnum Grove*, in *Plays*, II, 37.

6. Gareth Lloyd Evans, *J. B. Priestley—The Dramatist* (London, 1964), p. 166.

7. *Duet in Floodlight* (London, 1935), pp. 4–5.

8. *Plays*, II, x.

9. *Bees on the Boat Deck*, in *Plays*, II, 77.

10. George Billam and J. B. Priestley, *Spring Tide* (New York, 1936), p. 28.

11. *Rain Upon Godshill* (London, 1939), p. 31.

Chapter Twelve

1. *Plays* (London, 1950), III, x.
2. *Eden End,* in *Plays* (London, 1948), I, 122.
3. *Plays,* I, viii.
4. *Anton Chekhov* (London, 1970), p. 1.
5. *Three Plays and a Preface* (New York, 1935), p. xii.
6. *Nation,* CLVIII (February 5, 1944), 158.
7. *Three Plays and a Preface,* p. x.
8. Gareth Lloyd Evans, *J. B. Priestley—The Dramatist* (London, 1964), pp. 84-86.
9. *Anton Chekhov,* p. 72.
10. E. R. Wood, "Introduction" to J. B. Priestley, *Eden End* (London, 1974), p. ix; *Anton Chekhov,* p. 81.
11. *Anton Chekhov,* p. 82.
12. *Margin Released* (New York, 1962), p. 209; *Encore: The Sunday Times Book* (London, 1962), p. 95; quoted in Susan Cooper, *J. B. Priestley: Portrait of an Author* (London, 1970), p. 103.
13. *Particular Pleasures* (London, 1975), p. 139.
14. *Three Plays and a Preface,* pp. xii-xiii.
15. *Cornelius,* in *Plays,* III, 34.

Chapter Thirteen

1. *Man and Time* (London, 1964), p. 12.
2. *Rain Upon Godshill* (London, 1939), p. 42; subsequently identified parenthetically as RG.
3. *Time and the Conways,* in *Plays* (London, 1948), I, 136.
4. "Author's Note," *Three Time Plays* (London, 1947), p. viii.
5. *Plays,* I, ix.
6. *Margin Released* (New York, 1962), p. 207.
7. *Three Time Plays,* p. viii.
8. *Plays,* I, ix.
9. *I Have Been Here Before,* in *Plays,* I, 205.
10. As he wrote it, Priestley considered *Time and the Conways* "a dramatic expression of a philosophy" as opposed to the manipulation of time for theatrical effect in such plays as his own *Dangerous Corner,* Balderston's *Berkeley Square,* and Barrie's *Dear Brutus* (*New York Herald Tribune,* January 16, 1938). An American work which depends upon the contrivance of a time machine, Maxwell Anderson's *The Star-Wagon,* produced in New York in 1937 shortly after *I Have Been Here Before* opened in London, is another which could be added to the category which Priestley in *Man and Time,* p. 134, terms "the might-have-been plays."
11. *People at Sea,* in *Plays* (London, 1950), III, 78-79.

12. *Particular Pleasures* (London, 1975), pp. 126, 140; *The Long Mirror* (London, 1947).

13. *Particular Pleasures,* p. 140.

14. Rex Pogson, *J. B. Priestley and the Theatre* (Clevedon, Somerset, 1947), pp. 34, 37.

15. *The Times,* August 26, 1968, p. 15; August 22, 1974, p. 14.

Chapter Fourteen

1. *Plays* (London, 1949), II, viii.

2. *Mystery at Greenfingers* (London, 1938).

3. *Rain Upon Godshill* (London, 1939), p. 184.

4. *When We Are Married,* in *Plays,* II, 172.

5. Gareth Lloyd Evans, *J. B. Priestley—The Dramatist* (London, 1964), pp. 167, 158.

6. *Rain Upon Godshill,* p. 184.

7. *The Golden Fleece,* in *Plays,* II, 366.

8. *Midnight on the Desert* (London, 1937), pp. 137–38.

9. Priestley also appeared as himself in *Battle for Music,* a 1944 film written by Leigh Clowes about the London Philharmonic Orchestra's fight for survival during the blitz.

10. *The Rose and Crown* (London, 1947), p. 29.

11. *Ever Since Paradise,* in *Plays,* II, 453–54.

12. Evans, p. 170.

13. John Willett, ed. and trans., *Brecht on Theatre: The Development of an Aesthetic* (New York, 1964), p. 37.

14. Conversation with J. B. Priestley, Alveston, Warwickshire, August 13, 1972.

Chapter Fifteen

1. *Rain Upon Godshill* (London, 1939), p. 117; subsequently identified parenthetically as RG.

2. Quoted in Gareth Lloyd Evans, *J. B. Priestley—The Dramatist* (London, 1964), pp. 136–37.

3. *Plays* (London, 1948), I, ix.

4. David Hughes, *J. B. Priestley: An Informal Study of his Work* (London, 1958), pp. 157–58.

5. Evans, p. 140.

6. *Music at Night,* in *Plays,* I, 346.

7. *Four Plays* (New York, 1944), pp. v–vi.

8. *Johnson Over Jordan* (London, 1939), p. 135; subsequent references to this edition are identified parenthetically as JOJ.

9. James Agate, *Ego 8* (London, 1946), p. 82.

10. *Johnson Over Jordan,* in *Plays,* 277–78.

11. Agate, pp. 78, 82.

12. Morton Eustis, "On Time and the Theatre: Priestley Talks about Playwriting," *Theatre Arts Monthly*, XXII: 1 (January 1938), 54.

13. Priestley, in a letter to Agate, quoted in *Ego 8*, p. 94.

14. Eustis, p. 54.

15. *Margin Released* (New York, 1962), p. 207.

16. Jacquetta Hawkes and J. B. Priestley, *Dragon's Mouth* (New York, 1952), p. xi; subsequently identified parenthetically as DM; "Platform Piece: J. B. Priestley Discusses *Dragon's Mouth*," *Theatre*, 6: 150 (London, June 21, 1952), p. 10.

17. Ivor Brown, *J. B. Priestley, Writers and Their Work* series, No. 84 (London, 1964), pp. 32-33.

Chapter Sixteen

1. *Good Night Children*, in *Plays* (London, 1949), II, 274.

2. *Plays*, II, xi.

3. *They Came to a City*, in *Plays* (London, 1950), III, 201.

4. *Plays*, III, xi.

5. Ibid., pp. xi-xii.

6. *Desert Highway*, in *Plays*, III, 258.

7. Rex Pogson, *J. B. Priestley and the Theatre* (Clevedon, Somerset, 1947), p. 47.

8. *How Are They at Home?*, in *Plays*, II, 393.

9. *Plays*, III, xii.

10. *An Inspector Calls* (London, 1947), pp. vi-vii.

11. Ibid.

12. *An Inspector Calls*, in *Plays*, III, 269; subsequent references are to this edition.

Chapter Seventeen

1. *Rain Upon Godshill* (London, 1939), pp. 132-34.

2. E. R. Wood, "Introduction" to J. B. Priestley, *The Linden Tree* (London, 1976), p. xiii.

3. *Plays* (London, 1948), I, x.

4. Ibid.

5. *The Linden Tree*, in *Plays*, I, 450; subsequent references are to this edition.

6. Susan Cooper, *J. B. Priestley: Portrait of an Author* (London, 1970), p. 147.

7. Wood, p. xi.

8. *Margin Released* (New York, 1962), p. 205.

9. *Home Is Tomorrow*, in *Plays* (London, 1950), III, 389.

10. Gareth Lloyd Evans, *J. B. Priestley—The Dramatist* (London, 1964), p. 203.

11. *Summer Day's Dream,* in *Plays,* III, 422.

12. *The Olympians* (London, 1949), p. 45.

13. *Bright Shadow* (London, 1950), pp. 30–31. The play was presented in a small theater in the London suburb of Palmers Green a week after its first performance in Oldham.

14. Harold Clayton, "Note to Producers," in J. B. Priestley, *Treasure on Pelican* (London, 1953), p. 6. The play was televised in September 1951, before its first stage performance in Cardiff in February 1952.

15. *Treasure on Pelican,* p. 39.

Chapter Eighteen

1. *Theatre Outlook* (London, 1947), pp. 69–70.

2. Conversation with J. B. Priestley, Alveston, Warwickshire, August 13, 1972.

3. *The High Toby* (Harmondsworth, Middlesex, 1948).

4. *Private Rooms* (London, 1953), p. 23.

5. Donald FitzJohn, ed., "Introduction," *English One-Act Plays of Today* (London, 1962), p. viii.

6. *A Glass of Bitter* (London, 1954).

7. "Try It Again," *The Best One-Act Plays of 1952–53,* ed. Hugh Miller (London, 1954), p. 114.

8. Hugh Miller, *The Best One-Act Plays of 1952–53,* p. 5.

9. David Hughes, *J. B. Priestley: An Informal Study of his Work* (London, 1958), p. 192

10. *Mr. Kettle and Mrs. Moon,* in *When We Are Married and Other Plays* (Harmondsworth, Middlesex, 1969), p. 309. The play was first presented and published as *The Scandalous Affair of Mr. Kettle and Mrs. Moon;* see bibliography.

11. Conversation.

12. *The Glass Cage* (London, 1958), p. 54.

13. "Introduction," *Home Is Tomorrow* (London, 1949), p. ix.

14. Conversation.

15. *The Times,* September 16, 1957, p. 3.

16. Ivor Brown, *J. B. Priestley, Writers and Their Work* series, No. 84 (London, 1964), pp. 33–34.

17. Quoted in *The Times,* December 1, 1955, p. 3.

18. Conversation.

19. Ibid.

20. Iris Murdoch, *A Severed Head* (New York, 1963), p. 29; Iris Murdoch and J. B. Priestley, *A Severed Head,* in *Plays of the Sixties,* ed. J. M. Charlton (London, 1967), II, 22.

21. For an expanded discussion of the adaptation, see Albert E. Kalson, "*A Severed Head* from Novel to Play: Coarsening as the Essence of Adaptation," *Ball State University Forum* XVII: 4 (Autumn 1976), 71–74.

Chapter Nineteen

1. *A Writer's Life: J. B. Priestley: An Exhibition of Manuscripts and Books,* a catalogue, ed. Lucetta Teagarden (Austin, Texas, 1963), p. 13; subsequently identified parenthetically as WL.

2. "Danger of Versatility," *Outcries and Asides* (London, 1974), p. 190.

3. *Instead of the Trees* (London, 1977), p. 25; subsequently identified parenthetically as IT.

4. "Envoi," *Outcries and Asides,* p. 197.

Selected Bibliography

Compiled by Robert Petersen

PRIMARY SOURCES

Listed below are J. B. Priestley's published books. Each entry provides initially the facts of the first British publication, while information concerning the first American publication is indicated in parentheses. This task is complicated by Mr. Priestley's popularity, for his novels and plays frequently have run into multiple editions within a year or two of their initial publication. In addition, Heinemann initiated a collected edition in 1931 and has maintained it sporadically for the past forty years.

1. Fiction

Adam in Moonshine. London: Heinemann, 1927 (New York: Harper, 1927).

Benighted. London: Heinemann, 1927 (Entitled *The Old Dark House*. New York: Harper, 1928).

Farthing Hall, with Hugh Walpole. London: Macmillan, 1929 (Garden City, New York: Doubleday, Doran, 1929).

The Good Companions. London: Heinemann, 1929 (New York: Harper, 1929).

Angel Pavement. London: Heinemann, 1930 (New York: Harper, 1930).

The Town Major of Miraucourt. London: Heinemann, 1930.

Faraway. London: Heinemann, 1932 (New York: Harper, 1932).

Albert Goes Through. London: Heinemann, 1933 (New York: Harper, 1933).

I'll Tell You Everything, A Frolic, with Gerald Bullett. London: Heinemann, 1933 (New York: Macmillan, 1933).

Wonder Hero. London: Heinemann, 1933 (New York: Harper, 1933).

They Walk in the City: The Lovers in the Stone Forest. London: Heinemann, 1936 (New York: Harper, 1936).

The Doomsday Men, An Adventure. London: Heinemann, 1938 (New York: Harper, 1938).

Let the People Sing. London: Heinemann, 1939 (New York: Harper, 1940).

Black-Out in Gretley, A Story of and for Wartime. London: Heinemann, 1942 (New York: Harper, 1942).

Daylight on Saturday, A Novel About an Aircraft Factory. London: Heinemann, 1943 (New York: Harper, 1943).

Three Men in New Suits. London: Heinemann, 1945 (New York: Harper, 1945).

Bright Day. London: Heinemann, 1946 (New York: Harper, 1946).

Jenny Villiers, A Story of the Theatre. London: Heinemann, 1947 (New York: Harper, 1947).

Going Up, with Other Stories and Sketches. London: Pan Books, 1950.

Festival at Farbridge. London: Heinemann, 1951 (Entitled *Festival.* New York: Harper, 1951).

The Other Place, and Other Stories of the Same Sort. London: Heinemann, 1953 (New York: Harper, 1953).

Low Notes on a High Level, A Frolic. London: Heinemann, 1954 (New York: Harper, 1954).

The Magicians. London: Heinemann, 1954 (New York: Harper, 1954).

Saturn Over the Water. London: Heinemann, 1961 (Garden City, New York: Doubleday, 1961).

The Thirty-First of June. London: Heinemann, 1961 (Garden City, New York: Doubleday, 1962).

The Shapes of Sleep. London: Heinemann, 1962 (Garden City, New York: Doubleday, 1962).

Sir Michael and Sir George, A Tale of COSMA and DISCUS and the New Elizabethans. London: Heinemann, 1964 (Boston: Little, Brown, 1964).

Lost Empires. London: Heinemann, 1965 (Boston: Little, Brown, 1965).

Salt is Leaving. London: Pan Books Ltd., by arrangement with Heinemann, 1966 (New York: Harper and Row, 1975).

It's an Old Country. London: Heinemann, 1967 (Boston: Little, Brown, 1967).

Out of Town (Part I of *The Image Men*). London: Heinemann, 1968.

London End (Part II of *The Image Men*). London: Heinemann, 1968.

The Image Men. London: Heinemann, 1968 (Boston: Little, Brown, 1969).

Snoggle: A Story for Anybody between 9 and 90. London: Heinemann, 1971 (New York: Harcourt-Brace-Jovanovich, 1972).

The Carfitt Crisis and Two Other Stories. London: Heinemann, 1975 (New York: Stein and Day, 1976). Includes "The Carfitt Crisis," "Underground," "The Pavilion of Masks."

Found, Lost, Found, or The English Way of Life. London: Heinemann, 1976 (New York: Stein and Day, 1977).

My Three Favorite Novels. New York: Stein and Day, 1978. Includes *Angel Pavement, Bright Day, Sir Michael and Sir George.*

2. Drama

Dangerous Corner. London: Heinemann, 1932 (New York: Samuel French, 1932).

The Roundabout. London: Heinemann, 1933 (New York: Samuel French, 1933).

Laburnum Grove. London: Heinemann, 1934 (New York: Samuel French, 1935).

Eden End. London: Heinemann, 1934 (New York: Samuel French, 1935).

Duet in Floodlight. London: Heinemann, 1935.

Cornelius. London: Heinemann, 1935 (New York: Samuel French, 1936).

Three Plays and a Preface. London: Heinemann, 1935 (New York: Harper, 1935). Includes *Dangerous Corner, Eden End,* and *Cornelius.*

The Good Companions, adaptation with Edward Knoblock. London: Samuel French, 1935.

Spring Tide, written under the pseudonym Peter Goldsmith and in collaboration with George Billam. London: Heinemann, 1936 (New York: Samuel French, 1936, under own name).

Bees on the Boat Deck. London: Heinemann, 1936.

Mystery at Greenfingers. London: News-Chronicle Contest Edition, 1937. An edition by Samuel French came out later in the same year.

Time and the Conways. London: Heinemann, 1937 (New York: Harper, 1938).

I Have Been Here Before. London: Heinemann, 1937 (New York: Harper, 1938).

Two Time Plays. London: Heinemann, 1937. Includes *Time and the Conways* and *I Have Been Here Before.*

People at Sea. London: Heinemann, 1937.

When We Are Married. London: Heinemann, 1938 (New York: Samuel French, 1940).

Johnson Over Jordan, The Play, and All About It. London: Heinemann, 1939 (New York: Harper, 1939).

Three Plays. London: Heinemann, 1943. Includes *Music at Night, The Long Mirror,* and *They Came to a City.*

Desert Highway. London: William Heinemann, 1944.

Four Plays. London: Heinemann, 1944 (New York: Harper, 1944). Includes *Music at Night, The Long Mirror, They Came to a City,* and *Desert Highway.*

Three Comedies. London: Heinemann, 1945. Includes *Goodnight Children, The Golden Fleece,* and *How Are They at Home?*

An Inspector Calls. London: Heinemann, 1947.

The Rose and Crown: A Morality Play. London: Samuel French, 1947.

Three Time Plays. London: Pan Books, 1947. Includes *Time and the Conways, I Have Been Here Before,* and *Dangerous Corner.*

The Linden Tree. London: Heinemann, 1948.

The Linden Tree and An Inspector Calls. New York: Harper, 1948.

The High Toby: A Play for the Toy Theatre. Harmondsworth: Penguin Books, 1948.

The Plays of J. B. Priestley. Three volumes. London: Heinemann, 1948–1950 (Volume I entitled *Seven Plays of J. B. Priestley.* New York: Harper, 1950).

Home Is Tomorrow. London: Heinemann, 1949.

Bright Shadow. London: Samuel French, 1950.

Dragon's Mouth, A Dramatic Quartet in Two Parts, with Jacquetta Hawkes. London: Heinemann, 1952 (New York: Harper, 1952).

Private Rooms. London: Samuel French, 1953.

Mother's Day. London: Samuel French, 1953.

Try It Again. London: Samuel French, 1953.

Treasure on Pelican. London: Evans Bros., 1953.

A Glass of Bitter. London: Samuel French, 1954.

The Scandalous Affair of Mr. Kettle and Mrs. Moon. London: Samuel French, 1956.

The Glass Cage. London: Samuel French, 1958 (Toronto: Kingswood House, 1957).

A Severed Head, with Iris Murdoch. London: Chatto and Windus, 1964.

Time and the Conways and Other Plays. Harmondsworth: Penguin Books, 1969. Includes *Time and the Conways, I Have Been Here Before, An Inspector Calls,* and *The Linden Tree.*

When We Are Married and Other Plays. Harmondsworth: Penguin Books, 1969. Includes *When We Are Married, Bees on a Boat Deck, Ever Since Paradise,* and *Mr. Kettle and Mrs. Moon.*

3. Essays and Autobiography

Papers from Lilliput. Cambridge, England: Bowes and Bowes, 1922.

I For One. London: John Lane, 1923 (Freeport, New York: Books for Libraries Press, 1967).

Open House. London: Heinemann, 1927 (New York: Harper, 1927).

Apes and Angels. London: Methuen, 1928 (Entitled *Too Many People, and Other Reflections.* New York: Harper, 1928).

The Balconinny. London: Methuen, 1929 (New York: Harper, 1930).

Self-Selected Essays. London: Heinemann, 1932 (New York: Harper, 1933).

Midnight on the Desert: A Chapter of Autobiography. London: Heinemann, 1937 (New York: Harper, 1937).

Rain Upon Godshill: A Further Chapter of Autobiography. London: Heinemann, 1939 (New York: Harper, 1939).

Delight. London: Heinemann, 1949 (New York: Harper, 1949).

All About Ourselves, and Other Essays. Selected and introduced by Eric Gillett. London: Heinemann, 1956.

The Writer in a Changing Society. Hermon Ould Memorial Lecture, 1955. Aldington, Kent: Hand and Flower Press, 1956.

Thoughts in the Wilderness. London: Heinemann, 1957 (New York: Harper, 1957).

Margin Released: A Writer's Reminiscences and Reflections. London: Heinemann, 1962 (New York: Harper, 1962).

The Moments, and Other Pieces. London: Heinemann, 1966.

Essays of Five Decades. Chosen and introduced by Susan Cooper. London: Heinemann, 1969 (Boston: Little, Brown, 1968).

Over the Long High Wall: Some Reflections and Speculations on Life, Death and Time. London: Heinemann, 1972.

The Happy Dream: An Essay. Cheltenhan: The Whittington Press, 1976.

Instead of the Trees: A Final Chapter of Autobiography. London: Heinemann, 1977 (New York: Stein and Day, 1977).

4. Miscellaneous

The Chapman of Rhymes. London: Alexander Moring, 1918.

Brief Diversions, Being Tales, Travesties and Epigrams. Cambridge, England: Bowes and Bowes, 1922.

Figures in Modern Literature. London: John Lane, 1924 (New York: Dodd, Mead, 1924).

The English Comic Characters. London: John Lane, 1925 (New York: Dodd, Mead, 1925). Priestley wrote an Introduction for the 1963 John Lane reprint.

Essayists Past and Present, a Selection of English Essays, edited with introduction by J. B. Priestley. London: Herbert Jenkins, 1925 (New York: Dial Press, 1925).

The Book of Bodley Head Verse, chosen and edited by J. B. Priestley. Preface by J. C. Squire. London: John Lane, 1926 (New York: Dodd, Mead, 1926).

George Meredith. English Men of Letters Series. London: Macmillan, 1926 (New York: Macmillan, 1926).

The English Novel. London: Ernest Benn, Ltd., 1927.

Thomas Love Peacock. English Men of Letters Series. London: Macmillan, 1927 (New York: Macmillan, 1927).

English Humour. The English Heritage Series. London: Longmans, Green, 1929 (New York: Longmans, Green, 1929).

The Lost Generation: An Armistice Day Article. London: The Society of Friends, 1932.

English Journey. London: Heinemann in association with Victor
   Gollancz Ltd., 1934 (New York: Harper, 1934).
Four-in-Hand. London: Heinemann, 1934. Includes a novel, plays,
   stories, and essays.
Our Nation's Heritage, edited with introduction and epilogue by J. B.
   Priestley. London: Dent, 1939.
Postscripts. London: Heinemann, 1940.
Britain Speaks. New York: Harper, 1940.
Out of the People. London: Heinemann and Collins, 1941 (New York:
   Harper, 1941).
Britain at War. New York: Harper, 1942.
The Man-Power Story. London: The Ministry of Labour, 1943.
British Women Go to War. London: Collins, 1943.
Here Are Your Answers. Common Wealth Popular Library. London:
   Socialist Book Centre, 1944.
The New Citizen. London: The Council for Education in World
   Citizenship, 1944.
Letter to a Returning Serviceman. London: Home and Van Thal, 1945.
Russian Journey. London: The Society for Cultural Relations with the
   U.S.S.R., 1946.
The Secret Dream, An Essay on Britain, America, and Russia. London:
   Turnstile Press, 1946.
The Arts Under Socialism, being a lecture given to the Fabian Society.
   London: The Turnstile Press, 1947.
Theatre Outlook. London: Nicholson and Watson, 1947.
Journey Down a Rainbow, with Jacquetta Hawkes. London:
   Heinemann-Cresset, 1955 (New York: Harper, 1955).
The Bodley Head Leacock, edited with an introduction by J. B.
   Priestley. London: John Lane, 1957.
The Art of the Dramatist, A Lecture. London: Heinemann, 1957.
Topside, or The Future of England. London: Heinemann, 1958.
The Bodley Head Scott Fitzgerald, edited with introduction by J. B.
   Priestley. London: John Lane, 1958-60.
The Story of Theatre. Wonderful World Series. London: Rathbone,
   1959 (Entitled *The Wonderful World of the Theatre.* New York:
   Garden City, New York: Garden City Books, 1959).
William Hazlitt. Writers and Their Work, No. 122. London: Longmans,
   Green in association with The British Council, 1960.
Literature and Western Man. London: Heinemann, 1960 (New York:
   Harper, 1960).
Charles Dickens, a Pictorial Biography. London: Thames and Hudson,
   1961 (New York: Viking, 1962). Reprinted in 1969 as *Charles
   Dickens and his World.* Reissued in 1978 by Scribner's.
Man and Time. London: Aldus Books Ltd., 1964 (New York:
   Doubleday, 1964).

Trumpets Over the Sea. London: Heinemann, 1968.

All England Listened: The Wartime Broadcasts of J. B. Priestley, with introduction by Eric Sevareid. New York: Chilmark Press, 1968.

The Prince of Pleasure and His Regency, 1811–1820. London: Heinemann, 1969 (New York: Harper, 1969).

The Edwardians. London: Heinemann, 1970 (New York: Harper, 1970).

Anton Chekhov. International Profiles Series. London: International Textbook Company, 1970 (Cranbury, New Jersey: A. S. Barnes, 1970).

Victoria's Heyday. London: Heinemann, 1972 (New York: Harper and Row, 1972).

The English. London: Heinemann, 1973.

Outcries and Asides. London: Heinemann, 1974.

A Visit to New Zealand. London: Heinemann, 1974.

Particular Pleasures: Being a Personal Record of Some Varied Arts and Many Different Artists. London: Heinemann, 1975. (New York: Stein and Day, 1975).

English Humour. London: Heinemann, 1976 (New York: Stein and Day, 1977). Revised and expanded version of an earlier volume with the same title, 1929.

SECONDARY SOURCES

[ABBOTT, E. A.] *Flatland, A Romance of Many Dimensions,* by A Square. London: Seeley, 1885. The earliest work to influence Priestley's thoughts on time.

AGATE, JAMES.*The Amazing Theatre.* London: Harrap, 1939. Contains reviews of productions of Priestley's plays.

———. *First Nights.* London: Nicholson and Watson, 1934. Contains reviews of productions of Priestley's plays.

———. *Ego 8.* London: Harrap, 1946. Contains an exchange of letters with Priestley.

———. *Ego 9.* London: Harrap, 1948. Refers to Priestley and his plays.

———. *More First Nights.* New York: Benjamin Blom, 1969. Contains reviews of productions of Priestley's plays.

BENTLEY, ERIC. *What is Theatre?* New York: Atheneum, 1968. Compares Saroyan and Priestley.

BOULTON, MARJORIE. *The Anatomy of Drama.* London: Routledge and Kegan Paul, 1960. Uses Priestley's plays to illustrate dramatic concepts and devices.

BRAINE, JOHN. *J. B. Priestley.* London: Weidenfeld and Nicolson, 1978. A novelist's assessment of the major works of a fellow Bradfordian.

BREIT, HARVEY. *The Writer Observed.* New York: World Publishing Company, 1956. Contains an interview with Priestley which originally appeared in the *New York Times Book Review* in 1951.

BROWN, IVOR. *J. B. Priestley. Writers and Their Work*, No. 84. London: Longmans, Green in association with The British Council, 1957. Brief survey of Priestley's significant works.

BURGESS, ANTHONY. *The Novel Now*. London: Faber and Faber, 1967. Places Priestley in contemporary context.

COOPER, SUSAN. *J. B. Priestley: Portrait of an Author*. London: Heinemann, 1970. Appreciative critical biography.

DUNNE, J. W. *An Experiment with Time*. London: A. & C. Black, 1927. Discussion of precognitive dreams and theory of serialism in this work primarily, and the following works by Dunne as well, the most significant influences on Priestley's own time theories, the basis of *Time and the Conways*.

——. *The Serial Universe*. London: Faber & Faber, 1934.

——. *The New Immortality*. London: Faber & Faber, 1938.

——. *Nothing Dies*. London: Faber & Faber, 1940.

EUSTIS, MORTON. "On Time and the Theatre: Priestley Talks about Playwriting," *Theatre Arts Monthly*, XXII (January 1938), 45–55. Combines interview with critical essay.

EVANS, B. IFOR. *English Literature Between the Wars*. London: Methuen, 1949 (second edition). Provides a brief survey of Priestley's plays.

EVANS, GARETH LLOYD. *J. B. Priestley—The Dramatist*. London: Heinemann, 1964. Authoritative study of Priestley's drama.

HOBSON, HAROLD. *Theatre*. London: Longmans, Green, 1948. Contains reviews of productions of Priestley's plays.

——. *Verdict at Midnight: Sixty Years of Dramatic Criticism*. London: Longmans, Green, 1952. Contains reviews of productions of Priestley's plays.

HUGHES, DAVID. *J. B. Priestley: An Informal Study of His Work*. London: Rupert Hart-Davis, 1958. Appreciative critical study of Priestley as novelist, dramatist, essayist.

KALSON, ALBERT E. "*A Severed Head* from Novel to Play: Coarsening as the Essence of Adaptation," *Ball State University Forum*, XVII: 4 (Autumn 1976), 71–74. Demonstrates how Priestley's craftsmanship shapes the adaptation.

LINDSAY, JACK. "J. B. Priestley," *Writers of To-Day*, edited by Denys Val Baker. London: Sidgwick and Jackson, 1946.

LUMLEY, FREDERICK. *New Trends in Twentieth Century Drama: A Survey since Ibsen and Shaw*. London and New York: Oxford University Press, 1967. An earlier edition of this book was published by Rockliff in London in 1956. Suggests three stages in Priestley's dramatic development.

OUSPENSKY, P. D. *A New Model of the Universe*. London: Kegan Paul, 1931. Theory of recurrence influences Priestley's view of time and is the basis of *I Have Been Here Before*.

POGSON, REX. *J. B. Priestley and the Theatre*. Drama Study Books, No. 2. Clevedon, Somerset: Triangle Press, 1947. Discusses all of Priestley's plays from 1932 to 1947.

SIEPMANN, E. O. "Letter to Mr. Priestley from a Returning Service Man," *Nineteenth Century and After*, CXXXVIII (December 1945), 247–55. Review in form of a response to Priestley's *Letter to a Returning Service Man*, protesting Priestley's manner.

SMITH, GROVER, JR. "Time Alive: J. W. Dunne and J. B. Priestley," *South Atlantic Quarterly*, LVI (April 1957), 224–33. Exploration of time factor in Priestley's works.

SWINNERTON, FRANK. *The Georgian Literary Scene, 1910–1935*. London: Heinemann, 1935. Comments on Priestley's entry into the literary world.

TREWIN, J. C. *Drama, 1945–1950*. London: Longmans, Green in association with The British Council, 1951. Discusses Priestley's drama after the war.

———. *Dramatists of Today*. London and New York: Staples Press, 1953. Evaluates Priestley's position as contemporary dramatist.

WEST, ALICK. *The Mountain in the Sunlight: Studies in Conflict and Unity*. London: Lawrence and Wishart, 1958. Discusses Priestley's treatment of the middle class.

WILLIAMSON, AUDREY. *Theatre of Two Decades*. London: Rockliff, 1951. Discusses the British Theater during the period of Priestley's commercial success.

WILSON, COLIN. "A Hell of a Talent," *Books and Bookmen*, XXI (January 1975), 26ff.

WOOD, E. R. Introductions to Priestley's plays in "The Hereford Plays," Heinemann Educational Books series.
An Inspector Calls (London, 1965), pp. ix–xiv.
Eden End (London, 1974), pp. xii–xx.
The Linden Tree (London, 1976), pp. vii–xii.
Time and the Conways (London, 1964), pp. vii–xiii.
When We Are Married (London, 1971), pp. vii–xviii.
Useful introductions to individual plays in editions designed for schools.

A Writer's Life: J. B. Priestley: An Exhibition of Manuscripts and Books, ed. Lucetta Teagarden (The Humanities Research Center: The University of Texas, Austin, 1963). A catalogue of an exhibition of Priestley's works.

Reviews of Priestley's novels and plays in the *New York Herald Tribune, New York Times, Observer, The Times, Sunday Times, Times Literary Supplement*.

Index

Abbott, E. A., 22
Addison, Joseph, 103
Admass, 59, 107
Agate, James, 127, 128, 186, 188
Allen, Walter, 30
Amis, Kingsley, 105, 109
Anderson, Maxwell, 238n10
Arlen, Michael, 229
Arnold, Matthew, 54
Austen, Jane, 36, 45

BBC, 64–65, 116, 172, 193–94
Balcony, The (Genet), 100
Balderston, John L., 79, 238n10
Bardo, 186
Barrie, James, 79, 110, 113, 116, 120–21, 125, 162, 164, 238n10
Bauer, Harold, 18
Beckett, Samuel, 169
Belloc, Hillaire, 31
Bennett, Arnold, 30, 31, 50
Bergson, Henri, 74
Berkeley Square (Balderston), 79, 238n10
Billam, George, 142
Bliss, Arthur, 205, 213
Boyer, Charles, 189
Brahms, Johannes, 119, 158
Braine, John, 71, 109
Brecht, Bertolt, 66, 123, 177–78
Brideshead Revisited (Waugh), 40
Britten, Benjamin, 119, 188
Bridie, James, 116
Brontë, Charlotte, 34
Brown, Ivor, 30, 73, 192, 225
Bullett, Gerald, 39, 51
Burgess, Anthony, 30, 80, 87, 102, 103, 214, 230
Busoni, Feruccio, 18

Casals, Pablo, 18
Cat on a Hot Tin Roof (Williams), 134

Chaplin, Charlie, 66, 141
Chaucer, Geoffrey, 216
Chekhov, Anton, 121–22, 144–52, 175, 200, 206, 208, 230
Cherry Orchard, The (Chekhov), 122, 147–49, 151
Chesterton, G. K., 31, 39
Christie, Agatha, 92, 167
Churchill, Winston, 29
Circle, The (Maugham), 136, 138
City Lights (Chaplin), 66
Clockwork Orange, A (Burgess), 102
Collins, Wilkie, 41
Conrad, Joseph, 29, 31, 49
Contractor, The (Storey), 151
Cooper, Susan, 22, 30, 45, 73, 103, 208
Coward, Noel, 117, 127, 140, 178
Christofer, Michael, 184

Dear Brutus (Barrie), 79, 121, 238n10
Deighton, Len, 92
Dickens, Charles, 31, 32, 45
Dietrich, Marlene, 56
Doll's House, A (Ibsen), 121, 164
Don Juan in Hell (Shaw), 189
Doyle, Arthur Conan, 93
Dream Play, A (Strindberg), 187
Dumas (fils), Alexandre, 178
DuMaurier, Daphne, 174, 216
Dunne, J. W., 22, 24–27, 37, 54, 77, 86, 153, 158–59, 165

Elgar, Edward, 119, 206–207
Eliot, T. S., 116, 230
Elizabeth II, 230
Enrico IV (Pirandello), 222
Eustis, Morton, 188
Evans, Gareth Lloyd, 121, 124, 139, 148, 170, 181, 211
Eve of St. Venus, The (Burgess), 214
Every Good Boy Deserves Favour (Stoppard), 119

252

Experiment with Time, An (Dunne), 22, 24, 158

Faulkner, William, 29
Fielding, Henry, 32, 45, 230
Fields, Gracie, 174
Fields, W. C., 18
FitzJohn, Donald, 219
Flatland: A Romance of Many Dimensions (Abbott), 22–23
Fleming, Ian, 92
Forbes-Robertson, Jean, 164
Ford, Ford Madox, 31
Forester, C. S., 20
Francis, Kay, 56
Fry, Christopher, 116, 190

Galsworthy, John, 116, 121
Garbo, Greta, 56, 212
Gauguin, Paul, 54
Genet, Jean, 100
Georgian Literary Scene, The (Swinnerton), 20
Ghosts (Ibsen), 121
Go-Between, The (Hartley), 75
Golden Bough, The (Frazer), 226
Golden Bowl, The (James), 29
Goldsmith, Oliver, 200
Goldsmith, Peter (Priestley pseudonym), 142
Gosse, Edmund, 229
Great Dictator, The (Chaplin), 141
Greene, Graham, 20, 32, 58, 60
Gregory, Paul, 189, 190
Grock, 18
Guinness, Alec, 174
Gulliver's Travels (Swift), 103
Guthrie, Tyrone, 133–34

Hardwicke, Cedric, 139, 140, 189
Hardy, Thomas, 31
Harris, Jed, 162
Hartley, L. P., 75
Hawkes, Jacquetta, 20, 107, 119, 190–92
Hazlitt, William, 32
Henry Esmond (Thackeray), 33
Hepburn, Katharine, 108
Holland, Ruth, 39, 133
Hughes, David, 30, 56, 64, 73, 79, 180–81, 220

Huxley, Aldous, 31

Ibsen, Henrik, 121, 129, 131, 164, 178, 187, 230
It's a Battlefield (Greene), 58

Jamaica Inn (DuMaurier), 174
James, Henry, 29
Jane Eyre (Brontë), 34
Joyce, James, 29, 31
Jung, Carl, 73, 119, 125, 179–84, 190–91

Keaton, Buster, 56
Kennedy, Margaret, 127
Kitchen, The (Wesker), 151
Knoblock, Edward, 127–28
Kreisler, Fritz, 18
Kubelik, Jan, 18

Laughton, Charles, 189, 190
Lawrence, D. H., 29, 31
Lewis, Mary Holland Wyndham, 20, 167, 205
Light in August (Faulkner), 29
Liliom (Molnar), 188
Little Tich, 18
Look Back in Anger (Osborne), 109, 124–25, 221, 230
Lonsdale, Frederick, 117
Lucky Jim (Amis), 105, 109
Lyrical Ballads (Wordsworth), 33

Malayan Trilogy (Burgess), 80
Man and Superman (Shaw), 189
Mann, Thomas, 97
"Mario and the Magician" (Mann), 97
Marquis of Keith, The (Wedekind), 150
Marshall, Margaret, 147
Mary Rose (Barrie), 79, 113, 121, 164
Maugham, Somerset, 117, 127, 136, 178
Memory of Two Mondays, A (Miller), 151
Merry Widow, The (Léon and Stein), 18
Miller, Arthur, 117, 150, 151
Miller, Hugh, 220
Mr. Bolfry (Bridie), 116
Mitford, Unity, 68

"Modest Proposal, A" (Swift), 103
Molnar, Ferenc, 188, 219
Mosley, Oswald, 68
Moorehead, Agnes, 189
Murdoch, Iris, 103, 222, 225-28, 230
Myron (Vidal), 55

National Theatre, The, 21, 116-17
New Model of the Universe, A
  (Ouspensky), 22, 26-27, 159
Nietzsche, Friedrich, 27
Nightmare Abbey (Peacock), 44, 128
No Man's Land (Pinter), 159
Northanger Abbey (Austen), 45

O'Casey, Sean, 116, 127
Oedipus (Sophocles), 18, 131
Old Times (Pinter), 159
Olivier, Laurence, 141
O'Neill, Eugene, 117
Osborne, John, 71, 109, 116, 118,
  124-25, 220, 221, 230
Our Town (Wilder), 177, 179, 183
Ouspensky, P. D., 22, 26-28, 77, 84,
  159, 161, 162, 165
Outward Bound (Vane), 188

Pachmann, Vladimir de, 18
Peacock, Thomas Love, 44, 128
Peer Gynt (Ibsen), 187-88
Pendlebury, Richard, 18
Peter Pan (Barrie), 110, 116
Pickwick Papers, The (Dickens), 32
Piggott, Lester, 230
Pinter, Harold, 118, 159, 169
Pirandello, Luigi, 164, 220, 222
Piscator, Erwin, 178
Pogson, Rex, 165, 199
"Prelude, The" (Wordsworth), 37
Priestley, John Boynton, character
  types, 35-36, 37, 41-42, 119-20;
  common cause, 36-37, 46, 52, 60,
  66, 80, 98, 106, 175, 201, 209;
  influences, 32-37, 117-25, 136-37,
  140, 144-49, 153, 155, 159, 161,
  179, 186-87, 189; journalism, 19,
  20, 124; life, 17-21; politics, 17, 37,
  65, 172-74, 230-31; style, 231;
  time speculations and theories,

21-27, 67, 76, 77, 86, 102, 111,
153-65, 203

WORKS: AUTOBIOGRAPHIES;
REMINISCENCES; TRAVEL ACCOUNTS
English Journey, 21, 51, 57
Instead of the the Trees, 19, 229
Margin Released, 17, 31, 39, 42, 43,
  45, 46, 69, 229
Midnight on the Desert, 17, 21, 22,
  25, 31, 32, 51, 57, 65, 173-74
Rain Upon Godshill, 17, 21, 31, 61
Visit to New Zealand, A, 21

WORKS: CRITICISM; ESSAYS;
SOCIAL HISTORIES
Anton Chekhov, 146
Art of the Dramatist, The, 122-23
Brief Diversions, 19
Edwardians, The, 87
English Comic Characters, The, 20
Figures in Modern Literature, 20
George Meredith, 20
Journey Down a Rainbow (with
  Jacquetta Hawkes), 107
Literature and Western Man, 31, 87
Man and Time, 23-26, 238n10
Particular Pleasures, 164
Postscripts, 64, 194
*Prince of Pleasure and His Regency,
  The*, 87
Thomas Love Peacock, 20

WORKS: NOVELS; STORIES
Adam in Moonshine, 20, 33, 35, 36,
  39-43, 45, 46, 48, 54, 62, 76, 97,
  98, 103, 229
Albert Goes Through, 51, 55-56,
  91, 94
Angel Pavement, 30, 32, 48-50, 51,
  58, 69, 74, 99, 104, 149, 229
Benighted, 34, 43-44, 46, 53, 60,
  61, 69, 71, 128, 162
Black-Out in Gretley, 32, 64,
  67-69, 200
Bright Day, 17, 30, 37, 42, 64,
  73-76, 99-100, 119, 154, 229,
  230

Carfitt Crisis, The, 111-15, 225
Dangerous Corner (with Ruth Holland), 39
Daylight on Saturday, 30, 36, 64, 69-72, 124-25, 200
Doomsday Men, The, 34, 51, 59-63, 64, 69, 87, 89
Faraway, 21, 34, 51-54, 60
Farthing Hall (with Hugh Walpole), 39, 44-45
Festival at Farbridge, 34, 35, 42, 77, 79-82, 109
Found, Lost, Found, 110-11
Going Up, 111
Good Companions, The, 17, 20, 31, 32, 34, 45-48, 50, 51, 52, 54, 62, 69, 80, 97, 103, 109, 117, 127
"Grey Ones, The," 112, 221
"Guest of Honour," 113
I'll Tell You Everything (with Gerald Bullett), 39, 51
Image Men, The, 17, 32, 36, 42, 80, 87, 95, 102-109, 207, 230
It's an Old Country, 35, 36, 87, 93, 99-102
Jenny Villiers, 34, 77-79, 84, 95, 100, 113
Laburnum Grove (with Ruth Holland; "retold" by L. W. Taylor), 39
"Leadington Incident, The," 113
Let the People Sing, 36, 64, 65-67, 172
"Look After the Strange Girl," 113
Lost Empires, 42, 97-99, 100
Low Notes on a High Level, 35, 77, 82-84, 96, 110, 194
Magicians, The, 22, 34, 42, 77, 84-86, 88, 89, 95, 100
"Mr. Strenberry's Tale," 113
Other Place, The, 111-13
"Pavilion of Masks, The," 114-15, 219
Salt is Leaving, 31, 36, 42, 87, 92-94, 98, 209
Saturn Over the Water, 34, 35, 37, 38, 86, 87, 88-90, 92
Shapes of Sleep, The, 86, 87, 88, 90-92

Sir Michael and Sir George, 38, 87, 95-97, 103
Snoggle, 110
"Statues, The," 113
They Walk in the City, 36, 51, 56, 57, 58-59, 64, 91, 109, 111, 125
Thirty-First of June, The, 87, 94-95
Three Men in New Suits, 64, 72-73
Town Major of Miraucourt, The, 19, 51, 54, 55, 77, 86
"Uncle Phil on TV," 112
"Underground," 113-14
Wonder Hero, 36, 51, 56-58, 64, 91, 109

WORKS: PLAYS; SCRIPTS FOR FILMS
AND TELEVISION; LIBRETTO
Anyone for Tennis?, 165
Bad Samaritan, The, 136, 143
Bees on the Boat Deck, 136, 140-42
Bright Shadow, 205, 214-16
Bull Market, 166
Cornelius, 48, 121, 122, 144, 149-52, 186
Dangerous Corner, 20, 117, 119, 120, 121, 127, 128-35, 136, 138, 148, 153, 159, 201, 203, 215, 216, 220, 224, 229, 238
Desert Highway, 19, 189, 191, 193, 197-99
Doomsday for Dyson, 224
Dragon's Mouth, 119, 125, 189-92, 208, 217, 218
Duet in Floodlight, 117, 136, 140, 144
Eden End, 116, 119, 122, 125, 144, 145-49, 150, 153, 203, 206, 208, 223, 229
Ever Since Paradise, 118, 119, 120, 123, 166, 175-78, 223, 224
Foreman Went to France, The, 174
Fortrose Incident, The, 225
Glass Cage, The, 222-23, 225
Glass of Bitter, A, 219
Golden Entry, The, 225
Golden Fleece, The, 120, 166, 170-74, 217
Good Companions, The (with Edward Knoblock), 127-28

Good Night Children, 82, 193-94
High Toby, The, 218-19
Home Is Tomorrow, 125, 209-11,
    213, 215, 223, 224, 225
How Are They at Home?, 125, 193,
    199-200
I Have Been Here Before, 22, 27,
    114, 120, 124, 153, 159, 160-63,
    165, 166, 167, 185, 220, 238n10
Inspector Calls, An, 117, 193,
    200-204, 209, 213, 233
Johnson Over Jordan, 59, 119, 122,
    123, 125, 126, 149, 179, 184,
    185-89, 224
Laburnum Grove, 117, 120, 125,
    136, 138-40, 144, 145, 170, 171,
    225
Last Holiday, 166, 174-75
Linden Tree, The, 59, 105, 117,
    119, 120, 121, 144, 205,
    206-209, 215, 216, 230
Long Mirror, The, 164-65
Mr. Kettle and Mrs. Moon, 125,
    220-22, 223, 225
Mother's Day, 219
Music at Night, 119, 123, 125,
    179-85, 188
Mystery at Greenfingers, 166-67
Now Let Him Go, 224
Old Dark House, The, 43
Olympians, The, 119, 205, 213-14
Pavilion of Masks, The, 225
People at Sea, 163-64, 167, 191
Private Rooms, 219
Rose and Crown, The, 174-75, 218,
    219
Roundabout, The, 117, 136-37,
    138, 143
Severed Head, A (with Iris Mur-
    doch), 103, 222, 225-28
Spring Tide (with George Billam),
    120, 142-43, 168
Summer Day's Dream, 120, 123,
    125, 144, 205, 211-13, 214, 215
Take the Fool Away, 225
They Came to a City, 73, 120, 125,
    174, 193, 194-96, 209, 210, 211
Time and the Conways, 22, 27, 75,
    79, 119, 120, 126, 144, 153-60,
    163, 165, 166, 179, 182, 208,
    229, 238n10

Time Was, Time Is, 165
Treasure on Pelican, 205, 216-17,
    224
Try It Again, 219-20
When We Are Married, 17, 117,
    119, 139, 166, 167-70
White Countess, The, 118, 192

Proust, Marcel, 31, 54, 74-75

Rachmaninov, Sergei, 18
Rainbow, The (Lawrence), 29
Rice, Elmer, 188
Riceyman Steps (Bennett), 50
Richardson, Ralph, 141, 149, 186, 188
Richardson, Tony, 125, 221
Room at the Top (Braine), 109
Rossetti, Dante Gabriel, 160
Russell, Rosalind, 108

Schnitzler, Arthur, 219
Schumann, Robert, 119, 155
Seagull, The (Chekhov), 147
Secret Agent, The (Conrad), 29, 49
Shadow Box, The (Cristofer), 184
Shakespeare, William, 55, 78, 120,
    129, 133, 143, 211, 212, 228, 229
Shaw, George Bernard, 116, 117,
    118-19, 121, 127, 189
She Stoops to Conquer (Goldsmith),
    200
Sheridan, Richard Brinsley, 218
Sherlock Jr. (Keaton), 56
Six Characters in Search of an Author
    (Pirandello), 220
"Solitary Reaper, The" (Wordsworth),
    33, 34
Sophocles, 129, 131
Sound and the Fury, The (Faulkner),
    29
Spectator Papers, The (Addison and
    Steele), 84, 103
Squire, J. C., 20
Star-Wagon, The (Anderson), 238n10
Steele, Richard, 103
Stern, G. B., 127
Sterne, Laurence, 230
Stoppard, Tom, 119
Storey, David, 151
Strindberg, August, 129, 187
"Sudden Light" (Rossetti), 160

Swift, Jonathan, 103
Swinnerton, Frank, 20

Tairov, Aleksandr, 200
Taylor, L. W., 39
Tempest, Pat, 20
Thackeray, William Makepeace, 33, 45
Three Sisters, The (Chekhov), 122, 149
"Tintern Abbey" (Wordsworth), 62
To the Lighthouse (Woolf), 29
Trollope, Anthony, 31
Tudor, Antony, 188

Uncle Vanya (Chekhov), 147, 151
UNESCO, 21

Vidal, Gore, 55

Wain, John, 71
Walpole, Hugh, 30, 31, 37, 44, 127
Waugh, Evelyn, 40
Wedekind, Frank, 150
Wells, H. G., 30, 31
Wesker, Arnold, 118, 151, 220
Wild Duck, The (Ibsen), 130
Wilder, Thornton, 124, 177, 179
Williams, Tennessee, 117, 134
Wilson, Colin, 29, 31
Wood, E. R., 148, 205
Woolf, Virginia, 29, 54
Wordsworth, William, 33, 34, 37, 55, 62
Wuthering Heights (Brontë), 44

Ysaye, Eugène, 18

Zinkeisen, Doris, 219

DATE DUE